UNDERSTANDING PROGRAMMING
An Introduction
Using Java™

Scott R. Cannon

Utah State University

THOMSON
BROOKS/COLE

Australia • Canada • Mexico • Singapore • Spain • United Kingdom • United States

Computer Science Editor: *Kallie Swanson*
Editorial Assistant: *Aarti Jayaraman*
Technology Project Manager: *Burke Taft*
Executive Marketing Manager: *Tom Ziolkowski*
Director of Marketing Communications: *Margaret Parks*
Project Manager, Editorial Production:
   Kelsey McGee
Print/Media Buyer: *Vena M. Dyer*

Permissions Editor: *Sue Ewing*
Production Service: *Matrix Productions*
Copy Editor: *Frank Hubert*
Cover Designer: *Laurie Albrecht*
Cover Image: *Imtek Imagineering/Masterfile*
Cover Printing, Printing and Binding:
   Webcom
Compositor: *ATLIS Graphics & Design*

For more information about our products, contact us at:
Thomson Learning Academic Resource Center
1-800-423-0563

For permission to use material from this text,
contact us by:
Phone: 1-800-730-2214   **Fax:** 1-800-730-2215
Web: http://www.thomsonrights.com

Library of Congress Control Number: 2002027652

ISBN 0-534-38933-3

Brooks/Cole–Thomson Learning
511 Forest Lodge Road
Pacific Grove, CA 93950
USA

Asia
Thomson Learning
5 Shenton Way #01-01
UIC Building
Singapore 068808

Australia
Nelson Thomson Learning
102 Dodds Street
South Melbourne, Victoria 3205
Australia

Canada
Nelson Thomson Learning
1120 Birchmount Road
Toronto, Ontario M1K 5G4
Canada

Europe/Middle East/Africa
Thomson Learning
High Holborn House
50/51 Bedford Row
London WC1R 4LR
United Kingdom

Latin America
Thomson Learning
Seneca, 53
Colonia Polanco
11560 Mexico D.F.
Mexico

Spain
Paraninfo Thomson Learning
Calle/Magallanes, 25
28015 Madrid, Spain

Contents

Chapter 6   **More Control Structures   135**

Chapter 7   **Designing with Classes   167**

Preface

To the instructor

In every class, there will be bright students who find Java™ programming natural and intuitive. An instructor must be careful not to teach to just these students. The rest need and appreciate a text with a good teaching approach.

This text is not intended to be a definitive manual on Java. It is focused on teaching Java as a first language—using two principles: First, students learn best when they first see and appreciate an immediate *need*. Second, students learn best by *doing* and *experiencing*.

This text attempts to get students writing meaningful applications as early as possible. In practice, students don't really begin to appreciate Java programming as a useful problem-solving tool until they see loops and conditions. The book starts with a breadth-first approach in the first few chapters. Students are first taught *one* way to do I/O, *one* variable type, *one* way to do a condition, and *one* loop statement. Quickly, they begin coding useful and interesting programs with this subset of Java. There is no need to teach all there is to know about one concept before introducing the next—it just delays meaningful experience. Later, after the student has some experience and understands the kinds of useful applications that can be addressed, the text returns to other loop variations, other conditional statements, compound Boolean expressions, other data types, and so on. Because of this breadth-first approach, the text postpones detailed issues, such as nested combinations of **if** and **if-else** statements, mixed-mode expressions, exceptions, truncation, and so forth until after students have been given a solid start. Accordingly, the text tries to *avoid teaching mechanisms and concepts that allow errors students are not yet ready to understand.*

As you can see, this breadth-first approach is *spiral* in nature. A concept or method is first introduced in simplified form. Gradually, as the need for more capability is demonstrated, the primitive form is expanded on until the full concept is presented. This also means that the text may be spiraling in on several topics at the same time. For example, simplified conditions, simplified loops, and functions are presented before returning to more detail on conditions. The purpose is simple: get students writing meaningful programs as soon as possible. Experience then leads to motivation and understanding when more detail is presented.

Chapters are actually *teaching* units, not *topic* units. You will not find all there is to learn about a particular topic in one chapter. That may be ideal for a reference manual, but it is not always appropriate for a teaching text. Students may not be ready to appreciate (or even need) the whole topic. If you attempt to compare this text with traditional approaches, you may find that a chapter-by-chapter relationship is not particularly valid. For example, you may easily identify the chapter that covers loops in another text, but looping concepts and syntax are presented here over several chapters. There is a chapter covering program design and problem solving, but additional material on these concepts is also spread over the entire book. Methods of style, documentation, and software engineering are also presented throughout the text as the complexity of programs expands and the student is more capable of appreciating the need in larger software projects. In general, concepts attempt to build on needs demonstrated in previous examples and assignments.

Some of the more advanced topics in Java are presented in an introductory way, preparing students for future classes when these topics will be studied in more detail. Some advanced topics are not even broached—too much syntax and feature study tend to weaken a good foundation.

Java I/O

It has been said that Java is unique among programming languages in that "you need to know everything in order to do anything." This is particularly true with I/O. One traditional approach is to teach students to directly use standard Java library classes such as **PrintWriter**, **BufferedReader,** and the **AWT** or **Swing** packages. Unfortunately, they require a fairly good understanding of concepts that the beginning student is not ready for (e.g., exceptions and events). Consequently, *meaningful programs are significantly delayed.* Some common Java textbooks cover hundreds of pages before the student is capable of reading in two integers and outputting the sum!

This text provides three fairly simple classes to support disk and terminal I/O. These classes are wrappers around the aforementioned Java library classes and simplify the syntax and exceptions involved. The **IO** class (based on the **JOptionPane** class in **Swing**) gives students an easy-to-understand and easy-to-use approach to simple GUI windows for simple numeric and string I/O. The **DiskInput** and **DiskOutput** classes provide support for simple numeric and string disk file access. Consequently, students are quickly able to write meaningful programs.

These three classes are quite simple and straightforward. By the time students have completed Chapter 11, they know enough to write these classes themselves. The classes are also completely presented as listings with explanations in Appendix A.

Object-oriented programming

There are no two ways about it: Java is an object-oriented language. To teach Java, one must teach objects, instantiation, polymorphism, and inheritance. Without being able to take advantage of classes, libraries, beans, applets, packages, and so on from others, Java is just another language.

Unfortunately, a text that teaches Java strictly from an academic object-oriented view quickly runs into the "all before anything" problem mentioned earlier. A textbook can quickly bog down in terminology and concepts before the student writes the first program. Traditional Java textbooks have a very steep learning curve in early chapters.

This text takes what might be considered a "hybrid" approach. Static classes and "helper" methods are taught first as simple applications in themselves. After students become familiar with methods and parameters, the text introduces dynamic classes as objects requiring instantiation. Finally, the topic of instance variables is added. This approach leads to a simple understanding of the difference between static and dynamic, which is often a difficult topic for the beginning student.

Applets

Java is occasionally taught primarily using applets. In this text, applets are covered but not until Chapter 12. The applet approach not only delays meaningful programs, but it adds syntax and semantics that the student has little control over. Debugging becomes more difficult. Rather than understanding concepts, students begin to rely too much on "magic phrases."

Java 2

This text is based on Java Version 1.2 and makes use of the associated **Swing** library. Java 1.2 (or later) can be obtained from Sun Microsystems (www.java.sun.com). Chapter 12 (applets) is best taught with the support of a Java 1.2 compliant Web browser. If your school does not have one, *Opera* is free (www.opera.com).

Now a few pedagogical features

   You'll see this icon when an incorrect approach is demonstrated.

   This icon lets you know that a program or code fragment contains an error.

■ **Syntax Boxes** Syntax is presented with model forms, which are more rules of thumb than rules. This supports the spiral method of teaching—when additional syntax is presented for a construct or topic, it does not need to replace or contradict the simpler forms given earlier.

- **Examples** Few students are patient enough to wade through the study of a long involved example. Examples are paramount, however, because few students are abstract enough to solve new problems only by learning rules. I have tried to provide many example programs and code segments that are straightforward and to the point.

- **Learning by Experimentation** Some exercises require experimentation and creativity. Each chapter includes a few *Experiment* boxes containing suggestions for simple "what if" experiments to teach an important topic. These assignments encourage trial and experimentation.

- **Creative Challenge** Each chapter includes a few projects that may not have a simple or complete solution that can be implemented using what the student has been taught to that point. The purpose is to demonstrate the need for upcoming topics and to encourage self-study. They also encourage innovation and creative thinking.

To the student

The goal of this text is to help you begin writing meaningful and useful programs as early as possible. As a result, the simplified models and mechanisms presented in a chapter may not completely express all the capabilities of the Java language associated with the feature being described. They will, however, present enough of the capability of the language to significantly add to your ability to write more and more complex and useful programs. These simplified models are gradually expanded to more detail and capability as you progress.

Program examples are simple—complete when necessary, but only code fragments when not. Important examples are accompanied by *execution diagrams* showing how variables would change during execution. Examples of common programming mistakes and errors are marked with a road sign containing a bug figure or a *Wrong Way* message.

Paragraphs that contain helpful hints, important concepts, or rules of thumb are marked with a Concept margin note. Important vocabulary terms are marked in italics in a paragraph and marked with a Key Term margin note. Each chapter also includes shaded boxes containing "what if" experiments that ask you to try different tests with programs and just see what happens! The idea is that you need to learn by personal experience as well as by study.

Each chapter has a selection of possible assignment projects that utilize the tools learned from the chapter. Some of these assignments also demonstrate the need for the tools to be learned in the next chapter; at least one Creative Challenge project is posed at the end of each chapter. These problems may not have a simple solution using what you have learned to that point. They can usually be solved with some *creative* or *innovative* application of previously learned tools. Some may not have complete solutions at that point in your skills—in these cases, you will need to solve as much of the problem as you can and specify or describe the limitations of your solution. The purpose of these special problems is to help you understand and appreciate the need for the tools and skills you will learn in the next chapter.

The Java language is popular for a first programming course for a number of good reasons. For one, it is a practical and commonly used language that will support you in the rest of your degree study and into the commercial world. It is also a powerful language with a great deal of support in the practical world. In addition, the Java language supports models and methods that are very important to the development of large complex software systems that are becoming more and more common in the world. Finally, but perhaps most important, Java is closely tied to the Internet and the type of portable and distributed systems that are becoming so important.

Good luck! You will find that computer science is both challenging and a lot of fun.

Web access

The following Web site has been dedicated to this text. This site contains download files for all executable example programs, notes on errata, and other useful material.

www.brookscole.com/compsci

If you find mistakes or typos, please let me know: scott@cannon.cs.usu.edu

Acknowledgments

I wish to thank the following reviewers: Jim Ball, Indiana State University; Edward Delean, Northern Virginia Community College; Catherine LaBerta, Erie Community College; Mary Ann May–Pumphrey, DeAnza College; Kevin Sahr, Southern Oregon University.

Scott Cannon
Logan, Utah

List of Figures

Your First
Java Program

This chapter presents the fundamentals of creating your first simple program in the Java language. This includes a simple introduction to high-level languages, class variables, and declarations. In addition, you will learn how to do simple program input, calculations, and output. By the end of the chapter, you should be able to write and run complete Java programs that perform such tasks as calculating the area of a circle or solving similar equations.

1.1 Programming with high-level languages

KEY TERM
central processing unit

Prior to writing your first program, let's take a quick look at what a computer is and what it is capable of doing. Although there are many variations and types of computers, we take as our model the PC, or personal computer, that can be found in so many homes and schools (Figure 1.1). The PC in your school laboratory or home consists of five or six basic parts: the *central processing unit* (or CPU), internal memory, auxiliary or secondary memory, a keyboard and mouse input device, a monitor output or display device, and perhaps a printer.

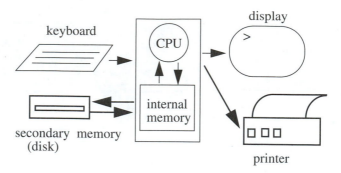

Figure 1.1 Basic components of a simple computer system

KEY TERM
volatile memory

Memory holds two types of information: programs and data. A program is just a sequence of instructions. The keyboard is used, under the control of the processor, to input or place these two types of information into computer memory. The processor is then later able to read a program and data from this memory and use them to produce useful results. Now, you might ask what the disk drive is. A disk is just another type of memory. Memory is classified into two simple categories: memory that loses stored contents when the power is turned off (*volatile* memory) and memory that retains values when power is removed (*nonvolatile* memory). Internal memory can be made of both volatile and nonvolatile sections; disk memory is nonvolatile.

The internal nonvolatile memory of a computer is usually read-only. In other words, it has been factory set to hold certain data. Often this is called ROM (read-only memory). Those sections of internal memory that are volatile are usually called RAM (random access memory). (Perhaps a more appropriate name would have been WRM for write/read memory, but that makes a more difficult acronym.) There are some newer forms of RAM memory that are also nonvolatile, but they are generally found in special computers.

Disks are particularly useful since the internal volatile memory of a computer is erased or lost when the power is turned off. Data and programs saved on a disk remain and are available when the computer is again started. Obviously, the monitor is used to display information from the memory, as is the printer; thus, they are output devices. A CD-ROM is a type of disk that is generally only written to once but later read many times.

KEY TERMS
assembly instruction, machine language

All processing done by a PC is handled or controlled by the CPU. Unfortunately, CPUs cannot perform very sophisticated operations. Even the most powerful CPUs are limited to the basic data-handling capabilities of add, subtract, multiply, divide, compare two values, move data or instructions to and from memory, and similar primitive operations. These commands are known as the basic *assembly instruction* set of the CPU or the CPU *machine language*.

Usually, the more powerful we claim a processor is, the faster it can perform these basic functions—usually on the order of many million operations per second. If processors are quite simple in their operation capability, how can computers perform amazingly difficult tasks such as designing aircraft or charting weather patterns? The complexity is not in the capability of the computer but in the capability of the computer programs!

A programmer's task is to devise a logical sequence of basic instruction-set commands that lead to the (more complex) desired result. The real power is in the mind and skill of the programmer. For example, the following set of Englishlike CPU commands (each representing a machine instruction) might represent a calculation for the circumference of a circle (using the formula $circ = 2\pi r$) for some hypothetical computer:

```
LOAD      radius
LOAD      pi
MULTIPLY
LOAD      two
MULTIPLY
STORE     circle
```

Here `radius`, `pi`, `two`, and `circle` are simply names used to represent the symbolic locations or addresses of where these values are stored in memory. (We have ignored for the moment how the values needed found their way into memory in the first place.) As you might expect, if the programmer must express these instructions in basic instruction-set operations (add, subtract, multiply, divide, compare, and move data), complex programs would be very difficult to write and very prone to mistakes. This was actually the case with the first computers! It didn't take long, however, for computer scientists to decide that there had to be a better way.

Another problem was evident to the first computer scientists. Each different CPU manufacturer usually has a slightly different basic instruction set for its particular family of CPUs. The machine language for an Intel CPU may represent the same primitive capabilities as those of the Motorola CPU in a Macintosh computer, but the encoding and implementation of these capabilities are different. As a result, a machine-language program written for an Intel CPU will not work in a Macintosh, and vice versa. Such a program was not portable. It could not be taken from one computer family to another and still work. The program had to be completely rewritten.

An important change in programming began when programs were written that could take a textual representation of a formula (representing many machine-language operations) and translate that representation into the appropriate basic instruction-set operations for a given CPU. For example, the circumference calculation might be expressed simply as:

$$circle = 2.0 * radius * pi;$$

KEY TERMS
compiler,
high-level language

It would then be the responsibility of this conversion program to transform the higher level formula into the appropriate basic instruction-set operations for the desired CPU. In reality, this conversion program is translating from one language to another. Programs that can do such translations are called *compilers*. If the syntax or forms of grammar used to express formulas and other operations are sufficiently powerful, they define what we call a *high-level language*. Java, Perl, Ada, and C++ are examples of high-level languages, and there are many others. A high-level language is in fact similar to English in many ways; there are grammar, punctuation, and syntax forms as well as semantic meaning to statements.

Now, don't confuse the compiler with the language it is designed to translate or the computer for which the translation is intended. For example, consider the C++ high-level language: The Microsoft C++ system contains a compiler to translate a C++ program into machine language for a computer with an Intel CPU. The Gnu C++ compiler might be used to translate the same C++ program into a different machine language for a SunSPARC CPU. If you have a C++ compiler for each different CPU, however, the original C++ program is now portable. To use a program from a Motorola CPU on an Intel CPU, you must recompile the program using an Intel-specific compiler.

Unfortunately, to execute a high-level language program on a new CPU, one must acquire an appropriate compiler and then translate (or compile) the program—often a costly and time-consuming process. The Java language extends the portability concept to the next higher level: A Java compiler translates a program into a general CPU language that has the basic characteristics of most CPUs but no characteristics that are specific to just one. A compiled Java program is then not really executable on any given CPU. However, the compiled Java program is very close to what a given CPU needs.

KEY TERM
interpreter

Next, Java provides an *interpreter,* or translator, for each particular CPU family. This interpreter provides a simple conversion of the general machine-level instructions into specific machine-level instructions for its associated CPU. This translation occurs as the Java program is being executed. We say the program is being interpreted.

KEY TERM
Java Virtual Machine

This interpreter is called the *Java Virtual Machine*. In other words, the Java language breaks the conversion process of producing a machine-level program into two steps: compilation and interpretation. The advantage of this approach over languages like C++ is that the compilation phase is general and appropriate for all CPUs, even those that will be invented next year. The translation phase for a specific CPU is actually quite simple and can be done automatically as the program is being executed. The user does not need to perform any special compilation on the machine he or she wishes to use. In other words, anyone with a Java Virtual Machine program can download or install compiled Java programs and run them immediately. (The situation is actually more versatile than that, and we will discuss several variations on this theme in future chapters.)

There are a number of other significant advantages to this approach—Java can be used for programs ranging from portable standalone application programs to dynamic Web pages and distributed systems. One significant advantage of Java over most other programming languages is that the compiler and interpreter are free. A Java system can be downloaded onto your home PC without cost via the www.java.sun.com Web site of the creator, Sun Microsystems.

You might ask why we simply don't use English as a programming language and eliminate the need to learn Java! That may work in science fiction movies, but we will need to wait for a future star date to see it happen. It would be very difficult to implement with today's technology. For one thing, the meaning of what we say in

English is often very dependent on context, inflection, and idioms. For example, saying "time passes" would imply one meaning if said during a high school reunion but have quite a different meaning if said by a football coach to his quarterback. Programming languages must be relatively context-free and unambiguous. The compiler must translate the exact meaning of your program without any extra information about the context of your request in the larger world environment.

1.2 A simple Java program

Your first few Java programs will follow the form given here:

```
public class class_name
{ public static void main (String[] args )
    {      declarations and statements
    }
}
```

Syntax form

The italicized words represent generic placeholders; you fill in the program name, definitions, declarations, and statements to accomplish a specific program purpose.

KEY TERM
class

At this point, let's start using Java terminology. Instead of *program*, we will use the term *class*. Although a class in Java is actually more than just a program, we will initially use the term *class* to refer to the programs we will be writing. Later, we will more appropriately distinguish between these two terms. With the exception of the class name, the italicized items are optional. The compiler will read this program from top to bottom and from left to right, just as we read English.

CONCEPT
file names must match class names

The name of the file we use to store this original source class must be the same as the chosen class name with the extension **.java**. For example, if the class were named *hello*, you would name the file holding this program source as **hello.java** on your disk.

KEY TERM
format

The *format* of a class is the style we use to organize the appearance of the class—that is, the spacing, indentation, and how we organize lines. The compiler, however, doesn't care how the class looks or is formatted; it must simply read correctly top to bottom and left to right. While the compiler might not care how you format your classes, certain standards have evolved that make a class easier to read by other humans (e.g., your course grader). For example, we line up a closing **}** directly under the opening **{**. It is perfectly correct to break a long statement into two lines as long as you do not break the statement in the middle of a word or other single item. Throughout the text, we will point out such standards when they become appropriate.

Let's take a look at each component of a class in turn. The first line, `public class` *class_name*, is where the class is named to distinguish it from other Java classes. A class name should be a single word beginning with a letter. (If you wish to use a phrase, connect the words with an underscore as shown.) The term `public` implies that other classes may be allowed to use or invoke this class in addition to a human user. This is a powerful concept we will return to. The contents of the class are enclosed within **{ }** symbols.

Inside the class block, the next line,

KEY TERM
method

```
public static void main (String[] args)
```

indicates where the class is to begin execution. This is called the main *method*. A method is simply a block or set of instructions to be executed. The statements of the main method are again enclosed within **{ }** symbols and will be executed in sequence. They represent what we wish our class to accomplish. (You will see later that a class may contain more than one method, but the main method is simply where a class begins execution.) We will return to the precise meaning of each word in the main method line later.

KEY TERM
comment

Before you begin writing your first class, you need to appreciate the concept of a *comment*. A comment is simply an English explanation to help you (and other programmers) understand your class. Comments are completely ignored by Java; they are only for human readers. A comment must begin with a double slash (/ /) and end with the end of a line. Here is an example:

```
// This program was written by Fred Jones
// on May 1, 2001.
```

Each high-level request for a calculation or other activity is called a statement. The braces **{ }** enclose the statements of the class that must be translated into machine instructions. You might envision a statement as being similar to a sentence in English. Just as there are different categories of sentences in English (declaratory, interrogative, etc.), there are several different types of statements in Java. They can be categorized into several groups, including:

- Input—a request to have the computer accept information from the keyboard or other input device.
- Output—a request to have the computer display information on the screen or other output device.
- Assignment—a request to have the computer store or assign a value to a location in memory. The value may be the result of a calculation.
- Condition—a request to have the computer choose between several different blocks of statements based on a comparison or test of memory values.

- Loop—a request to have the computer repeat a block of statements multiple times.
- Termination—a request to stop executing a class.

Naturally, there are many variations in each group. We will start by learning a statement from the last group:

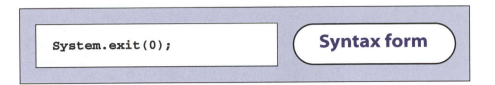

```
System.exit(0);
```
Syntax form

This statement always looks the same and has the same effect: terminate the program. In your first few programs, you will always place this statement as the last to be executed in your class. Notice that this statement ends with a semicolon. This is true of all Java instruction statements.

Let's now learn some simple statements in the first three groups (input, output, and assignment), and you'll find you can write useful Java programs.

1.3 Literal output

CONCEPT
code reuse

Program input and output can be a bit complex. Fortunately, Java allows us to take advantage of classes and methods previously written by others! We call this *code reuse*, and this feature of Java is extremely helpful. If a programmer comes across a problem to be solved (e.g., inputting a double number) and solves this problem with a segment of Java code, future programmers who need to solve the same problem can easily reuse this existing code segment without needing to re-solve the problem. We'll initially take that approach for program input and output (refer to Appendix A). Either download the file **IO.class** from the given Web site or copy the IO class from a disk location provided by your instructor. You could also copy the source for this class from the appendix into **IO.java** and compile—if you are careful. In either case, you will want to have a copy of this class in the same directory as the class you are currently developing.

The **IO.class** contains segments of code developed by another programmer to do simple input and output operations that are commonly needed in student programs. The Java Virtual Machine will automatically reuse these segments anytime your program refers to a statement preceded with IO. In effect, the **IO.class** file adds additional statements to the Java language! (Later in the text, we examine how these segments were written and how to develop your own reusable segments of code.) We will return to the reuse of classes written by others. Again, let's use proper Java terminology. Instead of saying "segments of code," we use the term *method*. Therefore, you might say that the IO.class provides methods for other classes to use or invoke.

Now back to output: An output statement in the **IO.class** can have a variety of forms—many of which you will see later on. Here is a statement that invokes a method from the **IO.class** to instruct the computer to display a message box containing information on the monitor:

```
IO.showMessage (message);
```

Syntax form

KEY TERM
literal

A message is simply a piece of text placed between quotation marks. We will call such a message a *literal*—*because we wish the computer to literally output the message as it appears.* A literal in Java can contain any character except the back slash and the double quote. These have special meanings that will be covered later. The double quote obviously indicates the end of the literal. Here is a complete class example:

Listing 1.I hello_world.java

```java
//  A simple Java class
public class hello_world
{  public static void main(String[] args)
   {  IO.showMessage("Hello world!");
      System.exit(0);
   }
}
```

This class (Listing 1.1) has only one statement: an output request that the computer display the literal message "Hello world!"

KEY TERM
program
development
environment

How you enter this class into memory, compile, and execute it will depend on the *program development environment* (PDE) available on your computer. Appendix A explains the simplest approach for Windows systems, but your instructor may provide another more elaborate PDE. A PDE is a set of programs that work together to allow you to enter a class into memory, save it to disk, accomplish editing changes, compile, and instruct the CPU to execute or interpret the translated class.

When the class is compiled, a new file is added to your directory. It has the same name but now with the extension **.class**. The **.java** file is the class source, while the **.class** file is the class executable. To execute your class, you (or others) only need the .class file. To make further changes to your class, you need to return to the source file and then recompile. In any case, when the above class is executed, the following appears on the display:

There are four items within this message box. First is the message or literal itself. The box is automatically sized to hold the requested message. To the left is an icon indicating that the message is informational. (You'll see other icon options in a few pages.) At the top is the box title; the default is "Message," but you'll see how to change that in the future. Finally, a button is presented to allow the viewer to dismiss the box and proceed with the program. By clicking the OK button (or pressing the Enter key), the box is dismissed and the class is allowed to proceed.

This is a trivial class of course. Let's take a look at a class that can do something worthwhile. Suppose we wish to write a class that could be used to calculate the area of a circle. To do this, we need to know how to instruct the computer to receive (or input) a number from the keyboard representing a radius, apply a formula for the appropriate calculation, and finally output the result of that formula to the display.

1.4 Double variables and declarations

KEY TERM
declaration

Before we write an instruction or statement to do input, we first must always declare a name to be associated with a memory location to be used to hold the value to be received. We reserve and label a memory location for a value through the use of *declarations*. There are several different types of values the Java language can immediately recognize. You'll see all of the standard types in later chapters and even see how to create new ones yourselves. To begin, however, we really need only one type. We will start with real or floating-point numbers—a number with an embedded decimal point. In Java, these are called **double** values. (The word *double* stands for "double-precision floating-point"; we'll return to precision later.)

KEY TERM
variable

The general form of a **double** declaration is given in the following box. The italicized *variable* is a label or name for a memory location in which we wish to hold a value. A **double** variable is simply a label or a name for a memory location that holds a number. The variable name then represents the contents of the memory location with that label. Computer scientists tend to be very terse, however. Rather than say "the value at the memory location labeled cost," we usually say "the value of cost" or, even shorter, just "cost." A variable (meaning the contents of the associated memory location) may hold only one value at a time:

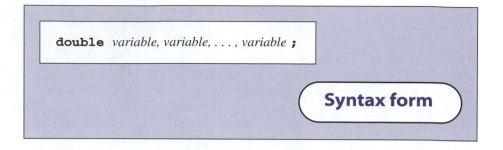

```
double variable, variable, . . . , variable ;
```

Syntax form

CONCEPT
a variable is
associated with a
location in memory

The ellipses in this form imply that a list of variables may be declared at the same time as long as the names are separated by commas. Some possible declarations are:

```
double cost, time;
double age, weight, height, color;
```

CONCEPT
a variable holds
one value

Some students find it easy to envision computer memory as a large collection of post-office boxes. Each box has a unique name associated with it and is capable of holding information. This analogy is excellent as long as you remember that a box (variable) *may hold only one piece of information at a time*. Each time a new value is placed into a variable, the old or previous value is lost or overwritten.

We may choose any name for a variable as long as three rules are followed. The name:

CONCEPT
variable name rules

1. must begin with a letter,
2. may consist only of letters, digits, and the underscore (_), and
3. may not be a reserved word.

KEY TERM
reserved word

(It is actually possible to begin a variable name with an underscore, but it can lead to confusion and is not recommended.) You probably remember that the name of a class must follow these same rules. A *reserved word* is one that has a predefined meaning for the language. For example, **main**, **void**, **static**, **double**, **public**, and **class** are the reserved words you have seen so far. We will identify more in further chapters (for a complete list, see Appendix B). In addition, many compilers limit the useful length of a variable name to 31 characters, so it is prudent to keep the name reasonably short. Look at the following possible declarations:

```
double age, cost, weight_95, class_number;
double temperature_fahr;
double thrust1, thrust2;
double mastertime, missedclients;
```

CONCEPT
name case

Be aware also that variable names are case sensitive! In other words, the following example declares four different **double** variables:

```
double Age, age, AGE, AgE;
```

CONCEPT
descriptive names

Since a class will need to be read and understood by other humans in addition to the computer, *always give variables names that in some way describe the nature or purpose of the value stored.* The compiler doesn't care what names you use, of course, but other programmers (and your course grader) will find your class much easier to understand if the names of variables describe what they are intended to hold.

1.5 Variable input and output

A statement used to receive a **double** value from the keyboard and place this value into a memory location labeled with a variable name has the form given in the following syntax form box:

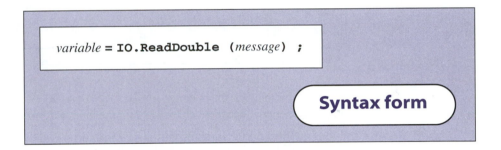

variable = **IO.ReadDouble** (*message*) **;**

Syntax form

The message of this statement is a literal that you wish to use to prompt the user for the value to be input. The variable is the destination of this value. When this statement is executed, a box will appear on the display showing the prompt and providing a place for the user to enter the value. A button is provided to allow the user to indicate that the number is complete. For example,

```
double age;
age = IO.ReadDouble ("Enter your age: ");
```

will result in the following message box. When the user clicks the OK button, the value entered within this box is assigned to the variable *age*.

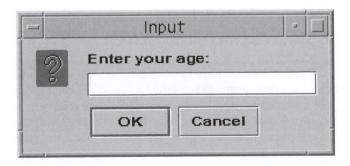

The icon for this box is a question mark—indicating the box represents a query and requires a user response. If the user makes a mistake while entering, the editing keys of the keyboard can be utilized. The number is not accepted and returned to your class until the user clicks OK. (We will ignore and not use the Cancel button for the moment.) A **double** number should contain a decimal point. If you leave the decimal point out, one will be assumed at the right side.

The value of a variable (or a constant) can be output with the following statement:

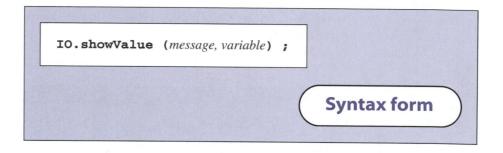

```
IO.showValue (message, variable) ;
```

Syntax form

In this statement, the message is used to annotate or describe the output. For example, a user who enters a value of 21.5 in the input box above:

```
IO.showValue ("You entered: ", age);
```

would produce the following display box:

1.6 Assignments and expressions

You now need to learn the statement used for formula calculations: the *assignment* statement. The general form is given in the following syntax form box. The variable on the left side is where we wish the result of a calculation to be placed. The expression on the right represents the calculation. The basic operators available for real number calculations are +, −, /, *, and of course, parentheses:

| variable **=** expression **;** |

Syntax form

KEY TERM
precedence

Expressions may contain variables and constants. A constant is simply a real number (with a decimal point) explicitly written into the expression. The order of *precedence* for the operators of an expression is the same as you learned in algebra: If parentheses are not used to indicate an operator order, multiplication and division are done first, followed by addition and subtraction. If an expression has two arithmetic operators at the same precedence, they are done left to right. In other words, the following assignment statement

```
cost = 2.0 + rate * 7.9 / (factor + 5.6);
```

implies that `factor+5.6` is to be calculated prior to being used in the division. In other words, the value of `factor` is to be added to 5.6, and that intermediate result will be used in the division. Next, the two operators `*` and `/` have the same precedence so the value of `rate*7.9` is to be calculated prior to division, and these two operations are done left to right. Finally, the `+` operator will be performed to add the value of 2.0 to the rest of the calculation. An expression may refer to the values currently assigned to variables or any explicit constants.

Naturally, using a variable in an expression implies that it previously was assigned a value or a value was read into it with an input statement. The above assignment statement would not make much sense if the variable `rate` and `factor` did not already contain values. If the compiler detects this might be the case when this statement is actually executed, it will usually give you a warning.

CONCEPT
use the decimal
point

Notice that each constant contains a decimal point. You will later learn about integer constants (and variables) that do not contain decimal points, but for now, all the problems we will initially need to solve can be done with **double** variables and real constants. If you forget and leave a decimal point out of a constant, you may not see the accuracy you expect in your calculations. The reason for this will be explained in Chapter 5.

Remember, the compiler (and thus the computer) does not consider the spacing of an expression. Adding blanks or tabs to group subexpressions would of course, have no effect. Take a quick look at the assignment statement below. Even though the spacing may seem to indicate otherwise visually, the `*` operator will be evaluated first:

```
time = age+delay * 7.9 ;//(delay*7.9)is still calculated first!
```

Here are some some possible assignment statements for a few simple geometry formulas:

$$area = 3.14 * radius * radius; \qquad\qquad a = \pi r^2$$

$$fraction = (height - length) / (height + length); \qquad f = \frac{H-L}{H+L}$$

$$coef = (volume - area) * (volume - area); \qquad c = (v-a)^2$$

The class for circle area might now look like that found in the following listing:

Listing 1.II

```
// Calculate the area of a circle given a radius value
public class circle_area
{  public static void main(String[] args)
   {  double area, radius;
      radius = IO.readDouble ("Enter a radius: ");
      area = 3.14 * radius * radius;
      IO.showValue ("The area for a circle of this radius is: ", area);
      System.exit(0);
   }
}
```

When this class is executed, the statements will be considered one at a time in the same order as they are written. The two double variables `area` and `radius` are first defined. Next the message `"Enter a radius: "` is sent to the output device (the display monitor). The computer then pauses and waits for the user to enter a real number that is then placed in the memory location reserved for the `radius` variable. A calculation is then performed; the value of pi as 3.14 is multipled by the variable `radius`, and that product is then multiplied again by `radius`. The result is then placed in the variable `area`. The last two statements output the message `"The area for a circle of this radius is: "` followed by the value in variable `area` and a carriage return. The following is what the user of this class might view as the class is executed.

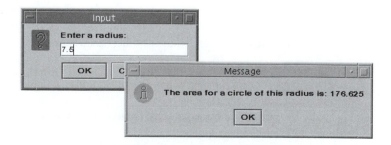

1.7 Class debugging

KEY TERMS
run-time, syntax, semantic bugs

Often, when programs are written, mistakes are made. Commonly, class development proceeds in an iterative fashion until we are convinced that the class is doing what we intended and is without mistakes (see Figure 1.2). There are three types of mistakes, or *bugs,* that may occur. These are *run-time* errors, *syntax* errors, and *semantic* errors.

Run-time errors occur when a class is executed with a statement that requires the CPU to do something it is not able to accomplish. One very common example of such an error is a request for division by zero:

```
temp = 0.0;
rate = 1.0 / temp;
```

Syntax bugs are errors in grammar or spelling while semantic bugs are errors in logic or meaning. An example of an English syntax error might be leaving a verb out of a sentence. A logic error might exist in a sentence that is grammatically correct but makes no sense:

The dog his paw.   (syntax or grammar error)

A paw ate the dog.   (good grammar, but illogical)

Of course, recognizing that the second sentence is illogical depends on your understanding of what the nouns *dog* and *paw* represent. If *paw* is your nickname for a tiger, it becomes reasonable.

Syntax errors are recognized by the compiler and result in error messages when your `.java` class is compiled. When a syntax error is detected, the compiler attempts to inform the programmer of the class line that contains the error and the nature of the error. Unfortunately, this is a very difficult task for some types of errors, and a programmer should always view error messages from the compiler as a best guess. Nevertheless, the actual error is usually at or just before the location specified. If more than one error is present, the compiler may become confused and not catch all the errors. In addition, the compiler may occasionally issue more than one error message for the same error if there is doubt as to the exact nature of the error. Consider the following programming attempt to calculate the volume of a box (Listing 1.III). (Line numbers have been added to the listing to help identify particular statements.)

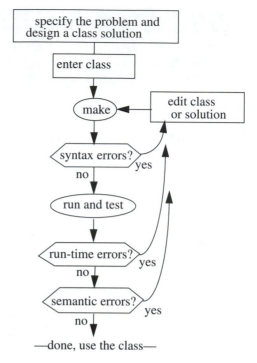

Figure 1.2   Class implementation cycle

Listing 1.III

```
1    // Calculate a box volume given height, length, and width (contains errors)
2    public class box_area
3    {  public static void main(String[] args)
4       {  double height, lenth, width, area, volume
5          height = IO.readDouble ("Enter height: ");
6          length = IO.readDouble ("Enter length: ");
7          width = IO.readDouble ("Enter width: ");
8          area = height + length;
9          volume = area * width
10         IO.showValue ("The volume is: ", volume);
11         System.exit(0);
12      }
13   }
```

BUG!

If you look closely, there are three syntax errors and one semantic or logic error present. First, the variable `lenth` declared in line 4 is not the same as the variable `length` used in the input and assignment statements of lines 6 and 8. Which statement is in error? The second and third errors are missing semicolons at the end of the declaration statement of line 4 and the assignment statement of line 9. The logic error is in the assignment statement of line 8 where height and length are added instead of multiplied. When this class is first compiled, the following error message was noted by one compiler:

```
circle_area.java:4: ';' expected.
        double height, lenth, width, area, volume
                                                 ^
```

This compiler found one of the syntax errors (the missing ';') on line 4 and aborted the compilation, allowing the programmer to correct the problem. Suppose we add a semicolon to the end of line 4 and recompile:

```
box_area.java:6: Undefined variable: length
    length = IO.readDouble ("Enter length: ");
    ^
box_area.java:8: Undefined variable: length
    area = height + length;
                    ^
box_area.java:9: Invalid type expression.
    volume = area * width
        ^
box_area.java:10: Invalid declaration.
    IO.showValue ("The volume is: ", volume);
            ^

4 errors
```

Whew! Now the compiler finds four errors! These are the compiler's best guess. Determining the exact nature of a syntax bug is often quite difficult for a compiler. Note that instead of recognizing that we misspelled the variable *lenth* in the declaration of line 4, the compiler assumes we forgot to declare the variable *length*. Notice also that the missing ; of line 9 is noted as an `Invalid type expression` error. In addition, the compiler finds an error on line 10—which is in fact correct!

The bottom line is this: If there is a syntax error, the compiler will always show at least one error message. One syntax error may, however, lead the compiler to list more than one message and may lead to error messages on subsequent lines in the class.

In general, the compiler error messages will be quite helpful in debugging your programs, but you must consider that they are only the compiler's best effort in interpreting the cause of syntax bugs and may not reflect their true nature.

There is a chance that when you enter a statement incorrectly, it may simply have another interpretation different from what you intended. For example, consider the following example of what the programmer intended to enter:

diameter = radius * 2.0;

and what was actually typed:

diameter = radius = 2.0;   **BUG!**

The second statement is obviously not what was intended, but it does not gener-ate a syntax error message! The reason is this statement has a valid interpretation (which will become apparent as you progress further in the course). So what can we conclude? If a statement is incorrectly formed for your intended meaning, you have a bug. If the malformed statement has a valid interpretation in Java, you will not nec-essarily see an error message. If there is no valid meaning, the compiler will issue at least one error message, but the suggested cause and location of the error may occa-sionally be off target from the true nature of the bug. Now suppose that, using these error messages as guides, we edit the class at this point to correct these syntax errors on lines 4 and 9 (correcting the spelling of length and adding the semicolons) and then again compile the class.

Listing 1.IV

```
1   // Calculate a box volume given height, length, and width (still contains errors)
2   public class circle_area
3   {  public static void main(String[] args)
4      {  double height, length, width, area, volume
5         height = IO.readDouble ("Enter height: ");
6         length = IO.readDouble ("Enter length: ");
7         width = IO.readDouble ("Enter width: ");
8         area = height + length;
9         volume = area * width;
10        IO.showValue ("The volume is: ", volume);
11        System.exit(0);
12     }
13  }
```

BUG!

The class now compiles without error messages, but that does not imply it is free of bugs. Notice that the logic error (line 8) was not detected. Naturally, the compiler has no idea as to the purpose or intent of the class—it simply translates a syntacti-cally correct class to do what you have told it to do. Compilers do not understand English. They cannot read your variable names and imply what they represent in na-ture. To the compiler, a variable name is only a sequence of characters. In addition, the compiler has no idea what the formula for the volume of a box should be in the first place.

Logic or semantic errors are usually found by program testing. In this particular case, we might hand calculate the volume of a set of known boxes (or *test cases*) and compare the results with those generated by the class. For this class, the comparison would indicate a logic error because the hand and class results would definitely not match. When the class of listing 1.IV is executed, suppose the user enters 4.0, 5.5, and 7.8, respectively, for height, length, and width. The resulting volume would show as 74.18.

Using a calculator, we expect the volume to be 171.6. The compiler is able to un-derstand and translate the instructions we have given, but they are not the instructions that lead to a correct volume calculation! The class does what we told it to do, not what we wanted or intended it to do.

Table 1.1   Execution table for the box-volume class

Statement	Height	Length	Width	Area	Volume
5 height = IO.readDouble(. . .	4.0	—	—	—	—
6 length = IO.readDouble(. . .	4.0	5.5	. . .	—	—
7 width = IO.readDouble(. . .	4.0	5.5	7.8	. . .	—
8 area = . . .	4.0	5.5	7.8	22	. . .
9 volume = . . .	4.0	5.5	7.8	22	171.6

If it is determined that a logic error is present, an execution table can be helpful in locating the source of the error. This table shows the expected values of variables at the end of important class statements as determined by hand with a calculator. Consider Table 1.1 for the above class for a box $4.0 \times 5.5 \times 7.8$ inches.

After completing this table by hand, you can compare it with the actual values of variables during class execution in one of two ways. First, if a tool called a "debugger" is available, it will allow you to step through class execution one statement at a time and display the values of selected variables at the end of each statement. In other words, a debugger can automatically generate the execution table for you. However, if a debugger is not available, you can simply add extra IO.showValue() statements to the class to output the values of variables at significant locations as class execution proceeds. For example, consider Listing 1.V:

Listing 1.V

```
1    // Calculate the area and volume of a box given height, length, and width (extra output)
2        public class circle_area
3        {   public static void main(String[] args)
4            {   double height, length, width, area, volume
5                height = IO.readDouble ("Enter height: ");
                 IO.showValue ("height: ", height);
6                length = IO.readDouble ("Enter length: ");
                 IO.showValue ("length: ", length);
7                width = IO.readDouble ("Enter width: ");
                 IO.showValue ("width: ", width);
8                area = height + length;
                 IO.showValue ("area: ", area);
9                volume = area * width;
10               IO.showValue ("The volume is: ", volume);
11               System.exit(0);
12           }
13       }
```

BUG!

When this class (Listing 1.V) is executed, the correct values are displayed for the entered height, length, and width (4.0, 5.5, 7.8), but the area is displayed as 9.5 while the table predicted 22! This gives us a clue to reexamine how area is calculated that helps to identify the semantic error. After correcting this semantic error and removing the extra `IO.showValue()` statements, the final class is given in Listing 1.VI:

Listing 1.VI

```
1   // calculate the volume of a box given height, length, and width (correct)
2   public class circle_area
3   {  public static void main(String[] args)
4       {  double height, length, width, area, volume
5           height = IO.readDouble("Enter height: ");
6           length = IO.readDouble ("Enter length: ");
7           width = IO.readDouble ("Enter width: ");
8           area = height * length;
9           volume = area * width;
10          IO.showValue ("The volume is: ", volume);
11          System.exit(0);
12      }
13  }
```

EXPERIMENT

What would happen if you entered something that was not a floating-point number? Run the above class and enter a name in response to the prompt.

There is much more to class debugging. In future chapters, we will not only consider more debugging concerns but also look at methods and approaches that tend to prevent us from making a variety of mistakes in the first place.

1.8 Example projects

Suppose a programmer wished to convert English feet measurements into metric meters. Now before attempting to write such a class, you first need to find the appropriate formula:

$$meters = feet \times 0.3048$$

As we logically think about the steps to arrive at a correct solution, we might come up with the following:

1. Input the number of feet to be converted from the user.
2. Calculate the number of meters for that many feet.
3. Display the calculated number of meters.

Naturally, we first need to declare any variables used by the class. It appears there are two, and the best descriptive names might be 'feet' and 'meters'. When the class wishes to input a value for 'feet', it is important that the user be prompted to know when to enter the correct value. When outputting the converted result in meters, it is best also to include the original number of feet for two reasons. First, it makes the output more self-documenting. Second, the user has a self-check to verify that the correct input was received. Writing the class is now a matter of using the appropriate Java syntax (Listing 1.VII):

Listing 1.VII

```
// Convert feet to meters
public class feet_to_meters
{   public static void main(String[] args)
    {   double feet, meters;
        feet = IO.readDouble ("Enter the number of feet to be converted to meters: ");
        meters = feet * 0.3048;
        IO.showValue ("The conversion in meters is: ", meters);
        System.exit(0);
    }
}
```

This approach of first logically thinking about the specific steps to be accomplished before worrying about how to express them in Java represents a peek at basic class design methods. We will return to this issue. Keep in mind for now that a class can be divided into two problems. First, what steps are needed to arrive at a correct solution? Second, how should these steps be coded into Java?

Take a look at still another example. Suppose we now have a much more complex formula to apply. For example, let's calculate the surface area of a truncated or clipped right-circular cone (illustrated in the following figure):

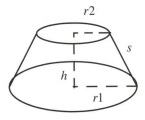

The formula from a good geometry text is the following:

$$area = \pi[r1^2 + r2^2 + (r1 + r2)s]$$

The steps needed for this class are similar to the previous one. In fact, having written this type of class before, this new class should be easy. You will find that solving a problem using an approach that worked for other similar problems makes many programs fairly easy to write:

1. Input the radii, side length, and height.
2. Calculate the associated area using the given formula.
3. Display the area.

It appears the class will need four variables for input, and you might choose the names `minor_radius`, `major_radius`, `height`, and `side`. The answer or result might be named `surface_area`. Rather than try to code this entire complex formula in a single assignment statement, let's break it into subexpressions. Looking inside the braces, we'll call the first `sum_of_squares` and the second `radii_product`.

Once again, the user should be adequately prompted for what the class expects for input. Since this class will be more difficult to understand and read by another, we'll make more use of comments (Listing 1.VIII).

Listing 1.VIII

```
// Calculate total surface area of a truncated right-circular cone
public class cone_area
{  public static void main(String[] args)
    {  double minor_radius, major_radius;          // cone top and bottom radii
       double height, side;                        // cone height and side length
       double surface_area;                        // total cone surface area
       double sum_of_squares, radii_product;       // sub-expression values in formula
   // prompt user and input needed variables
       major_radius = IO.readDouble ("Enter major radius: ");
       minor_radius = IO.readDouble ("Enter minor radius: ");
       height = IO.readDouble ("Enter cone height: ");
       side = IO.readDouble ("Enter side length: ");
   // calculate area formula using sub-expressions
       sum_of_squares = major_radius*major_radius + minor_radius*minor_radius;
       radii_product = (major_radius + minor_radius) * side;
       surface_area = 3.14 * (sum_of_squares + radii_product);
   // display results
       IO.showValue ("Total surface area: ", surface_area);
       System.exit(0);
    }
}
```

Using this class, the user could enter a major radius of 4.0, a minor radius of 5.75, a height of 3.5, and a side of 3.91. If so, the total surface area will display as 273.7609.

1.9 Summary

KEY TERMS Several terms were introduced in this chapter that are important for you to understand:

1. *central processing unit (CPU)*—the brains of a computer where actual calculation and processing take place.

2. *volatile memory*—memory (usually internal) that loses its contents when the power is turned off. Nonvolatile memory (usually disk) retains its contents when the power is removed.

3. *assembly instruction, machine language*—the primitive machine operations that a CPU is constructed to perform.

4. *compiler*—a class that is able to translate a textual source class in a high-level language into another class consisting of lower level assembly language instructions.

5. *high-level language*—a programming language that allows the expression of operations and formulas for calculations in a manner closer to a more human way of expressing the steps of a problem.

6. *interpreter*—a program that interprets general assembly-language code that is not specific to any one CPU architecture.

7. *Java Virtual Machine (JVM)*—the program that interprets a compiled Java program for a particular machine.

8. *class*—at this point in your career, a class is a program.

9. *format*—the visual style or layout of a class or statement.

10. *method*—a segment of code within a class to accomplish a task.

11. *comment*—a textual message preceded by the // symbol and used for human-readable documentation.

12. *literal*—a textual message enclosed within quotation marks.

13. *program development environment (PDE)*—a program or set of programs to aid in entering, editing, compiling, and other operations associated with producing a class.

14. *declaration*—a statement specifying the name of a variable to be associated with a particular type of data. (You will later see that other things can also be declared.)

15. *variable*—a symbolic name associated with a location in memory and used to store a value.

16. *reserved word*—a word specifically set aside to have a built-in meaning to the compiler.

17. *precedence*—the order in which operators in an expression are evaluated when not specified by parentheses.

18. *run-time errors*—errors caused by instructing the computer to do something it is not physically capable of doing.

19. *syntax errors*—errors in spelling and grammar detected by a compiler.

20. *semantic errors*—errors in logic or intent not usually detected by the compiler.

CONCEPTS   There were several syntax forms to remember in writing your first Java programs. First, the general form of your first Java programs will be the following:

```
public class program_name
{  public static void main (String[] args )
   {   declarations and statements
   }
}
```

Real or decimal variables used in a class must first be declared using a statement in the form: **double** *variable, variable, . . . , variable* **;**

Values can be output using a statement in the form: **IO.showValue(***message, value***)** **;**

Read values can be input to **double** variables using a statement in the form: *variable* **= IO.readDouble(***message***);**

Variable names must not be reserved words and must begin with a letter or underscore. They may contain letters, digits, and the underscore and should usually be fewer than 31 characters in length. Letter case is significant.

Variables may be assigned the results of calculations using a statement in the form: *variable* = *expression* **;**

The operators *, /, +, and – are available along with parentheses. Operator precedence dictates that * and / are performed before + and – when parentheses do not indicate otherwise. When equal-precedence operators occur without overriding parentheses, they are performed left to right. Constants may be used in assignment statement expressions. A constant is always written with a decimal point at this time in your career.

The following facts, tips, and helps are useful to remember:

- Variables should always be named descriptively.

- A variable may hold only one value. If a new value is stored into a variable using an assignment or input statement, the previous value is overwritten.

- If a syntax error is present, the compiler will issue an error message, but messages may not always accurately describe the nature or location of the true mistake. A statement that represents something different from what the programmer intended to write, but which nevertheless represents some other valid Java construct, will not usually result in an error message.

- Semantic errors can be located with a debugger or an execution table using test data for which the programmer predicts the correct answers manually.

Table 1.2   Example segments

`double age, weight;`	establish two real variables with these names.
`age = IO.readDouble();`	input a value into `age`.
`cost=5.6+4.2*3.0;`	multiply 3.0 times 4.2, add the result to 5.6, assign to `cost`.
`IO.showValue("the value is: ", cost)`	output the message followed by the value of `cost` on a line.

■ You may write a long statement on more than one line as long as you do not break the statement in the middle of a word, literal, or other item.

Keep in mind that in following the strategy of this text, you have not learned all the ways of inputting data, performing calculations, and displaying results. You have basically learned one way. On the other hand, you are now in a position to write quite a variety of useful classes with this small set of knowledge.

1.10 Exercises

Short-answer questions

1. Memory that loses its contents when the power is removed is _____ memory.
2. Memory that retains its contents when the power is removed is _____ memory.
3. A statement that identifies a variable name to a class is known as a _____ statement.
4. The act of preparing a class for execution is called a _____.
5. Text enclosed within quotation marks is known as a _____.
6. A word that has a predefined meaning in a Java class and cannot be used as a variable name is known as a _____ word.
7. Explain the difference between a semantic and a syntax error.
8. If a new value is assigned to a variable, the old value is _____.
9. Draw the box that would be displayed as a result of the following input or output statement:
   a. `IO.showMessage ("programming is fun!");`
   b. `cost = IO.readDouble ("enter the cost:");`
   c. `IO.showValue ("the cost is:", cost);`
10. Which of the following are valid variable names?
    a. `temperature`
    b. `cost_of_living`
    c. `$deposit`
    d. `side2`
    e. `weight_`
    f. `percent%_raise`

11. Propose valid variable names for the following information:
  a. the cost of a new car
  b. the number of yards gained in a football game
  c. the square root of the variable `distance`
  d. the average value of a list of scores
  e. the time required to pay off a loan

12. Declare appropriate variables to be used in the calculation of the number of square feet in a triangular residential lot.

13. Express the following formulas as an assignment statement (or perhaps a group of assignment statements with subexpressions):

  a. $x = \dfrac{ay^2 + 3}{(4 - a)}\pi$

  b. $val = (x + y)(x - y)$

  c. $cost = (rate)(value - 1)$

14. Based on the given values in the variables listed, show what values would be assigned as a result of the following statements:

value	cost	markup	price
7.5	8.1	10.0	

  a. `price = value + cost * markup;`
  b. `price = (value+cost) * markup / 2.0;`
  c. `price = value + cost * markup + value / 2.0;`

15. When prompted by a class to enter a **double** value, what will occur if the user fails to enter a decimal point?

16. Explain a possible reason a compiler syntax error message may be associated with the line following the statement in which the error actually occurs.

17. Briefly explain why a compiler may not detect semantic errors in a class.

18. Briefly explain how semantic errors are normally detected.

19. List the reserved words presented in this chapter.

20. What is the purpose of comments in a class?

Projects

1. Write and test a complete Java class to input the dimensions of a rectangular building lot and then calculate and output the total square footage. Be sure to use appropriate prompting messages to the user and good annotation messages to describe the output.

2. Write and test a complete Java class to input a radius and then calculate the volume of the corresponding sphere. The formula is $vol = \dfrac{4}{3}\pi r$.

3. Write and test a complete Java class to calculate the area of a general trapezoid.
The formula is $area = \frac{1}{2}(a+b)h$.

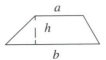

4. Write and test a complete Java class that can be used to convert a weight in the English pound system to an equivalent weight in the metric kilogram system. There are 2.2 lb in 1 kg.

5. Write and test a Java class to calculate and output an employee paycheck. Your class should input two numbers: the number of hours worked and the hourly rate.

6. Write and test a Java class to convert Fahrenheit temperatures to Celsius.The formula is: $\frac{5}{9}(f-32) = c$.

7. Using an earth radius of 6356.912 km and the speed of sound in dry air at 0°C of 331.36 m/sec, write and test a Java class to determine how long it would take a loud noise to travel a percentage of the earth's circumference. The input to this class should be a decimal number less than or equal to 1.0. For example, an input of .25 should produce the time it would take a loud noise to traverse 25 percent of the earth's circumference.

8. Write and test a Java class to calculate an estimated mass for the earth. In other words, how many kilograms is the earth? You may assume the earth is spherical with a radius of 6356.912 km and a mean density of 5.522 gm per cubic cm. Refer to Project 2 for the formula for spherical volume. Notice that you will need to perform conversions to ensure that the units of the formula you use are all the same.

9. Creative Challenge: Modify the class of Project 2 so that it calculates the volume of three different spheres, not just one. The class will need to prompt for three different radii and output three different volumes. You have not yet been taught an efficient way of programming a solution to this problem, but it can be done with what you already know. Be creative.

10. Creative Challenge: Modify Project 5 to allow for overtime pay. Employee pay should be calculated as the number of hours worked times the hourly rate with time and a half for overtime (the hours worked over 40). For example, consider the following:

hours worked and hourly rate: 37.5 5.75

pay should be: $215.625

Since this employee worked less than 40 hours, the pay is only 37.5 times 5.75. Now if the employee had worked more than 40 hours, overtime would need to be considered:

hours worked and hourly rate: 47.5 5.75

pay should be: $294.6875

Simple Choice and Repetition

What can we do when different conditions call for different formulas in a class? This chapter presents the fundamentals of making choices in a class using alternatives. In addition, methods for repeating instructions are introduced. By the end of the chapter, you should be able to write classes that process many sets of input data and test input data values to determine which instructions need to be executed.

2.1 The conditional statement

At the end of the previous chapter, one assignment required a programmer to calculate employee paychecks (Project 10). Take a minute and review that problem. . . The difficulty with this task is that there are two different formulas: one for employees with no overtime and one for employees with overtime. The only methods of solving this problem were (a) to write two different programs or (b) to apply both formulas blindly in one class and present the user with a correct and an incorrect answer! The user then had to examine an employee timecard and determine which class to run or which answer to accept.

KEY TERM
conditional
statement

High-level languages are perfectly capable of allowing choices to be specified. That is the purpose of the *conditional statement*. The conditional statement allows a class to examine data and choose an appropriate set of instructions for execution. The general form is the following:

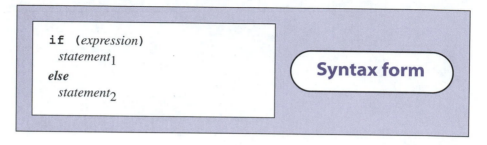

```
if (expression)
    statement₁
else
    statement₂
```

Syntax form

The **if** and **else** are additional reserved words (see Appendix C). The meaning of the condition is simple: If the given *expression* is true, the first *statement* is executed. If the *expression* is not true, then the second *statement* is executed. In other words, only one of the two statements is ever executed. What can these statements be? Any Java statement is allowed; output, input, and assignment statements from the previous chapter are usable as are other **if** statements. (You will see later that another form of the **if** statement is also available as well as other types of conditional statements.)

KEY TERM
flow of control

The flow of execution, or *flow of control*, through the **if** statement is represented by the diagram of Figure 2.1.

KEY TERM
relational
expression

Most commonly, the expression used in an **if** statement is a *relational expression*. This means that the relationship between two variables or constants (or perhaps simple arithmetic expressions) is tested. There are six relational or comparison operators that can be used. Four are introduced here. (You'll see the other two after you learn more about other data types.)

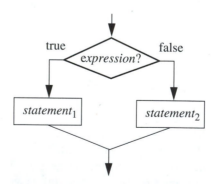

Figure 2.1   Symbolic representation of flow of control through the **if** statement

CONCEPT
relational
operators

Some relational operators

>greater than

<less than

>=greater than or equal to

<=less than or equal to

For example, consider the following relational expressions:

$a < b$ true if the value of a is less than that of b

$x >= (y+2.0)$ true if x is greater or equal to the value of $(y+2)$

$z > 25.0$ true if z is greater than 25

We are now ready to construct some complete **if** statements. Consider the following simple example:

```
if (a <= b)
    IO.showMessage ("a is less than (or equal to) b");
else
    IO.showMessage ("a is greater than b");
```

This method fragment will output the first message if the value of the variable a is less than or equal to the current value of variable b. The second message would be output when the value of variable a is not greater than nor equal to b (or when a is greater than b).

With the conditional statement, we can revisit the employee pay problem with a much more practical solution. If you remember, an employee's pay is calculated from one of two formulas. If the employee works less than or equal to 40 hours, the pay is calculated with the formula $pay = hours \times rate$. If the employee works overtime, time and a half is paid for the hours over 40 and the second formula is applied: $pay = (40 \times rate) + (overtime \times 1.5 \times rate)$, where overtime is of course, the hours worked over 40 (Listing 2.I).

In this listing, a comment is used to document the name of the class and provide a brief description of its purpose. In general, a good programmer will provide comments at the top of each class to document the name of the class, clarify the purpose and intent of the class, and provide other useful documentation such as the name of the programmer and the date. We will discuss more about documentation later in the text.

Now, there are two conditions or **if** statements in this class. The user is first prompted to input the hours worked and then the pay rate. After these values are input and stored in variables hours and rate, the number of overtime hours are calculated as hours −40. If this value is greater than 0 (meaning the employee worked overtime), the overtime formula is applied to calculate pay. If not, the regular formula is applied for pay. After pay has been calculated, it is output to the user. Finally, overtime is again tested in the second **if** statement, and one of two messages is added to the output to indicate whether the employee did or did not work overtime (Listing 2.1).

Listing 2.1

```
// A class to calculate paychecks
public class calculate_pay
{   public static void main(String[] args)
    {   double hours, pay, rate, overtime;
        hours = IO.readDouble ("enter hours worked:");
        rate = IO.readDouble ("enter pay rate:");
        overtime = hours - 40.0;
// employees working more than 40 hours receive overtime
        if (overtime > 0.0)
            pay = (40.0 * rate) + (overtime * 1.5 * rate);
        else
            pay = hours * rate;                  // no overtime paid for this employee

        IO.showValue ("pay is: ", pay);

        if (overtime > 0.0)
            IO.showMessage (" overtime worked");
        else
            IO.showMessage (" no overtime worked");
        System.exit(0);
    }
}
```

If we use this class for an employee who did not work overtime, the output might look like this:

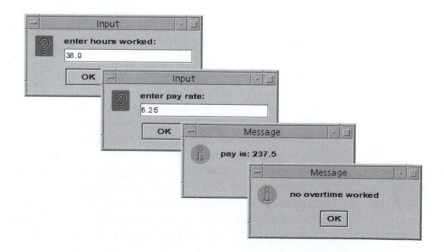

An employee who did work overtime would cause the class to use the overtime formula and produce the "overtime worked" message box.

EXPERIMENT

What would happen if the user clicks the Cancel button in one of the input boxes? Why do you think this occurs?

CONCEPT
use proper
indentation

Since a class often needs to be read by more than one programmer, we are concerned with using a consistent and readable style. Just as giving variables descriptive names is considered good style, proper class indentation is very helpful in making it obvious which statements belong to the *true* and *not true* segments or clauses of a condition. Note that the two output statements in Listing 2.I are indented, and the **if** and **else** are aligned in good paragraph notation. This helps to show the human reader which statements are subordinate.

If one of the two statements is not needed in the **if**, a semicolon by itself can be used to indicate an empty or null statement. (You'll see later that there is a simpler method to solve this problem.) For example:

```
if (a < b)
    IO.showMessage (" a is larger");
else
    ;
```

2.2 Statement blocks

You probably noticed that the class of Listing 2.I made the same decision twice to check for overtime. Actually, we can combine blocks of statements by enclosing them inside { }, or brace symbols. This indicates we wish the entire block to be treated as a single *compound* statement. For example, all the statements of the main method are enclosed inside braces; a method consists of a single compound statement. Let's go back to the employee pay class of Listing 2.I. It might make more sense and make the class more readable if we were to test if hours is greater than 40 and then calculate using the overtime or regular formula depending on the answer. Listing 2.II is an example of such a modified class.

Listing 2.II

```
// A class to calculate paychecks (2nd version).
//   Contains blocked statements
```

```
public class calculate_pay2
{  public static void main(String[] args)
   {   double hours, pay, rate, overtime;
       hours = IO.readDouble ("enter hours worked:");
       rate = IO.readDouble ("enter pay rate: ");

       if (hours > 40.0)
       {   overtime = hours - 40.0;
           pay = (40.0 * rate) + (overtime * 1.5 * rate);
           IO.showValue (" pay (with overtime) is: ", pay);
       }
       else
       {   pay = hours * rate;
           IO.showValue (" pay (no overtime) is: ", pay );
       }
       System.exit(0);
   }
}
```

EXPERIMENT

What would happen if a semicolon were added immediately after the else in Listing 2.II?

This class is somewhat easier to read because the two different ways of calculating pay and the associated output messages are nicely compartmentalized. For example, if we wish to modify the section dealing with overtime, we would be less concerned about how that modification might affect the section dealing with regular pay. The idea here is to avoid allowing modifications in one section of a class to introduce errors in another. We will return to this concept repeatedly throughout this text.

You will notice that we are beginning to see quite a number of nested { } symbols. As we discussed in Chapter 1, keeping an opening { symbol directly aligned over the associated closing } symbol will help you keep track of correct nesting.

If a user of this class were to enter 45.0 for hours worked and 7.25 for pay rate, the output box would show the following:

Now suppose you inadvertently left the braces out of the false section of the above **if** statement:

```
if (hours > 40.0)
    {   overtime = hours - 40.0;
        pay = (40.0 * rate) + (overtime * 1.5 * rate);
        IO.showValue (" pay (with overtime) is: ", pay );
    }
else
    pay = hours * rate;
    IO.showValue (" pay (no overtime) is: ", pay);
```

Even though you have indented appropriately, only the 'pay=...' assignment statement is considered as the false section of the **if**. In this case, the bottom output statement would be executed regardless of the **if** expression because it is now outside (or after) the **if**. This is not a syntax error, but it is certainly a semantic error because that is not what was intended.

Once again, there is another form of the **if** statement, and there are more conditional statements. Rather than spend time on them here, let's get right into class looping. We'll come back to conditions.

2.3 The while statement

At the end of Chapter 1, an assignment was made for a class to calculate the volume of three different spheres (Creative Challenge 9). The only straightforward method of solving this problem was to duplicate the statements needed for a single sphere three times! For example, refer to Listing 2.III:

Listing 2.III

```
// A class  to calc. the volume of 3 spheres
public class sphere_volume
{   public static void main (String[] args)
    {   double volume, radius;

        radius = IO.readDouble ("Enter radius: ");
        volume = (4.0 / 3.0) * radius * radius * radius * 3.14;
        IO.showValue ("volume is: ", volume);

        radius = IO.readDouble ("Enter radius: ");
        volume = (4.0 / 3.0) * radius * radius * radius * 3.14;
        IO.showValue ("volume is: ", volume);

        radius = IO.readDouble ("Enter radius: ");
        volume = (4.0 / 3.0) * radius * radius * radius * 3.14;
        IO.showValue ("volume is: ", volume);

        System.exit(0);
    }
}
```

This approach is of course, very impractical if the number of different data to be processed is large. A simpler approach is to instruct that certain statements (or compound statement blocks) are to be repeated using the **while** statement:

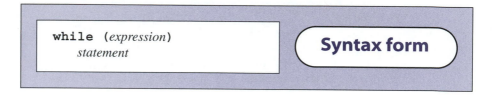

```
while (expression)
    statement
```

Syntax form

CONCEPT
the while
statement

When a **while** statement is encountered during the execution of a class, it instructs the CPU to repeatedly execute the associated *statement* as long as the *expression* is true. The same relational operators you learned to use with the **if** expression can be used in the **while** expression. The flow of execution through a **while** statement might be symbolically represented with the diagram of Figure 2.2.

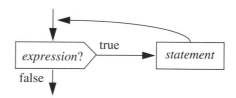

Figure 2.2 Symbolic representation of the flow of execution through a **while** statement

KEY TERM
loop

Note from Figure 2.2 that the *expression* is tested first. If true, the associated *statement* is executed. Control returns back to retest the *expression*, and the cycle continues. This is called a *loop*. Nearly all useful programs contain some type of loop, and we will return to this mechanism often in this text. For example, the following will output the numbers 1, 2, 3, 4, 5, 6, 7, 8, 9:

```
n = 1.0;
while (n < 10.0)
{   IO.showValue ("n is: ", n);
    n = n+1.0;
}
```

EXPERIMENT

What would happen if you use the wrong comparison operator? Change the relational operator from < to > and try the above class.

2.4 Introduction to analysis and design

CONCEPT
write the user's
manual first

Let's return to the problem of finding the volume of a number of different spheres. Rather than fixing the number of volume calculations to be three, we will extend the problem and let the user instruct the class when all spheres have been calculated. We will often begin the design of a class by writing the *user's manual* first. These are the instructions that would be given to a user to help them properly operate the class. After all, if we cannot describe how the class is going to interact and perform, we really don't know what to write! Writing the manual first is part of our class analysis and design. We will return to this concept later. For now, if we choose to name our class CALCVOL2, this might be our manual:

> When the CALCVOL2 class is run, it will begin by prompting you to enter a radius. Respond by typing the radius value and press the Enter key. The class will then display the volume for the sphere with this radius using the formula $volume = \frac{4}{3}\pi(radius)^3$ and again prompt you for a radius for another calculation. When you have processed all radii, enter a value of −1.0 for a radius. This will indicate that you are finished, and the class will terminate.

With this user's manual, we know just what the interaction will look like when the class is executed. Something like the following dialog sequence:

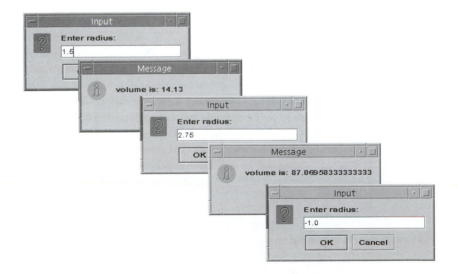

2.5 Use of loops

The **while** statement is used to generate a class loop for a variety of reasons. In general, all class loops can be classified as *indefinite* or *counted*.

Indefinite loops

KEY TERMS
indefinite loop,
sentinel

The next job is to write a class that acts as described in the user's manual written earlier. Consider Listing 2.IV. Since you cannot predict how many times the statement block of the **while** will repeat simply by looking at the class, this is known as an *indefinite loop*. The number of repeats depends on how many radii the user wishes to process. When an indefinite loop depends on the user entering a special value to indicate that the class should stop looping, this special value is known as a *sentinel*. Obviously, a sentinel must be a value that would not normally occur in the list of values being read and processed. An indefinite input loop that terminates upon reading a sentinel value has the following general model:

```
variable = IO.readDouble ( prompt ) ;
while  ( expression comparing variable with sentinel )
{    calculation or other use of variable ;
     variable = IO.readDouble ( prompt ) ;
}
```

CONCEPT
the sentinel loop

If the variable used in the testing expression was not input first, it would not have a known value at the first test, and the behavior of the loop may be unpredictable. Similarly, if the variable was not filled with new input at the bottom of the repeated block, it could never change and cause the loop to terminate. If this loop executed once, it would execute an infinite number of times!

KEY TERM
infinite loop

There is a special term for a loop that never terminates—an *infinite loop*. Consider the following small indefinite output loop example:

```
range = 7.0;
while (range > 5.0)
{    value = range * 2.0;
     IO.showValue ("value is: ",value);
}
```

Notice that the value of variable `range` never changes inside the repeating block of statements. When executed, the CPU will continually (or infinitely) compute and output the value of `range*2`. When this occurs, you can usually interrupt or abort the class if the loop contains an input or output statement by clicking the Cancel button or by pressing Ctrl+C.

Another common mistake made by beginning programmers is to place a semicolon after the parentheses as follows:

```
while (range > 5.0) ;
{   value = range * 2.0;
    IO.showValue ("value is: ",value);
}
```

Remember that the semicolon by itself can be an empty or null statement. In the above example, it is this empty statement that is being repeated—another infinite loop. The compiler of course, does not consider that you properly indented the block of statements; the block will be treated as following the loop, not as a part of it.

Using this mechanism or model of an indefinite loop, we can now write the class to calculate sphere volumes (Listing 2.IV):

Listing 2.IV

```
// A class to calculate sphere volumes with a user-controlled indefinite loop.
public class sphere_loop
{   public static void main (String[] args)
    {   double radius, volume;

        radius = IO.readDouble ("enter radius values (-1 to stop): ");
        while (radius > 0.0)
        {   volume = (4.0 / 3.0) * radius * radius * radius * 3.14;
            IO.showValue ("the volume is ", volume);
            radius = IO.readDouble ("enter radius values (-1 to stop): ");
        }
        System.exit(0);
    }
}
```

EXPERIMENT

What would happen if you enter two radii on the same line before clicking the OK button? Listing 2.IV asks the user to enter one radius value at a time.

Counted loops

KEY TERM
counted loop

When the number of times a loop repeats can be determined by looking at the class, it is known as a definite or *counted loop*. Suppose we wish to rewrite the **sphere_loop** class so that it always processes five spheres. In other words, we do not expect the user to enter anything special to stop the loop; it always repeats exactly five times. Before writing this new class, let's consider first the following simple definite loop to output the word "Hello!" five times as shown in Listing 2.V.

Listing 2.V

```
// A class to output  "Hello" 5 times
public class hello_loop
{   public static void main (String[] args)
    {    double count;
        count = 0.0;
        while (count < 5.0)
        {   IO.showMessage ("Hello!");
            count = count + 1.0;
        }
        System.exit(0);
    }
}
```

When this class is executed, it will produce five consecutive output boxes showing the word "Hello!" First, look at the assignment statement count = count + 1.0;. While that would give a heart attack to an algebra teacher, this is not algebra but a class assignment instruction. It indicates that 1.0 is to be added to the old value of count, and this new value is to be placed back into the variable count. This is often called an accumulating or an incrementing assignment statement. (Actually, this is so common in Java that there is a special operator for this action. We'll come back to that issue later. For now, incrementing a variable in this way will help you become more aware of the difference between algebra and assignment statements.)

Let's look at how the loop works. The class first initializes a variable (in this case count) to zero. Each time the bottom of the loop is reached, the class adds 1.0 to this variable, and the CPU jumps back to the top of the loop. The **while** loop tests this variable to determine whether the loop should be repeated. The execution table for this segment is given in Table 2.1.

In general, any block of statements could be made to repeat five times by placing it inside the above loop. To change the number of iterations, you simply change the test expression to compare against a different number limit. Look at the following diagram:

```
count = 0.0;
while (count < Max)
{
                          ⎛ whatever statements are placed here ⎞
                          ⎝ will be executed exactly Max times  ⎠

count = count + 1.0;
}
```

Let's go back to the problem of processing exactly five different spheres: We will copy the statements from the original class (that processed only one sphere) and use them to replace the output statement in the definite loop segment (see Listing 2.VI). (After copying, we'll clean up the class by changing the class name and the comments.)

Table 2.1   Execution table for listing 2.V

Statement	Count	Expression	Output
count = 0.0	0.0	—	—
while (count < 5.0)	0.0	true	
IO.showMessage("Hello!");	0.0		Hello!
count = count + 1.0	1.0		
while (count < 5.0)	1.0	true	
IO.showMessage("Hello!");	1.0		Hello!
count = count + 1.0	2.0		
while (count < 5.0)	2.0	true	
IO.showMessage("Hello!");	2.0		Hello!
count = count + 1.0	3.0		
while (count < 5.0)	3.0	true	
IO.showMessage("Hello!");	3.0		Hello!
count= count + 1.0	4.0		
while (count < 5.0)	4.0	true	
IO.showMessage("Hello!");	4.0		Hello!
count = count + 1.0	5.0		
while (count < 5.0)	5.0	false	

Listing 2.VI

```
// CALCVOL; a class to calc. sphere volumes using
// a definite loop for 5 iterations

public class calc_volumes
{ public static void main (String[] args)
   {        double count, radius, volume;

// loop for 5 iterations
         count = 0.0;
         while (count < 5.0)
         {   radius = IO.readDouble ("enter radius: ");
             volume = (4.0 / 3.0) * radius * radius * radius * 3.14;
             IO.showValue ("volume is: ", volume);
             count = count + 1.0;
         }
         System.exit(0);
   }
}
```

EXPERIMENT

What would happen if you forgot to increment the counting variable? Remove the count=count+1.0 statement and try the class.

Summing and counting

A common use of the loop is to sum a series or list of values. Let's use an indefinite loop to input a list of positive values. The loop should terminate when the sentinel value of −1.0 is read. Each time a new value is input, that value will be added to the sum of all the previous values (Listing 2.VII). Notice that prior to adding values into the variable sum, it is first initialized to zero. In this manner, the first time the statement

```
sum = sum + number;
```

is executed, the zero in sum will be added to the first number prior to storing a new value into the sum variable. Each successive time this statement is executed, sum will be replaced by the previous sum value plus the new value just input.

Listing 2.VII

```
// A class to sum a list of positive numbers
public class sum_loop
{   public static void main (String[] args)
    {   double number, sum;
        sum=0.0;

        number = IO.readDouble ("enter a positive value (ending with -1): ");
        while (number > 0.0)
        {   sum = sum + number;
            number = IO.readDouble ("enter a positive value (ending with -1): ");
        }
        IO.showValue (" sum is: ", sum);

        System.exit(0);
    }
}
```

Table 2.2   Execution table for listing 2.VII and inputs 5.0, 7.5, 2.1, −1

Statement	Expression	Number	Sum
number = IO.readDouble (. . .		?	0.0
while (number > 0.0)	true	5.0	0.0
sum=sum+number		5.0	5.0
number = IO.readDouble (. . .		7.5	5.0
while (number > 0.0)	true	7.5	5.0
sum=sum+number		7.5	12.5
number = IO.readDouble (. . .		2.1	12.5
while (number>0.0)	true	2.1	12.5
sum=sum+number		2.1	14.6
number = IO.readDouble (. . .		−1.0	14.6
while (number>0.0)	false	−1.0	14.6
IO.showValue ("sum is . . .		−1.0	14.6

Here is an example execution of this class.

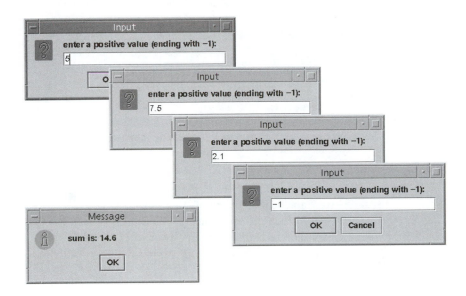

The execution table for the application class in Listing 2.VII, assuming the same list, is given in Table 2.2.

CONCEPT
initialization

There is a shorthand method of declaring and initializing a variable in one statement. Instead of the earlier declaration and an assignment statement to set sum to zero, the following would be equivalent:

```
double sum = 0.0;
```

In general, any variable name in a declaration statement can be followed by an assignment symbol = and an initial value. You should remember that this initial value is stored for the variable only once, when it is set up or allocated.

Let's now combine two things we have learned: summing and counting. Suppose the average of values read is to be displayed instead of the sum. We can add another variable called count that is initialized to 0.0 at the top of the class. Each time a new value is read and summed, we will simply add 1.0 to count. At the end of the indefinite loop when the sentinel is read, sum will contain the total of all values read, and count will contain the number of values read. Obviously, the average of all values can then be calculated (Listing 2.VIII):

Listing 2.VIII

```
// A class to sum and average a list of positive numbers
public class average_loop
{  public static void main (String[] args)
   {  double number, average, sum=0.0, count=0.0;
```

```
    number = IO.readDouble ("enter a positive value (ending with -1): ");
    while (number > 0.0)
    {   sum = sum + number;
        count = count + 1.0;
        number = IO.readDouble ("enter a positive value (ending with -1): ");
    }

    average = sum / count;
    IO.showValue (" average is: ", average);

    System.exit(0);
    }
}
```

Notice that this class would run into problems if the very first number entered were the sentinel value of −1. In that case, the **while** loop would not even be entered. When the assignment statement to calculate average was reached, count would be zero and a run-time error would occur because division by zero is not possible. (What would you do to prevent this run-time error from occurring in this situation?)

KEY TERM

condition variable, or flag

Occasionally, the condition that should cause a loop to terminate is more complex than a single condition or comparison of values. At times, a loop should be terminated when any one of a set of possible conditions becomes true. In these situations, it is often convenient to use a *condition variable* (sometimes called a *flag*). A condition variable is simply a variable that is initialized to a predetermined value. The loop is set to terminate when the condition variable changes. We will use 1.0 as the predetermined value. When the loop should stop, we will change this value to zero. Within the loop, as many **if** statements as are needed are used to test the several conditions that might cause the loop to terminate and change the condition variable if any of these conditions are true.

For example, suppose a loop is needed to sum an indefinite list of positive values until either (a) a sentinel value of a negative number is encountered or (b) the sum becomes greater than 100. This loop should terminate if either of these conditions is true. To accomplish this, we will define a condition variable called done and initialize it to one. Each time a value is read, it will be tested as a possible sentinel. Within the loop, each new value of the running sum will be tested to check for a value greater than 100. We will assume the first value read is never the sentinel:

```
double done = 1.0, sum = 0.0, value;

value = IO.readDouble("enter a value (-1 to finish): ");
while (done > 0.0)
{   sum = sum + value;
    if (sum > 100.0)        // check for sum limit
        done = 0.0;
    else
    {   value = IO.readDouble("enter a value (-1 to finish): ");
```

```
        if (value < 0.0) // check for sentinel and clear 'done'
            done = 0.0;
        else ;              // or else do nothing
    }
}
```

Keep in mind that there are other statements used in class looping, just as there are conditional statements in addition to the `if`. Before we examine these other statements, let's first gain some experience in applying loops and conditions in relevant and practical programs.

2.6 Nested conditions and loops

What if we have a need to express more than two choices or alternatives in a class? For example, suppose there were three different formulas for calculating employee pay from the previous example:

1. If an employee works 40 hours or less: $pay = hours \times rate$

2. From 40 to 60 hours: $pay = (40 \times rate) + (overtime \times 1.5 \times rate)$

3. Over 60 hours: $pay = (40 \times rate) + (overtime \times 2.0 \times rate)$

In other words, employees are paid time and a half for overtime if they work between 40 and 60 hours but are paid double-time for all overtime hours if they work more than 60 hours. We need to express these three choices in a class. One method of using the `if` statement to make multiple choices is to *cascade* the choices. Figure 2.3 is a symbolic diagram of these three cascaded choices.

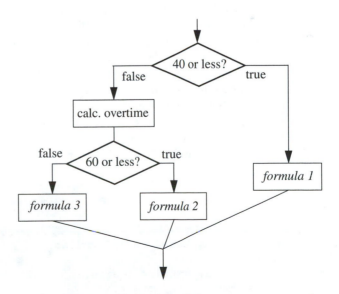

Figure 2.3   Cascading two `if` statements to make three choices.

In each choice of this diagram, the number of hours worked is compared with increased limits. This same diagram might also be represented in a skeletal Java form. In this form, we simply substitute ovals containing the symbolic English of needed operations:

```
if (hours <= 40.0)
{
```

> use formula 1

```
}
else
{   if (hours <= 60.0)
    {
```

> use formula 2

```
    }
    else
    {
```

> use formula 3

```
    }
}
```

This type of skeletal segment allows the programmer to ensure that the braces are properly placed and that the appropriate true and false sections of each choice are in the correct locations. Later, it is a simple matter to remove the ovals and fill in the specific statements associated with each symbolic English statement. This skeletal diagram can easily be converted to a Java class, which is shown in Listing 2.IX.

Now, you may be thinking that some of the braces in Listing 2.IX are not really necessary, which is true. You may decide at this point to eliminate any brace pairs that enclose only a single statement. It would not be wrong, however, to leave them in place. Suppose that during a future modification or class upgrade, you needed to change formula 1 and replace it with several statements. If the braces are already in place, the potential for introducing an error is much less than if you now need to recognize they need to be inserted.

Listing 2.IX

```
// A class to calculate pay based on 3 formulas
public class calc_pay3
{   public static void main (String[] args)
    {   double hours, pay, rate, overtime;
        hours = IO.readDouble ("enter hours: ");
        rate = IO.readDouble ("enter pay rate: ");
```

```
if (hours <= 40.0)
{   pay = hours * rate;
}
else
{   overtime = hours - 40.0;
    if (hours <= 60)
        {   pay = (40.0 * rate) + (overtime * 1.5 * rate);
        }
    else
        {   pay = (40.0 * rate) + (overtime * 2.0 * rate);
        }
}
IO.showValue ("pay is: ", pay);
System.exit(0);
    }
}
```

Notice that the careful indentation and placing of braces help the reader follow the logic and intention of the class. Consider how difficult it would be for another programmer (or the grader for your class!) to follow this class if no indentation was used and if the braces were not consistently placed.

Suppose a class is needed to output a table of powers for the numbers 1.0 to 10.0. For each number, the square, cube, fourth, fifth, and sixth power are to be output in a form similar to the following:

table of powers

N	2	3	4	5	6
1.0	1.	1.	1.	1.	1.
2.0	4.	8.	16.	32.	64.
3.0	9.	27.	81.	243.	729.
4.0	16.	64.	256.	1024.	4096.
5.0	25.	125.	625.	3125.	15625.

KEY TERM
concatenate

The calculation of this table can easily be accomplished with nested definite loops. However, it would be quite clumsy to output this table with a display box for each number! Here's a peak at a Java feature that is quite useful—we'll cover this in much more detail later, but we'll introduce it here. You have learned that real numbers may be stored in **double** variables. There is also a variable type to hold literals or messages: **String** variables.

> **String** *variable_name* **;**
>
> **Syntax form**

The following **IO** class methods can be used to join, or *concatenate*, a second message or double value onto the end of a **String** variable.

```
String_variable = IO.concatenate (String_variable, message);
String_variable = IO.concatenate (String_variable, value);
```

Syntax form

KEY TERM
carriage return

Another useful feature to remember is that each time a display box command encounters the special sequence of two characters "\n" in a message, it will start a new line in the display. This sequence is called the *carriage return*. By building an output message in a series of concatenation steps, we can delay generating an output display box until the entire message is ready.

Now, let's return to the powers table. First, there must be a segment to print the table title and headings. Next we will need to output five lines, one for each value of *N*. Let's consider the outer loop that will be responsible for these five lines of the table.

```
String output ="table of powers \n";
output =IO.concatenate(output," N   2    3    4    5       6 \n");
N = 1.0;
while (N <= 5)
{
```

generate a display of 6 powers of N
and concatenate onto **output**

```
    N = N + 1.0;
}
```

Let's now consider the responsibility of the nested oval. This can be accomplished with another loop: one iteration for each power of *N*. Each successive power of *N* is just *N* times the previous power. The first value output is N^1, which of course is just *N*. The loop must output six values and then an end of line:

```
count = 0.0;
power = 1.0;
while (count < 6.0)
{   power = power * N;
    output = IO.concatenate (output, "    ");
    output = IO.concatenate (output, power);
    count = count+1.0;
}
output = IO.concatenate (output, "\n");
```

This is often an effective way to approach nested loops and is known as *top-down design*. We will return to this topic in the next chapter. When using nested loops, it is often helpful to the reader if you place a comment at the end of each loop indicating which expression is controlling the loop. The completed class is written by doing a little pasting and adding declarations for the variables utilized (Listing 2.X).

Listing 2.X

```
// A class to generate a table of powers for N = 1 to 5
public class power_table
{  public static void main (String[] args)
   {  double count = 0.0, power = 1.0, N = 1.0;
      String output =  "table of powers \n";
      output = IO.concatenate (output, "   N     2      3       4       5       6 \n");
      N = 1.0;

      while (N <= 5)
      {  count = 0.0;
         power = 1.0;
         while (count < 6.0)
         {  power = power * N;
            output = IO.concatenate (output, "  ");
            output = IO.concatenate (output, power);
            count = count+1.0;
         }
         N = N + 1.0;
         output = IO.concatenate (output, "\n");
      }

      IO.showMessage (output);
      System.exit(0);
   }
}
```

The execution of this class produces a display like the following. The columns are not quite aligned, but it is not too bad for our first try at multiline output displays!

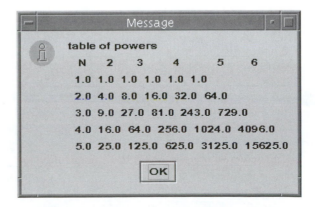

2.7 Example project

Suppose a grading class is needed to calculate the average grade for a list of 25 students. Each student has anywhere from 2 to 10 different grades. The class is to output a summary table indicating the number of As, Bs, Cs, Ds, and Fs. We will use a flat grading scale where As are 90 and above, Bs are 80 up to less than 90, and so on.

The input data are organized so that each individual student is represented by a list of numbers on a single line. The first number is a student ID, and the rest of the numbers are grades ending with a sentinel value of −1.0. For example, here is some possible input (for the first four students):

```
2345 89.4 91.3 67.8 83.5 75.2 -1.0
3456 75.0 57.6 81.0 65.0 -1.0
4567 98.2 93.4 81.2 79.3 87.5 88.5 95.6 97.4 -1.0
7890 73.0 65.8 83.5 87.2 -1.0
  .  .  .
```

The output might be a display box containing something like the following:

```
grade summary:   A 4, B 6, C 10, D 4, F 1
```

Let's start with the declarations for variables we think we might need for the class:

```
double A=0.0, B=0.0, C=0.0, D=0.0, F=0.0; // grade counts
double ave, sum, grade, grade_count;// grade calculation vars
double ID;                           // student ID number
double count;                    // loop counter for 25 students
```

Using the top-down approach, let's first look at a segment that could be used to process the entire list of students. The actual work of processing a single student will be left as a symbolic oval:

```
count = 0.0;
while (count < 25.0)
    {
```

(process a student to calculate "average" grade.)

(determine grade and increment the appropriate grade count.)

```
        count = count + 1.0;
    }
```

(build output message to display grade data.)

Now we need to flesh out the first oval that has the job of processing a single student. The first input number is the student ID, and the rest of the numbers are a sentinel list of grades. We will use a summing loop to add them and count the number of grades. The average is then this sum divided by the grade count:

```
ID = IO.readDouble ("enter ID: ");
grade_count = 0.0;
sum = 0.0;
grade = IO.readDouble ("enter a grade (end each student's list with -1):");
while (grade > 0.0)
{    sum = sum + grade;
     grade_count = grade_count + 1.0;
     grade = IO.readDouble ("enter a grade: ");
}
ave = sum / grade_count;
```

Notice that we reset sum to zero at the top of the loop rather than in the declaration. That is because it needs to start over for each of the 25 students, not just the first. Now let's flesh out the second oval. We will use a sequence of nested **if** statements to test which grade category this average falls within and then increment that category:

```
if (ave >= 90.0)
    A = A + 1.0;
else if (ave >= 80.0)
    B = B + 1.0;
else if (ave >= 70.0)
    C = C + 1.0;
else if (ave >= 60.0)
    D  = D + 1.0;
else F = F + 1.0;
```

The final class is now written by pasting these segments in the appropriate places (Listing 2.XI):

Listing 2.XI

```
// Calculate 25 average student grades, report summary
public class grade_summary
{   public static void main (String[] args)

    {    double A=0.0, B=0.0, C=0.0, D=0.0, F=0.0;    // grade counts
         double ave, sum, grade=0.0, grade_count;     // grade calculation vars
         double count;                                // loop counter for 25 students
         String output;                               // output message variable

         count = 0.0;
         while (count < 25.0)                          // loop over 25 students
         {   grade_count = 0.0;
```

```
                sum = 0.0;
                grade = IO.readDouble ("enter a grade (end each student's list with -1): ");
                while (grade > 0.0)                         // loop through list of grades
                {    sum = sum + grade;
                     grade_count = grade_count + 1;
                     grade = IO.readDouble ("enter a grade: ");
                }                                           // end of (grade > 0.0) loop
                ave = sum / grade_count;                    // calc this student's grade
                if (ave >= 90.0)                            // add a count to appropriate
                    A = A + 1.0;                            //    grade category
                else if (ave >= 80.0)
                    B = B + 1.0;
                else if (ave >= 70.0)
                    C = C + 1.0;
                else if (ave >= 60.0)
                    D  = D + 1.0;
                else F = F + 1;
                count = count + 1.0;                              // bottom of (count < 25) loop

        }

        output = "A's ";                                    // build output message
        output = IO.concatenate (output, A);
        output = IO.concatenate (output, "   B's ");
        output = IO.concatenate (output, B);
        output = IO.concatenate (output, "   C's ");
        output = IO.concatenate (output, C);
        output = IO.concatenate (output, "   D's ");
        output = IO.concatenate (output, D);
        output = IO.concatenate (output, "   F's ");
        output = IO.concatenate (output, F);
        IO.showMessage (output);
        System.exit(0);
    }
}
```

2.8 Summary

KEY TERMS   Several new terms were introduced in this chapter:

1. *conditional statement*—an expression that is either true or false, often used in an **if** statement.

2. *flow of control*—the flow of execution or the order in which statements are executed.

3. *relational expression*—a true/false condition using the relational operators.

4. *relational operators*—<, >, <=, >= (more to be learned later).

5. *loop*—the repeated execution of a statement or block of statements.

6. *indefinite loop*—a loop where the exact number of iterations or repeats cannot be predicted by examining the class code.

7. *sentinel*—a special input value that indicates an indefinite loop should terminate.

8. *infinite loop*—a loop that never finishes or exits.

9. *counted loop*—a loop that uses an incrementing variable to maintain a running count of the number of loop iterations.

10. *condition variable*—a class variable used in a loop condition to represent the combination of several different relations and which is tested and changed using multiple **if** statements within the loop. Also known as a flag.

11. *concatenate*—joining one item (**String**, literal, message) onto the end of another.

12. *carriage return*—a special character sequence of "\n" indicating a new line.

CONCEPTS   The syntax forms introduced in this chapter covered two new statements: the **if** and the **while**.

```
if ( expression )
    statement
else
    statement
```

```
while ( expression )
    statement
```

Most commonly, the expression tested for the **if** and **while** is a relational comparison. Four relational operators for comparison expressions were introduced.

>   greater than

<   less than

>=   greater than or equal to

<=   less than or equal to

A common use of the **while** is for a loop that is used to process an indefinite list of input values ending with a sentinel value. This loop has the following form:

```
variable = IO.readDouble (message);
while (expression comparing variable with sentinel)
{    calculations or processing;
     variable = IO.readDouble (message);
}
```

Another use of the `while` is for a loop that executes a counted or definite number of times. This loop has the following form:

```
count = 0.0;
while (count < number of iterations )
{    calculations or processing;
     count = count + 1.0;
}
```

It is possible to initialize a variable as part of a declaration statement by following the variable name with an assignment operator and a value.

Two important tips to class development were given:

1. To make a class more readable, indentation of nested statements and alignment of opening and closing braces should be consistent.

2. A good first step to designing a class solution is to first write the user's manual defining how the class and user will interact and what the class will produce or calculate from the input.

Table 2.3   Example segments

`if (age <= 56.0)`
`   IO.showMessage ("young");`
`else`
`   IO.showMessage ("old");`
	if age is less than or equal to 56, output young; otherwise output old.

`sum = 0.0;`
`while (sum < 10.0)`
`   sum = sum + 1.0;`
	Start sum at 0.
	While sum is less than 10, continue to add 1.0 to sum.

`age = IO.readDouble ("enter age: ");`
`while (age < 25.0)`
`{ IO.showMessage ("valid age");`
`   age = IO.readDouble ("enter age: ");`
`}`
	Read a value for age.
	While input values are less than 25, output `valid age`. When not less, continue ...

2.9 Exercises

Short-answer questions

1. A statement that a class uses to choose between two alternative formulas is called a _____ statement.
2. A true/false test of a pair of values or variables is called a _____.
3. A loop that repeats a fixed or predetermined number of times is called a _____ loop.

4. A loop where the exact number of repeats or repetitions is not known is called a _____ loop.

5. To aid in class design, the user's manual is often written (before or after) the class.

6. If the user is to first enter the count for a list of values (followed by the values themselves), the programmer would use a _____ loop.

7. If the user is to enter a sentinel value at the end of an indefinite list of values, the programmer would use a _____ loop.

8. List and explain the four relational operators presented in this chapter.

9. Will the following comparisons return true or false? Assume $a = 4.0$ and $b = 3.0$:
   a. $(a < b)$
   b. $(a >= b)$
   c. $(a > b)$
   d. $(a < 4.0)$
   e. $(a >= 4.0)$

10. Draw a symbolic diagram or flowchart of a class segment that could be used to output the message "pass" or "fail" for a given test score. Assume 65 and above is a passing score.

11. Draw a symbolic diagram or flowchart of a class segment that could be used to output a letter grade for a test score. Assume 90–100 is an A, 80 up to less than 90 is a B, 70 up to less than 80 is a C, and so on.

12. What would be a good sentinel value for the following indefinite-list input data?
   a. a list of student ages
   b. a list of mean temperature differences between consecutive days
   c. a list of daily gas mileage rates for a company car
   d. a list of daily checking account balances

13. Give a section of code that could be used to
   a. output the word "yes" if the variable cost is less than 0.0 (otherwise do nothing).
   b. output the word "yes" if the variable cost is greater than 0.0 but not greater than 100.0 (otherwise do nothing).

14. Give a section of code that could be used to output the word "yes" if the variable cost is greater than 100.0 or output the word "no" if cost is less than or equal to 100.0.

15. Give a section of code that could be used to input and sum a list of exactly 25 values.

16. What would be the output result of the following class segments?
   a. double n;

```
n=0.0;
while (n<10.0);
{    IO.showValue ("n is: ", n);
     n = n+2.0;
}
```

   b. double n, k;

```
        String output = " ";
        n=0.0;   k=0.0;
        while (n<4.0)
        {   while (k<2.0)
            {   output = IO.concatenate (output, n);
                output = IO.concatenate (output, ", ");
                output = IO.concatenate (output, k);
                output = IO.concatenate (output, "\n");
                k = k+1.0;
            }
            n = n+1.0;
        }
        IO.showMesssage (output);
```

17. Describe the nature of the following syntax errors:

   a. if x > y IO.showMessage ("yes");

```
        else IO.showMessage ("no");
```

   b. if (x >= y)

```
        IO.showMessage ("yes");
        y = y+1.0;
        else IO.showMessage ("no");
```

18. Give a class segment using a condition variable that could be used to sum input values until (a) the sum was greater than 100.0 or (b) a negative sentinel value was input.

19. Give a class segment of nested `if` statements that could be used to output the word "YES" if the variable `age` is (a) less than 100.0 and (b) greater than 25.0. If neither condition is true, the segment should output the word "NO".

20. Give a class segment to input an indefinite list of positive values ending with a negative sentinel value and then output the maximum value read.

Projects

1. Write a class to input a test score in the range 0 to 100.0 and then output the message "passing" if the score is above 65.0 or the message "failing" if the score is less than or equal to 65.0.

2. Modify the class written for Project 1 so that the class will process an entire list of test scores. Assume the test scores will be entered one per line and that the list will end with a negative sentinel score.

3. Modify the class written for Project 2 so that the number of test scores processed and the average of all test scores are output just before the class terminates.

4. Write and test a class to output a letter grade for a given test score using the criteria of Short-Answer Question 1.

5. Modify the class written for Project 4 so that letter grades are output for a list of test scores. Assume test scores will be entered one per line and that the list will end with a negative sentinel score.

6. Modify the class written for Project 4 so that letter grades are output for a list of exactly five test scores. Assume test scores will be entered one per line. After the fifth test score has been processed, the class should automatically terminate.

7. Write and test a complete class to input and sum a list of numbers until any one of the following conditions is true: (a) the sum exceeds 100.0, (b) a negative value is input, or (c) a maximum of 25 numbers have been summed. When the loop terminates, output the sum.

8. Write a class to calculate and output the minimum, maximum, and average of a list of positive test scores. Assume the scores will be entered one per line and that the list will end with a negative sentinel score.

9. Creative Challenge: Project 6 assumes that test scores are all positive. Suppose a class were needed for scores that could take on any value: positive, zero, or negative. Write a class to solve the general problem of finding the average of a list of values (positive, zero, or negative). Assume any value is possible and any number of values may be entered. You have not yet been taught a simple way of solving this problem, so be as creative as you can with what you know. You may need to place some extra requirements on the user or some additional constraints on the class, but get as close to the ideal solution as you can.

10. Creative Challenge: Write a class to calculate the square root of a number N. A square root can be approximated by making an initial guess of the root. This initial guess can be checked by squaring and comparing against the number N. Obviously, the initial guess will probably be quite wrong. A better guess can be calculated from this initial guess using the following formula:

$$nextguess = 0.5\left(lastguess + \left(\frac{N}{lastguess}\right)\right)$$

where N is the number for which a square root is to be calculated. Use 1.0 as your initial guess. This formula allows a previous guess at the root (*lastguess*) to be improved (*nextguess*). Repeat this calculation until the difference between two successive guesses is less than 0.005.

Helper Methods

As we begin to write more complex and involved applications, you will begin to find that they are harder to design, implement, and manage. This chapter presents methods of modularizing complex applications into smaller and more manageable units called methods. Proper use of methods will significantly reduce your workload as a programmer.

3.1 Modular programming concepts

There are many analogies to computer programs in the world around us. Consider the following simple recipe for my wife's homemade rolls:

> Dissolve 1 cup hot water, $\frac{1}{2}$ cup sugar, and $\frac{1}{2}$ cup oil in large bowl.
> Add 3 well-beaten eggs, 2 teaspoons salt, 2 cups flour and mix well.
> Add 1 tbs yeast dissolved in $\frac{1}{4}$ cup warm water and $2\frac{1}{2}$ cups additional flour.
> Mix until well blended. Let sit for 1 hour then cover and refrigerate overnight.
> Roll onto floured board and cut into 2.5-inch circles. Dip into melted butter and fold.
> Let rise on ungreased baking sheet for 2 hours.
> Bake at 400 degrees for 10 minutes or until lightly browned.

The idea of the recipe is that by carefully following the instructions step by step, you can make rolls. If a friend has this set of instructions, we could ask them to make some rolls simply by saying, "Please make rolls," rather than going to the bother of instructing them in each individual step. In essence, we have modularized the action of making rolls, and we might even give this module a name: `makeRolls()`. The parentheses in the name are used here to differentiate this as a *method module* and not a variable. Now if I have a similar recipe for making jam called `makeJam()` and one for making apple butter called `makeAppleButter()`, my wife might leave me a note saying:

Please:

```
makeRolls();

makeJam();

makeAppleButter();
```

Thank you.

This of course implies that I am politely instructed to (a) apply the recipe instructions for making rolls, then (b) apply the recipe instructions for making jam, and finally, (c) apply the recipe instructions for making apple butter. In other words, the line `makeRolls()` implies that I am to use or execute the instructions of this module. In computer science, asking a class to execute the instructions of a method is known as calling or invoking the method. The note is a request that the instructions of the `makeRolls()` module are to be called, followed by calling the `makeJam()` module, followed by calling the `makeAppleButter()` module.

The note would be rather complex and harder to understand if all the required instructions of each recipe were given. Rather, they are modularized into three distinct and independent methods. These methods also represent reusable modules. Next week, my wife might leave a note asking that only rolls be made. Rather than restate the instructions, she would just reuse the method name `makeRolls()`.

KEY TERM
helper method

This analogy is related to computer programs in that we can modularize a block of instructions into a distinct and independent process and give it a representative name. Each time we wish the block of instructions for a method to be executed, we can invoke the method by referring to it by the given method name. Such methods that support `main()` are called *helper methods* in this text. First, we will examine how helper methods are written in Java and then how such methods can be used to simplify and better manage the creation of complex applications and classes.

The `main()` programs we have written so far have all been methods themselves. To write helper methods in Java, we follow a similar format but give these additional methods new names. The name `main()` is reserved for the first method to be executed when the class is run. Refer back to the first syntax form box of Chapter 1 (repeated here for convenience).

CONCEPT
defining methods

Notice that there is a location between the `public class` line and the `public static void main` line where definitions may be placed. (You will see in a later chapter that methods may be placed in other locations, but there are concerns we do not wish to address just yet.) Formally, a method is a kind of definition. When you write or specify a method, we say you are "defining" the method.

```
public class class_name
{ definitions and declarations
  public static void main (String[] args )
     {     declarations and statements
     }
}
```

Syntax form

3.2 Top-down design with methods

The general format you will use to define a helper method is given in the following syntax form box:

```
access static type method_name ( parameters )
{ declarations and statements
}
```

Syntax form

As in other chapters, the items in italics are to be replaced with specific items of the programmer's choosing. The *access* defines who is able to invoke or call this method. For now, we will use the keyword **public**—indicating any other method may invoke this method. (You'll see later that there are instances where you will wish to restrict who may use the method.) We will initially use the reserved word **void** for the method type (as we have done with the main() methods or classes we have written so far).

CONCEPT

a convention for naming methods

The name given to a method (*method_name*) must follow the same rules as those for a variable name. We should give methods names that describe in some way what the purpose of each method is. It is usually very helpful to begin a method name with a lowercase letter but to capitalize other words within the name. This has become a common convention in Java. In that way, it is immediately obvious which class names are associated with variables and which are associated with methods. Notice also that a method name is always followed by a set of parentheses.

The *parameters* item in the syntax form is new. Parameters are optional and not every method will have them. The parentheses are required, however, even if there are no parameters inside. (We will return to parameters.)

This concept of modularization can be very helpful when designing a complex application class. While writing the `main()` method, a programmer can refer to a module of instructions using a method name. Rather than deal with the details of how these module instructions are to be written, a programmer often simply refers to the method *abstractly* and continues with the bigger picture of writing the `main()` method instructions. In other words, a programmer may replace a pseudocode oval in a preliminary design with a method.

For example, suppose an application class is needed to display important proprietary information to a client. In this case, let's assume a company has just developed a new nonstick frying pan coating called Tufflon. The application might first require the client to accept an agreement to hold the information confidential prior to displaying the data. After the data are displayed, the application might again remind the client that the information is confidential.

The programmer might begin with a general English outline of the steps this class needs to take:

1. Get the client's agreement.

2. Display the information.

3. Remind the client not to share the information.

Since each of these steps probably represents many statements, the programmer might choose to use a method for each one. In addition, the first and third steps also represent processes that might be useful in future application classes. The `main()` method can now be written using chosen method names:

```
public class ProprietaryInfo
{
```

```
                                          needed method definitions
```

```
    public static void main(String[] args)
    {   verifyAgreement();
        displayInfo();
        remindDoNotShare();
    }
}
```

Notice that whenever a method is invoked or called, the name of the method is followed by a set of parentheses. This is important and allows the compiler to know you wish a method to be invoked and that you are not referring to a variable.

The smaller problems associated with each method can now be worked on separately. (In fact, they could be worked on by three different programmers.) In effect, the programmer has applied a divide-and-conquer strategy, dividing a complex problem into separate modules and then attacking each module independently. The three methods might be written as follows:

```
public static void verifyAgreement()
{  String agree = "This information is proprietary \n";
   agree = IO.concatenate (agree, "By choosing OK, you agree \n");
   agree = IO.concatenate (agree, "to hold this information confidential");
   IO.showMessage (agree);
}

public static void displayInfo()
{  String info = "The secret to getting Tufflon to stick to a frying pan \n";
   info = IO.concatenate (info, "is to first coat the metal with #4 glue");
   IO.showMessage (info);
}

public static void remindDoNotShare()
{  IO.showMessage ("Remember, do not share this information!");
}
```

These method bodies should be placed after the class definition as in Listing 3.I:

Listing 3.I

```
// An application class to display a proprietary information message
public class ProprietaryInfo
{
    public static void verifyAgreement()
    {  String agree = "This information is proprietary \n";
       agree = IO.concatenate (agree, "By choosing OK, you agree \n");
       agree = IO.concatenate (agree, "to hold this information confidential");
       IO.showMessage (agree);
    }
    public static void displayInfo()
    {  String info = "The secret to getting Tufflon to stick to a frying pan \n";
       info = IO.concatenate (info, "is to first coat the metal with #4 glue");
       IO.showMessage (info);
    }
    public static void remindDoNotShare()
    {  IO.showMessage ("Remember, do not share this information!");
    }
    public static void main (String[] args)
    {  verifyAgreement();
       displayInfo();
       remindDoNotShare();
       System.exit(0);
    }
}
```

EXPERIMENT

What would happen if parentheses are left off a method call?

3.3 Methods that return a value

CONCEPT

returning values

Often, a method is used to perform some task or process *and then return a result* for the main method (or other calling method) to use. This is accomplished by (a) specifying the *type* of result to be returned and (b) using the **return** statement to cause a value (of the specified type) to be handed back to the main method (or some other calling method). You will learn of many different types in a later chapter. For now, the only types you are familiar with are **double** and **String**. The **return** statement is simple; it consists of the reserved word **return** and the single value or expression result to be returned:

> **return** *expression* ;
>
> **Syntax form**

The expression is commonly placed within parentheses, but that is not required. For example, suppose we need an application that can be used to calculate the monthly payments on a range of loan periods (number of months to payoff). The user is expected to provide the loan amount and interest rate and the range of loan periods (from 0 to 72 months). The class is to generate a table of monthly payments. A programmer might start with the following first design:

> Get the loan amount. Be sure it is a positive value.

> Get the loan interest rate. Be sure it is a positive value.

> Get the starting period. Be sure it is a positive value.

> Get the ending period. Be sure it is a positive value.

> Output the monthly payment for each loan period from start to end.

The programmer would notice that the first four steps are very similar and might use a single helper method to accomplish these steps. The next step might then be to refine the outline using Java code and use methods for these first steps that represent details that have not yet been worked out. The first four steps might call a method named getPosAmount() as shown next. (We'll ignore the last pseudocode oval for now.)

```
amount = getPosAmount();
rate = getPosAmount();
startperiod = getPosAmount();
endperiod = getPosAmount();
. . .
```

Notice that the instructions associated with the getposAmount() method are being reused! Instead of restating these instructions four different times, we simply call the method four times. Our class is significantly smaller than it would have been had we repeated the instructions. A possible implementation of the getPosAmount() method is given in Listing 3.II. Notice that the type of the helper method is not **void** but **double**, indicating that the method is to do a job *and return a decimal answer to the calling class.* The value to be returned is specified in the **return** statement.

Listing 3.II

```
// getPosAmount()  Inputs and returns a positive value
public static double getPosAmount()
{   double temp;
    temp = IO.readDouble ("Enter a positive value: ");
    while (temp < 0.0)
    {  temp = IO.readDouble ("**Negative value, enter a positive value: ");
    }
    return (temp);
}
```

This method prompts for and inputs a value from the user and then places the value into variable temp. If the value is less than zero, the method responds by warning the user of an entry error and reprompts for another value in a loop. This loop continues to reprompt and accept a new value until the user finally enters a positive value. This value (in variable temp) is then returned. An example of the execution of this method would look like this:

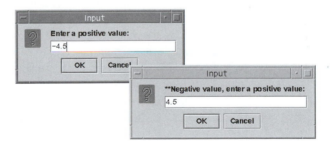

The code of this method could be copied into each of the main() method sections corresponding to steps 1 through 4 of the English outline, but look how much smaller and simpler the application would be when the code is made general in a method that is reused for each of these four steps.

EXPERIMENT

What would happen if the calling program does not assign or use the returning value of a method?

3.4 Helper method parameters

Frequently, a method needs some additional information to complete its task. For example, suppose the statement of the problem is refined to more carefully ensure that valid input is being used: The loan amount must be between 0 and 30,000. The interest rate must be between 0 and 1.0. The starting period must be between 1 and 71. The ending period must be between the starting period and 72. The first design might be:

Get the loan amount. Be sure it is between 0 and 30,000.

Get the loan interest rate. Be sure it is between 0 and 1.0.

Get the starting period. Be sure it is between 1 and 71.

Get the ending period. Be sure it is between starting period and 72.

Output the monthly payment for each loan period from start to end.

KEY TERM
argument

The first four steps again involve getting a value from the user, but now we are interested in verifying that it lies within a known range. These four steps are still similar, but they have different values that define a correct range. Values that are to be passed to a method for use in doing the required job are called *arguments*. Argument values are passed to a method when it is called simply by placing them inside the parentheses after the method name. These arguments then are automatically copied into the method before it begins execution (as will be illustrated in a moment).

What about the actual table calculation? Let's also call a method for this last design pseudocode oval. This last method will need to know the starting period and the ending period to produce a table:

```
amount = getValueBetween (0.0, 30000.0);
rate = getValueBetween (0.0, 1.0);
startperiod = getValueBetween (1.0, 71.0);
endperiod = getValueBetween (startperiod, 72.0);
calcTable (startperiod, endperiod);
```

CONCEPT
use of method
return value

In each step, the method is called and passed values to be used in the statements of the method. The single value returned by the method is then stored into an appropriate variable. Actually, *the value returned by a method can be used in any expression just as the value of a constant might be used.* The following line would output the value returned by the method call (but fail to save it for later use):

```
IO.showValue("the value is: ", getValueBetween(0.0, 30000.0) );
```

The next instruction would multiply the value returned by a method call by 5.0, add 3.0, and save the result in variable demo:

```
double demo = getValueBetween (0.0, 30000.0) * 5.0 + 3.0;
```

These two instructions are only for demonstration; of course they have no use in the loan class that is being developed.

A method is written to accept values being passed into it from a list of arguments by defining the variables that are to receive these values between the parentheses of the method heading or title. Refer back to the syntax form box for methods at the beginning of this chapter. These variables are known as parameters (as mentioned previously). Listing 3.III gives the getValueBetween () method needed by the programmer in the design above. We'll ignore the code for the calcTable () method for now or leave it as an exercise for the student.

When the getValueBetween () method is called, the first argument in the call is copied into the first parameter, the second argument is copied into the second parameter, and so on for as many parameters as are defined. The number of argument values passed to a method must match the number of corresponding parameters listed in the method definition. At this point in your career, an argument may be a constant, a variable, or even an expression. The variable name of a parameter may be the same as or different from the corresponding argument.

Listing 3.III

```
// Loan payment table calculator
public class LoanTable
{
    // getValueBetween()   Inputs and returns a value that is between
    // parameters min and max.
    // IN:        min -- the minimum acceptable input
    //            max -- the maximum acceptable input

    public static double getValueBetween (double min, double max)
      { double temp, accept;
        String message = "Enter a value between ";
        message = IO.concatenate (message, min);
        message = IO.concatenate (message, " and ");
        message = IO.concatenate (message, max);
        temp = IO.readDouble (message);
        accept = 1.0;
        while (accept > 0.0)
        {   if (temp >= min)
                if (temp <= max) accept = 0.0;
                else ;
            else ;
            if (accept > 0.0)
            {   temp = IO.readDouble ("** illegal value, enter again: ");
```

```
          }
        else ;
      }
    return (temp);
  }


  public static void calcTable (double startperiod, double endperiod)
  { . . .   // to be written
  }


  public static void main (String[] args)
  {  double amount, rate, startperiod, endperiod;

     amount = getValueBetween (0.0, 30000.0);
     rate = getValueBetween (0.0, 1.0);
     startperiod = getValueBetween (1.0, 71.0);
     endperiod = getValueBetween (startperiod, 72.0);
     calcTable (startperiod, endperiod);
  }
}
```

In this listing, the parameter variables that are to accept the argument values being passed to the helper method (when it is invoked) are declared inside the parentheses following the method name in the place where the method is actually written or defined. When a method is invoked or called, argument values are placed inside the parentheses to be passed to the method and used.

Thus, when a method begins, the parameters will already contain initial values—copies of the argument values passed to the method when it was invoked. When this method getValueBetween() is called, there must always be two values between the parentheses. The first value will be copied into the variable min, and the second value will be copied into the variable max. Consider Figure 3.1. This figure is an attempt to diagram the action of calling the method getValueBetween(). The top section diagrams what occurs when the method is called. If variable x is 5.5 and y is 7.8 when this method is called, these two values are copied into min and max, respectively. If the user enters 2.3 into temp, the method outputs the message ** il-legal value, enter again: and awaits another user input. If the second time the user enters 6.5, which is between min and max, the value is accepted. The bottom section shows what occurs when the method returns the value of temp (6.5) back to the main method to be copied into the variable z.

Notice that the opening and closing braces of Listing 3.III are carefully lined up one above the other. Statements that are part of the same block are indented the same amount. Subordinate statements that are part of an **if** statement are indented beyond the parent **if**. These are part of good programming style, as we have mentioned. They definitely make the class much easier for others to read and follow.

KEY TERM
comment header

Notice also that the parameters of the helper method have special comments associated with them at the top of the method. In general, a good programmer is expected to place a block of comment lines at the top of each and every method. This comment block should, at a minimum, document and describe (a) what is expected to be passed into the method as parameters, (b) what the method is to accomplish, and (c) what the method is expected to return for the calling method to utilize. Naturally, the programmer may not know exactly what the values of the parameters and arguments will be when the method is executed. However, he or she can still document what these parameters and the return value will represent and what the legal range of each should be. This is typically called the *comment header*.

The method parameters are labeled with the word IN within this comment header of Listing 3.III. This is to remind the reader that the method only receives copies of the corresponding arguments when the method is called. For example, in the diagram of Figure 3.1, the values of 5.5 and 7.8 are passed from the variables x and y in the main method into the method parameters min and max. If the method were to change the value of variable min for some reason, this would *have no effect on the variable x in the main method.*

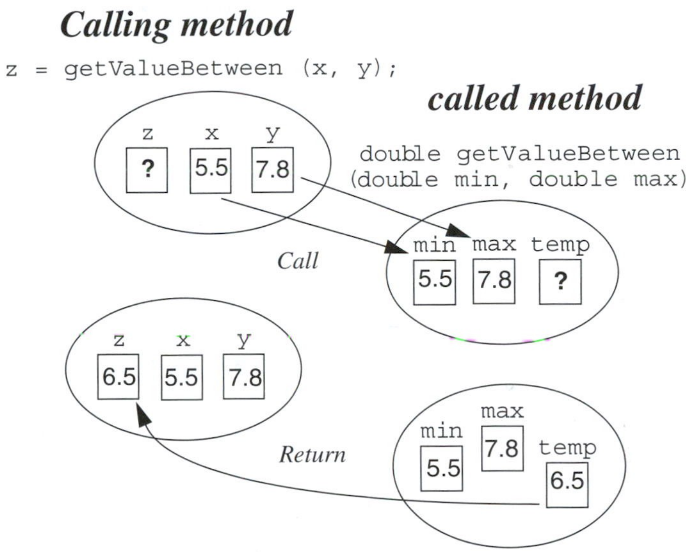

Figure 3.1 Parameter passing and method value return

3.5 **Scope of variables**

CONCEPT

method variables are local

Note that in Figure 3.1, the getValueBetween() and calling method variables are shown inside separate ovals. The purpose is to illustrate that these are separate methods, and *each has its own separate set of variables.* Normally, the only variables that a method statement should reference are those that are declared in the same method. (There are methods of declaring variables that both can share, but this is a future topic. In addition, those methods are often avoided in a well-designed class.) Remember that main() is also a method and the same rule applies; the main() statements cannot not reference any of the variables declared in any of the methods. The means of sharing values is by passing arguments into parameters and by methods returning values:

```
public static double SomeMethod (Double x)
{   double y;
    y = z * x;                  // not valid: z is not in this method!
    return (y);
}
public static void main(String[] args)
{   double a, b;
    a = 5.9;
    y = a;                      // not valid: y is not in this method!
    b = SomeMethod (a);
    . . .
```

CONCEPT
deallocation of
local variables

What if a `main()` method and a helper method have variables of the same name? They are separate and distinct. What happens to helper method variables when the method returns? They are removed from program memory. In other words, *new memory space for method variables is allocated each time the method is called and deallocated when the method exits.*

Consider the example of the following section of code. Both the `main()` method and the helper method have a variable named `cost`. The value of the `main()` method `cost` is passed into the helper method to become the value of the method's variable cost. Even though the helper method changes its own value of `cost`, that change has no effect on the `main()` method cost.

```
public static void SomeMethod (double cost)
{   cost = 7.2;
    IO.showValue ("In SomeMethod(), cost is: ", cost);
}
public static void main (String[] args)
{   double cost;
    cost = 15.5;
    SomeMethod (cost);
    IO.showValue ("In main(), cost is:", cost);
}
```

The output of this code would be display boxes showing the following:

```
In SomeMethod(), cost is 7.2
In main(), cost is 15.5
```

3.6 Constants

CONCEPT
declaring constants

Often a value used within a method is always a constant. For example, the numeric value of *pi* doesn't change. Rather than write this numeric constant into each expression calculation in a large class, it is often simpler to declare a name or identifier to be associated with each value that will not change. This is accomplished by using the qualifier **final** as in the following syntax form box:

---

final *type identifier* = *value* ;

Syntax form

CONCEPT
naming constants

An identifier is just a name that follows the same rules you learned for variable names. To help you remember that this is a special identifier that will never change in value, it is a good idea to use a name in all capital letters:

```
final double PI = 3.14159;
```

The identifier PI can now be used throughout the method in which it is declared. If the method were ever to attempt to change the value associated with this name, a compile-time error message would result.

```
PI = 3.0;
```
WRONG!

Names that are associated with **final** constants must be initialized at declaration with the value they are intended to represent. They may never subsequently be assigned another value. Suppose a class needs to contain several summing loops, each for a list of the same number of values. This loop count could easily be defined in a **final** variable and referred to by each loop:

```
final double  LOOPCOUNT = 25;
double count1, count2, count3 ;
. . .
while (count1 < LOOPCOUNT);
. . .
while (count2 < LOOPCOUNT);
. . .
while (count3 < LOOPCOUNT);
. . .
```

Now, if the class is ever modified to change to another size list, only the declaration and initialization for LOOPCOUNT need to be updated. Otherwise, the new programmer making the modification would need to search throughout the method looking for all situations where this value was referenced (and hope that all were identified).

In general, a good programmer will identify all the constants in a class and declare **final** identifiers for each. Throughout the application class, these constants are referred to by name. Modification of the class at a later date becomes much simpler, and the class becomes much more readable and self-documenting for others. For example, suppose an application has many different loops that must all execute 25 times. A programmer wisely defines a **final** identifier LOOPCOUNT and references it in each loop condition. Now suppose the programmer needs to change all these loops to execute 50 times. Rather than edit each of the many loops, he or she can edit only the single line that declares and initializes LOOPCOUNT.

Naturally, if a constant is declared within a method, it may only be referenced inside that method, just as with other variables. Suppose a constant is needed throughout an entire class. Does it need to be redefined within each? The answer is no. If you reexamine the syntax form box at the beginning of this chapter, you will see that definitions may be placed after the **public class** line. A definition can be a constant declaration as well as helper methods. Since these declarations are not within any one method, they become *global* to the rest of the class that follows; any method below the global definitions in the class can reference these identifiers. These are called *global constants*.

In the following example file, the globally defined constant PI can be referenced and used in any of the class methods: method1(), method2(), or the main() method.

```
public class Demo
{   final double PI = 3.14159;   // a globally-defined constant

    public static void method1 ()
    {  . . .
    }
    public static void method2 ()
    {  . . .
    }
    public static void main(String[] args)
    {  . . .
    }
}
```

If **final** identifiers can be declared globally, why can't regular variables also be declared globally? Well, they can—it just isn't a good idea at this point. For the moment, you will find that your application classes are easier to write and debug if you avoid global variables. There will be a purpose and need for them in later chapters.

Can you intermix method and constant declarations? Well yes, but it may not be a good idea. The simplest form to follow is to first declare all constants, then define all helper methods, and then define the main() method. A reader should have a good idea of where to look to find your constant declarations.

3.7 **Example project**

An interesting problem is encountered when trying to determine how many different combinations or committees of people can be chosen from a group. The formula associated with the number of ways r people can be selected from a group of n is the following:

$$C(n, r) = \frac{n!}{(n-r)!r!}$$

Here the ! math symbol indicates a factorial. The factorial of a number is defined as follows:

$$x! = x(x-1)(x-2)(x-3) \ldots 1$$

So, 5! would be 5(4)(3)(2)(1), or 120. Now, suppose a committee of three is needed out of a group of seven people:

$$C(7, 3) = 7! / (7-3)! \, 3! = 5040 / ((24) \, 6) = 5040 / 144 = 35$$

In other words, there are 35 different committees that can be formed from a group of seven people. An application class to determine combinations would be simple to write if a helper method were available to perform these calculations. If such a method were available, the main() method could resemble the following:

```
public static void main (String[] args)
{   double group_size, committee_size, combinations;


                                   ( prompt user and perform inputs. )


    combinations = combi (group_size, committee_size);


                                   ( echo inputs and display the result. )


}
```

All the main() method does is get input values from the user, call the combi() helper method for the calculation, and display the answer. The helper method itself must in turn calculate three different factorials. The simple approach is to write a factorial() helper method and just call it three times in an expression:

```
public static double combi (double group, double committee)
{   double combinations;
    combinations = factorial (group) /
        (factorial (group - committee) * factorial (committee));
    return (combinations);
}
```

A factorial can be calculated with a loop that counts down until a value of 1 is reached. For each count of the loop, a running product is calculated for decreasing values of the argument n:

```
public static double factorial (double n)
{   double product = 1.0;
    while (n > 1.0)
    {   product = product * n;
        n = n - 1.0;
    }
    return (product);
}
```

Now, let's improve the main() method a bit so that it continually prompts the user for input and performs calculations until the user responds to indicate no further committee calculations are needed. We will also add an **if** statement to verify that the group size is larger than the size of the committee. The entire project with appropriate method header comments would look like Listing 3.IV:

Listing 3.IV

```
// Combinations calculations application class
// Prompts the user for a group and committee size and then calculates
//   number of different committees that can be formed.
public class Combinations
{
    // factorial()  Returns the factorial of the argument n.
    // IN:  n is a positive integer
    public static double factorial (double n)
    {   double product = 1.0;
        while (n > 1.0)
        {   product = product * n;
            n = n - 1.0;
        }
        return (product);
    }

    // combi()  Returns the number of different of committees
    // that could be formed from group
    // IN:  group is a whole-number value greater than committee;
    //        committee is a positive whole-number value.
    public static double combi (double group, double committee)
    {   double combinations;
        combinations = factorial (group) /
        (  factorial (group - committee) * factorial (committee));
        return (combinations);
    }
```

```
public static void main(String[] args)
{   double group_size, committee_size, combinations;
    double done = 1.0;
    while (done > 0.0)
    {   group_size = IO.readDouble ("enter the size of the group: ");
        committee_size = IO.readDouble ("enter committee size: ");
        if (group_size >= committee_size)
        {     combinations = combi (group_size, committee_size);
              IO.showValue ("Possible number of committees is:", combinations);
        }
        else
              IO.showMessage (" ** illegal values; group must be larger");
        done = IO.readDouble ("another calculation? (enter 1 for yes, 0 for no ");
    }
    System.exit(0);
}
}
```

In this class, the helper methods are defined above the main method, but the order really doesn't matter. Here is an example execution for a group of 27 and a committee of 8:

Now, however, suppose we try a very large group and a very small committee. There should be quite a few possible combinations:

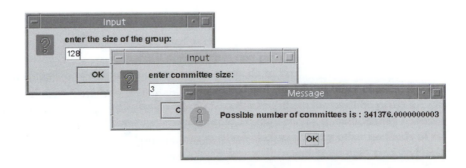

How is that possible? Not only is the number smaller than we expected, it isn't even a whole number! We'll return to this particular problem in Chapter 5. At this time, we'll simply point out that there are limits to the accuracy and range of **double** numbers represented in a Java application. In this particular case, we've exceeded that capability.

Another problem occurs when a group or committee size is entered as something other than a whole number. The class accepts this nonsensical input and dutifully outputs a nonsensical answer! The bottom line is this: We are becoming aware that **double** variables and values have limitations and may not be appropriate in all programming problems. There is a growing need for more capability in expressing data. Fortunately, there are additional variable types that address these concerns. We'll return to this problem.

EXPERIMENT

What would happen if the user enters values such as 5.5 or 9.3? The above class would be in error. How would you check the parameters of the `combi()` method to verify that they were whole numbers? (Chapter 6 will examine this problem.)

3.8 Library classes and helper methods

KEY TERM
packages

Many of the simpler methods you might need in a class have been written before. Such methods are commonly organized into a predefined class. Groups of these classes can be placed in one or more system libraries and made available to class developers. These libraries are usually called *packages*. We'll use the terms package and library interchangeably. All Java development systems provide a set of standard packages and usually also provide one or more specialized libraries of useful methods.

You may think of a package as just a file containing a set of predefined classes and associated helper methods that are generally useful across a variety of applications. Rather than storing the source code version of these classes, libraries usually store only a precompiled version, but that is not particularly important to the following discussion.

Common Java packages

There are numerous library classes and associated helper methods that perform a variety of tasks. As you learn more of the Java language, more of these classes and methods will be introduced. Each development environment usually has a library manual or other such documentation to indicate how these methods are to be used and what they are intended to return.

Packages are organized as a directory structure in Java. This gives a hierarchical representation of the various packages available and helps to organize how different libraries are related. All Java systems have a basic directory set, but not all systems have all packages. New packages are being added all the time. Many libraries are developed by private companies or individuals. Some packages must be purchased, and others are free. Older packages are being replaced with newer packages.

KEY TERM
default library

A basic *default library* of classes and helper methods is available to all Java applications. Nothing special needs to be done to a Java class to utilize this library. (Other libraries must be explicitly referenced so that the Java run-time environment or interpreter knows where to look to find a particular class or method that you are referencing.) For example, the following statement has been used in each application we have written so far:

```
System.exit(0);
```

This is a call to the helper method `exit()` belonging to the **System** class of the default library. If your were to use the following statement

```
exit(0);
```
(WRONG!)

the compiler would look for a helper method of this name within your application class. Since you didn't define this method, it would not be found, and a syntax error would be shown. To specify that you wish the `exit(0)` method defined within the library class `System` to be used, you simply preface the method with the library class within which it is defined. When the compiler encounters this statement, it knows to look in the appropriate library for the needed helper method.

The Math class

The **Math** class is also a part of the default library and contains a variety of useful mathematical functions.Some of the more common helper methods of this library are listed in Table 3.1.

Table 3.1   A few useful Math class helper methods

Method	Argument(s)	Returns (double)
abs()	any number	the absolute value of the argument
sqrt()	any number	the square root of the argument
cos()	any number (in radians)	the cosine of the argument
sin()	any number (in radians)	the sine of the argument
tan()	any number (in radians)	the tangent of the argument
ceil()	any number	the first whole number larger than or equal to the argument
floor()	any number	the first whole number smaller than or equal to the argument
log()	any positive number	the natural log of the argument
exp()	any number	the natural exponent of the argument
pow	any two numbers	the first argument raised to the power of the second argument

The constant `PI` is also available from the `Math` library:

```
IO.showValue ("the value of pi is:", Math.PI);
```

OK, let's do an example with the **Math** library. Suppose you are a known distance from a tall building. Listing 3.V gives an example class that calculates the height of a building and the distance from the observer to the top, given the ground distance from an observer to the building and the angle the observer must look up to see the top. (To convert from degrees to radians, multiply by π and divide by 180.) The formulas are:

$$ht = base \times \tan(angle)$$

$$dist = \sqrt{base^2 + ht^2}$$

Note that even though both the method `calcHypot()` and the `main()` method have variables declared with names `base`, `angle`, and `dist`, they are separate and distinct variables (Listing 3.V):

Listing 3.V

```
// application to calculate the height of a building or tower
public class BuildingHt
{   final static double PI_RADIANS = 0.01745;// pi / 180.0

// calcHypot() A method to calc. and return the hypotenuse
// of a right triangle.
//   IN:     base; the base of the triangle
//           angle; an angle in degrees between the base and hypot.
   public static double calcHypot (double base, double angle)
   {   double radians, ht, dist;
       radians = angle * PI_RADIANS;
       ht = base * Math.tan(radians);
       dist = Math.sqrt (base*base + ht*ht);
       return (dist);
   }

   public static void main(String[] args)
   {   double base, angle, dist;
       base = IO.readDouble ("enter base distance to tower:" );
       angle = IO.readDouble ("enter angle (in degrees):") ;
       dist = calcHypot (base, angle);
       IO.showValue (" distance from observer to top: " , dist);
   }
}
```

Here's an example of this application class for a building that is 1000 feet away and the angle of sight to the top of the building is 60 degrees:

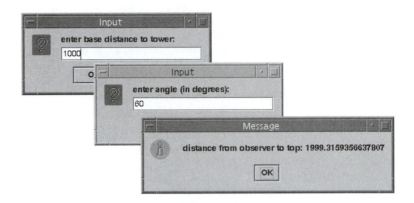

Personal libraries

You can create your own libraries. Your application class can reuse any of the classes (with their associated helper methods) in the same directory as long as the library class is declared **public** and the methods of the library class are declared **public** and **static**. The keyword **public** implies that a method or a class is available for reuse by any other class. The keyword **static** implies that the methods are always available. (There are more formal definitions, but these will suffice for now.) The **IO** class is just such a library. A library class may or may not have a main() method. If it does, it can also be used as an application class by itself. If not, it can only be used as a library of helper methods and constants for other application classes.

For example, suppose we have developed the following class to assist in converting U.S. dollars into the foreign florin currency (Listing 3.VI):

Listing 3.VI

```
// a library class for the conversion of dollars to or from florins
public class Florins
{   public final static double CONVERSION = 3.79;//(I just made this constant up)
    public static double toFlorins (double dollars)
    {   return (dollars * CONVERSION);
    }
    public static double fromFlorins (double florins)
    {   return (florins / CONVERSION);
    }
}
```

If the compiled class file for this source is in our current directory, we can easily convert from dollars to florins in our application class. We can also use the defined CONVERSION constant because it is also **static** and **public**:

```
double dollars = IO.readDouble ("enter dollar amount: ");
IO.showValue ("in florins: ", Florins.toFlorins(dollars));
IO.showValue ("the conversion rate is: ", Florins.CONVERSION);
```

Specialized libraries

When a library class is used or referenced that is not in the default library or in the current directory, you need to indicate to the compiler where the library file can be found. This is done with the keyword import at the very top of a Java class:

```
import package_name ;
```

Syntax form

As has been mentioned, libraries are organized in a hierarchical manner. A package name consists of a hierarchical path and a specific package file. This hierarchical path is usually not the same as a Windows or UNIX directory path, but the two are related. The provider of the library or package will tell you what package name to use with the keyword **import**.

For example, the java.util.Calendar library class contains a set of universal constants for days of the week and months of the year:

```
import java.util.Calendar;
. . .
IO.showValue ("Friday is the " + Calendar.FRIDAY +
    "th day of the week");
```

You will see more of this in later chapters when we use more specialized libraries.

3.9 Summary

KEY TERMS   Terms associated with methods that were introduced in this chapter are the following:

1. *helper method*—a module of Java statements that can be invoked from the main() or other method using the name of the method.

2. *argument*—a value to be passed to a method (when the method is invoked) and represented by a corresponding parameter.

3. *parameter*—a special method variable that is initialized with a corresponding argument value when the method is invoked.

4. *comment header*—a block of documenting comments at the top of a method definition that clarifies the use of parameters and the intent of the method.

5. *package*—a collection of useful classes and methods that can be invoked or reused in an application class.

6. *default library*—a set of Java packages common to all Java systems that is automatically referenced by the Java compiler and run-time interpreter.

CONCEPTS

In this chapter, you learned that one method of simplifying a complex class is to modularize operations into *helper methods* that break a problem into more manageable pieces. Each problem piece can then be attacked separately. At this point in your experience, the general form of a helper method is:

```
access static type method_name ( parameters )
{   declarations and statements
}
```

Several important concepts were presented concerning the use of methods. The *access* of a method determines what other methods may invoke it. If a method is **public**, all other methods are allowed to use it. If a method does not return a value, the type is **void**. If it returns a decimal number, the type can be **double**. The value returned by a method can be utilized in any expression similar to how a simple constant is used.

Variable values can be passed to a method as arguments. The arguments passed to a method must match the number and order of parameters a method expects. Method parameters must be declared within the parentheses following the method name in the head or top of the actual implementation.

Identifiers declared inside a method are local to that method and cannot be referenced by the `main()` method (or other methods). Each time a method is called, its local variables are reallocated or created. When a method exits, its local variables are deallocated or destroyed.

Libraries or packages consist of prewritten classes and methods that are generally useful for a variety of programming problems. If a method to be referenced is not in the default libraries, a Java class may require an **import** statement at the top to indicate where the library containing this method may be found.

Identifier names can be declared to hold constant values through use of the **final** declaration qualifier. Such **final** identifiers declared immediately after the **class** definition become globally accessible to all methods in the class. **Public** final identifiers that are globally accessible are also available to other classes.

Several important tips regarding good programming practice were presented. It is important to choose descriptive names for methods to improve the readability of a class. Constants should be defined using the **final** qualifier for a declaration. This allows constants to be symbolically named in a class and makes the class more readable. In addition, later modifications to constants can be made in a central location.

Although constants are often declared to be globally accessible, regular variables should be avoided at this point. Make it a practice to share information with a method only through arguments/parameters and returning method values.

It is a common convention in Java to name helper methods using two or more words—the first word in lowercase letters and all subsequent words capitalized. It is also helpful to form constant identifiers using all capital letters. Following such conventions allows a programmer to quickly determine the nature of an identifier. By way of review, we now have four conventions for naming:

```
double cost;                    //variables in lower case
public class MyApp             //classes capitalize each word
final double PI = 3.14;        //constants in all caps
public static void myMethod() //methods capitalize all but first word
```

Table 3.2   Example segments

`cost = costCalc (5.4);`	Call `CostCalc` and pass the value 5.4. The returning value is to be assigned to `cost`.
`return (age);`	The current method will return the value of `age` to the calling class or method.
`final  double FACTOR = 1.0;`	FACTOR represents the constant 1.0.
`public static double costCalc (double x)` `{ 'double y;`	y and x are only accessible or visible within this method.

3.10 Exercises

Short-answer questions

1. The value to be passed to a method is known as a _____.
2. A variable that receives a copy of a value when a method is called is known as a _____.
3. Briefly explain the difference between *arguments* and *parameters*.
4. A _____ _____ is used to document the use of parameters and the intent of a method.
5. The _____ _____ is a collection of useful methods that are common to all Java systems and automatically referenced by the system.
6. To access an available method or class in a specialized library, the _____ statement file must be included at the top of the application.
7. To specify a method that returns a double value, the method definition should use the word _____ prior to the method name.
8. May variables declared inside a method be referenced or used inside the `main()` method as well?
9. Explain where methods should be declared or defined.
10. Explain where global constant identifiers are typically declared or defined.

11. Give an example statement that could be used in a class to calculate the square root of the variable `distance` using the **Math** library class

12. If a method does not return a value, with what *type* must the method be declared?

13. Identify and explain the syntax error in the following:

```
public static double someMethod (double cost)
{   double cost;
      . . .
}
```

14. Is it possible for two distinct variables in a class to have the same name? Explain.

15. The following method is intended to calculate the payments on a car loan given the number of months to payoff and the interest rate:

```
public static double Payment
              (double num_months, double interest_rate)
              { . . .
              }
```

Show how this method could be used to calculate and output the payments on a 52-month loan at 9 percent. Remember, 9 percent is 0.09.

16. Briefly explain what you would expect to happen if a method has two parameters declared, yet the `main ()` method attempts to call the method with only one argument.

17. Briefly explain the four conventions for naming classes, helper methods, variables, and constants.

18. Suppose an application used for student grading has a maximum of 50 points for each assignment and test. This constant is used throughout the class in all associated helper methods. Declare a globally accessible constant for this value and show how it would be initialized.

19. The following application would like to calculate the cube root of a variable. Suppose there is a Java class called **Roots** with a `cubeRoot ()` helper method that accepts a `double` and returns a `double` (as the cube root). Suppose the **Roots** class (and helper method) is referenced with the following package name:

```
java.special.roots
```

What must be added to the following application so that `cubeRoot ()` is accessible?

```
public static void main (String[] args)
{   double value;
    value = IO.readDouble ("enter value: ");
        IO.showValue ("the cube root is: ", cubeRoot (value));
}
```

20. Briefly explain why it is good practice to use header comments at the top of a method. Propose three different types of information that might be documented in header comments.

Projects

1. Write an application to input a list of numbers representing angle measurements in degrees. Output a table of sines and cosines. The input list should terminate with a negative value. The following input list

   ```
   0.0 5.0 10.0 20.0 30.0 45.0 90.0 -1.0
   ```

   would produce output similar to the following table:

   ```
   angle     sine          cosine
   0.0       0             1.0
   5.0       0.08716       0.99619
   10.0      0.17365       0.98481
   20.0      0.34202       0.93969
   30.0      0.5           0.86603
   45.0      0.70711       0.70711
   90.0      1.0           0
   ```

2. Write an application that inputs a sentinel list of positive angles in degrees and outputs the corresponding angles in radians. Use a helper method named `Radians()` for the conversion.

3. Write a method named `sumOfWholeNums()` that accepts a whole number *num* as a parameter and then calculates and outputs the sum of whole numbers from 1 to *num*. Use this method to output the sums of whole numbers from (a) 1 to 10.0, (b) 1 to 25.0, (c) 1 to 75.0, and (d) 1 to 100.0. For example, the following `main()` method might be used:

   ```
   public static void main(String[] args)
   {   SumOfWholeNums (10.0);
       SumOfWholeNums (25.0);
       SumOfWholeNums (75.0);
       SumOfWholeNums (100.0);
       System.exit(0);
   }
   ```

4. If a person falls from a building of height *h* feet, the altitude *A* of the unfortunate victim at any time *t* can be calculated with this formula:

$$A = h - \frac{32t^2}{2}$$

Write a helper method named `fallTable()` that accepts a building height as a parameter and then outputs a table of victim altitudes for every second of fall (until the victim hits the sidewalk and has a negative altitude). Test this method in an application class that calls `fallTable()` from `main()`.

5. Write a helper method named `convertTemp()` that accepts a Fahrenheit temperature and returns the equivalent temperature in Celsius. Use this method to convert the Fahrenheit temperatures 60.5, 32.0, 0.0, and −5.0 to Celsius. For example, the following `main()` method might be used:

```
public static void main(String[] args)
{   double temp1 = convertTemp (60.5);
    double temp2 = convertTemp (32.0);
    double temp3 = convertTemp(0.0);
    double temp4 = convertTemp (-5.0);
    . . .

}
```

The formula for temperature conversion is $cel = \left(\frac{5}{9}(fahr - 32)\right)$

6. Write an application to solve Creative Challenge problem 9 of Chapter 1 using a method to calculate the volume of a sphere.

7. Write an application to solve Creative Challenge problem 10 of Chapter 1 using a method that accepts pay-rate and hours-worked parameters and returns the appropriate paycheck value. Remember that employees working more than 40 hours receive time and a half for overtime.

8. Assume student grades will be input into an application with one student per line for 20 lines. Each student line will consist of five different grades. The output of the application should consist of (a) the maximum average, (b) the minimum average, and (c) the grand or overall average of the class. Use a helper method named `studentAve()` to input a student's information and return the average of those five grades.

9. Write a method named `loanCost()` that accepts three parameters: the amount of a loan `principal`, the number of months a payment is to be made (`period`), and the interest `rate`. The method should calculate and return the cost of the loan (or the difference between the principal and the total amount to be paid back to the bank). The formula is

$$cost = principal - period \times payment$$

where `payment` is the monthly payment:

$$payment = \left[\frac{rate}{1 - (1 + rate)^{-period}}\right] \times principal$$

Use this method in an application that inputs two loans and outputs the difference in cost between the two loans.

10. Creative Challenge: Suppose an *X*-,*Y*-coordinate system is used to mark the position of a hiker on a map. This two-number position represents the number of miles east (*X*) and north (*Y*) of a central location. If the hiker walks a given distance in a particular compass direction, he or she will be at a new *X,Y* position on the map. Write an application class with useful helper methods that accepts an initial *X,Y* position and then a list of compass directions and distances. The list should terminate with a negative distance as a sentinel. Output the final *X,Y* position of the hiker. For example, the input might be similar to the following

```
125.7    -45.8
5.9      270
10.3     84
-1
```

which would indicate that the hiker began at 125.7 miles east and −45.8 miles north (which is 45.8 miles south) of the central location. The hiker then traveled 5.9 miles in a direction of 270 degrees and then 10.3 miles in a direction of 84 degrees. Remember that compass directions are in degrees, which need to be converted to radians before calling any of the trig. library methods:

$$radians = \frac{degrees \times \pi}{180}$$

Problem Solving and Method Design

Understanding the syntax and rules of Java is only a small part of programming. Problem solving or program design is a vital skill for a programmer. This chapter doesn't introduce any new Java but rather revisits the problem-solving process and presents some modeling and conceptual aids.

4.1 Learning to solve programming problems

The problem solving or class design part of programming cannot (unfortunately) be expressed as a set of rules or fixed steps. It involves analytical as well as creative thinking—logic and imagination. There is no one type of person who is able to learn method design. True, method design comes easier to some, but it can be learned and applied by a fairly wide range of people.

It is not strictly a *left-brain* versus *right-brain* endeavor. Those with a more analytical nature may develop method design abilities in a somewhat different manner than those with a more creative or imaginative nature. Once learned, however, both personality or intellect types are often very effective programmers. It is not uncommon to see a computer science major with a minor in art or music. It is also common that the best students in a computer science class are business, humanities, or social science majors.

Now, some students may initially struggle with method design. Occasionally, a student will have a mind-set against "story" kinds of problems, perhaps from a bad algebra class experience. Once over this little hump, however, they do quite well and often become quite accomplished programmers.

So how does one initially learn method design skills? For most of us, they are learned by *example* and by *experience*. We learn the steps that can be used to solve a certain problem and then apply that experience to future similar problems. We begin to see combinations or sequences of these simpler method designs in more complex problems. We begin to find that new problems are only variations of problems we have solved in the past.

There is no one thought process universally employed to solve programming problems. There are a few mechanisms, tools, and concepts that will aid many of you with method design—and we'll look at these in this chapter. These are only aids, and there is no substitute for good examples and striving to design and program variations of these problems.

4.2 Useful thought processes

Method design or class problem solving is similar to working with a faulty three-burner stove. Suppose you move into a new apartment that has a three-burner stove. For lunch that day, you wish to cook tamales and chili. You place the tamales in one pot on burner 1 and place the chili in a second pot on burner 2. After turning on both burners, you go study while your lunch heats. After a while, you return to find both pots still cold because the stove is broken. You quickly check burner 3 and find that at least that burner still works.

KEY TERM
decomposition

Now you have a problem. There are two pots to heat but only one burner. As an experienced computer scientist, you apply an important principle: *decomposition*. You break a complex problem into a set of simpler problems that can be solved one at a time. Concentrating on just heating the tamales, you move them from burner 1 to burner 3 and heat.

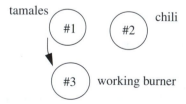

Now you are left with just half the problem: how to heat the chili. *As a computer scientist*, you move the chili from burner 2 to burner 1 *because that is a problem you have solved before!*

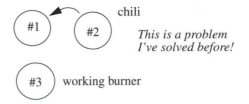

A silly example of course, but it illustrates two useful thought processes: decomposition and using previous experience.

4.3 Basic components

Look for ways to apply your experience. Let's focus on the body of a class and ignore the boilerplate syntax at the top for a moment. Those details and the declarations of variables you have used can be added last.

CONCEPT
basic components

Here is a very important concept: *All programming problems can be solved with a sequence of only six components*. The first three are trivial:

1. input: collect information or data from the outside world.
2. process: calculate or process existing information or data.
3. output: display information or results to the outside world.

A component is one or more Java statements. Think about the class of Chapter 1 to calculate the area of a circle (Listing 1.II). The executable sections were:

```
radius = IO.readDouble ("enter a radius: ");  // output prompt
                                              // and input data

area = 3.14 * radius * radius;        // process or use the data

IO.showValue ("the area is " , area); // output results
```

You have already mastered basic design for each of these three components. You know how to prompt the user to indicate what the class wants. You know how to input values from the user into variables. You understand how to implement a formula. You know how to output results to the user.

Suppose you must design a class to convert feet to meters (Listing 1.VII). You quickly recognize that this is again a variation of your previous experience. What about a class to calculate the square of pi? This class doesn't need to input any information from the outside world because the value of pi doesn't change. The other two statements (process and output) are still needed, however, and are just variations of what you have done before. You are now prepared to solve a wide variety of simple class problems based on your experience with the above circle class.

4.4 Compound design

Now, most programming problems are not simple sequences of the three basic components. They are compound—containing conditions and/or loops. The last three components are:

4. indefinite loop

5. definite loops

6. conditions

Loop designs

Anytime a class needs to process more than a couple of similar inputs or values, a loop is indicated. In Chapter 2, you saw examples of two different kinds of class loops. The first was the indefinite loop. This type of loop was used when the number of repetitions depended on some value calculation or a sentinel input when the loop actually ran. You learned this type of loop was associated with a condition variable. We'll call this component 4:

```
get or calculate the first value of the variable;
while (expression comparing variable with a sentinel value)
{   components to be repeated;
    get or calculate the next value of the variable;
}
```

KEY TERM
pseudocode

Here we used italics and English to represent details to be filled in later. This is known as *pseudocode*. For example, suppose the problem is to calculate the areas of a list of circles. For each circle, the user supplies a radius. After the list of radii has been input, the user inputs a negative number as the sentinel:

```
radius = IO.readDouble ("enter radius: ");
while (radius > 0.0)
{

            calculate and output area using radius.

    radius = IO.readDouble ("enter radius: ");
}
```

If it is helpful to more distinctly separate pseudocode from the actual Java code being designed, draw an oval around it. We didn't bother with the details of the pseudocode—those are basic component details to be left for later. We'll come back to that, and we know we have solved a problem like that in the past.

Now suppose the problem is to calculate and output volumes for a list of boxes. The user is to input height, length, and width for each box. After the list, the user is to input a negative number as a sentinel. OK, this is just a variation of the sentinel loop:

```
height = IO.readDouble ("enter height: ");
if (height > 0.0)
{
```

> *input a width and length.*

> *calculate and volume using height, width and length.*

```
    height = IO.readDouble ("enter height: ");

}
```

Suppose the problem is to calculate the squares of integers from 1 on as long as a square is less than 1000. Again, its' only a variation. The condition variable is calculated rather than input:

```
n = 1.0;
square = n * n;
while (square < 1000.0)
{   IO.showValue ("square is ", square);
    n = n+1;
    square = n * n;
}
```

You might recognize that the first calculation of square when n was 1 didn't really require a multiplication, but it made the class easier to understand. We'll come back to that later. With this fourth sentinel construct (and the first three trivial basic components), you have the experience to solve an even wider variety of programming problem variations.

The second type of repetition was the *counted loop*, which is component 5. This was used whenever a loop was to repeat a specific number of times—that is, when the class would know how many times to repeat a set of components before the loop began:

```
initialize or set the counter variable to 0
while (variable  <  maximum)
{   components to be repeated
    variable = variable + 1.0;
}
```

Suppose that the programming problem is to input a set of exactly five boxes and output the calculated volumes:

```
count = 0.0;
while (count < 5.0)
```

```
{
```

> *input a height, width and length.*

> *calculate a volume using height, width, and length.*

> *output the volume.*

```
    count = count + 1;
}
```

Summing can be done with either loop variation. This is accomplished by initial-izing a summing variable to zero prior to the loop. Within the loop, each new calcu-lation or value is added to the running sum.

```
sum = 0.0
while (. . .
{
sum = sum + value;
}
```

Conditions

As you remember, a condition or `if` statement is used whenever a decision or choice must be made. This is component 6. The decision is made by comparing two values or variables using the `>`, `<`, `>=`, and `<=` operators:

```
if ( compare two values )
{   components to be executed if comparison is true
}
else
{   components to be executed if comparison is false
}
```

As you remember, either of the two sections—the true or false components—could be empty and represented with a single semicolon. Suppose we again look at the problem of calculating a paycheck. An overtime formula is used if an individual works more than 40 hours and a standard formula if not:

```
hours = IO.readDouble ("enter hours: ");
if (hours <= 40.0)
{
```

> *calculate pay using overtime formula.*

```
}
else
```

```
{

```
> *calculate pay using regular formula.*

```
}
IO.showValue ("pay is ", pay);
```

If you think about it, all other conditions' examples you have seen are variations of this solution.

4.5 Top-down design

Your study of the previous chapters has given you examples and experience with the six basic components of a programming problem solution. Some future problems you will see may require quite a large sequence of these six components. You will learn alternative ways of specifically expressing these components and the data or variables they use in more compact ways appropriate to more complex problems in future chapters.

The concept of the six basic components is quite fundamental. *Every programming problem can be solved with a sequence of the six components.* Notice, however, that the two loop components and the condition component contain nested components themselves, which may in turn be other sequences. This possibility of loops within loops or conditions that are within loops within conditions (etc.) makes class problem solving nontrivial!

Beginning a design

Start by making sure you know how to solve the problem with paper and pencil. Make up a set of input data and work through the data to generate expected output. If you can't do this step, it doesn't make sense to proceed with method design. Save the results of this work because you'll need them later to compare against your class results.

Now you are ready to start with the method design. The approach most often used to solve these nontrivial problems is to *start with a design that ignores the details of nested components.* The beginning design is only a sequence of the foregoing six components. Next, we continually refine the solution by replacing vague components with less vague components until the solution is in Java.

Start by looking for the overriding structure in a component or problem. First, ask yourself if a component is really a straight sequence of smaller or finer components and express these one after the other. If your pseudocode or description of the component includes words such as *next* or *then*, you may have a straight sequence. Expand your component into a sequence of components. Once you find that the sequence doesn't readily expand any further, consider each component with the following three sets of questions:

1. *Is this component processing more than one set of data?* A component needs a loop if it needs to process more than one set of data or repeatedly calculate more than one set of results. If it needs a loop, *can you determine how many times the loop must execute?* This is true if the statement of the problem indicates the number of data sets to be processed or the number of output results to be produced. It is also true if you are able to calculate this number with a paper and pencil from currently known information prior to asking this question. A positive response indicates a definite loop; a negative response calls for an indefinite loop.

2. If it does not need a loop, *does this component have alternatives?* A component needs a condition if there are alternative components that are to be executed based on previously input or calculated data.

3. If it is not a loop or a condition, *does this component require information from the user?* If so, it is an input. *Does this component display information or prompts to the user?* If so, it is an output. *Does this component involve a formula or math calculation?* If so, it is a process component.

Based on the answers to these questions, the next design of the class can be given. Let's review the structure of the compound components for indefinite loops, definite loops, and conditions. An indefinite loop can be expressed with the following pseudocode:

```
get or calculate the first value of the variable;
while ( expression comparing variable with a sentinel value )
{   components to be repeated
    get or calculate the next value of the variable;
}
```

A definite loop has the following structure:

```
count = 0.0;
while ( count < maximum )
{   components to be repeated
    count = count + 1.0;
}
```

Naturally, there is nothing special about the variable name count. Another name could be used.

A condition has the following pseudocode structure:

```
if ( compare two values )
{   components to be executed if comparison is true
}
else
{   components to be executed if comparison is false
}
```

Once we have the next design, we can attack a particular pseudocode component to further refine vagaries into specifics by repeatedly considering the same three question sets—as applied to that specific component. When no further pseudocode remains, we have a final design solution. The final work of adding variable declarations and other boilerplate is usually quite mechanical and requires little imagination.

A class solution starting with a correct first design has an excellent chance of leading to a correct class. A solution starting with an incorrect first design has no chance of leading to a correct solution.

Example

Let's do a fairly complex example (at least for this point in your career). A pharmaceutical company sells six different cold medications and needs a class to help a doctor with dose calculations. The company would like to have a doctor first input a patient weight. Next the doctor will input a list of drugs with each entry consisting of the drug number followed by the dose rate (mg per lb of body weight for a prescription). If a patient is over 120 lb, the dose is calculated as the dose rate times the patient weight. Otherwise, the dose is 120 times the dose rate. Finally, the class should also output the average dose for the list of drugs entered.

If we cannot do this with pencil and paper, we have little chance of writing a correct class, so let's do a self-test. Suppose the doctor enters the following input:

115	(patient weight)
56	2.1
86	0.3
75	1.4
97	0.9
68	2.3
39	1.8

If you arrived at the following manually determined output for this future class, you are ready to proceed. If not, go back and study the problem description. (Remember, this patient weighs less than 120 lb.)

dose for drug 56 is 252

dose for drug 86 is 36

dose for drug 75 is 168

dose for drug 97 is 108

dose for drug 68 is 276

dose for drug 39 is 216

average dose is: 176

We could start with a single oval:

> Get the patient weight, then input the list; calculate and output doses, then output the average dose.

Not very helpful. Now, start the decomposition process. First, we note that this is a straight sequence of three components:

> Get the patient weight.

> Input the list; calculate and output the correct dose for each drug.

> Calculate then output the average for all drugs.

The first and last ovals look easy. Analyze the middle oval by asking the following questions:

Is this component processing more than one set of data? Yes. This component is a loop because multiple drugs need to be processed. This loop will also need to do summing for calculated doses so that an average can be output.

Can I determine how many times the loop must execute? There are exactly six drugs, so the loop must be definite.

Based on these answers, the middle oval can be expanded. Using our experience from previous similar programs, we'll include the obvious details for controlling the loop. Since this is the first time we have used actual code, we'll call this our first design:

> Get the patient weight.

FIRST DESIGN

```
count = 0.0;
while ( count < 6.0)
{
```

> components to be executed for each drug

```
count = count + 1.0;
}
```

> Calculate then output the average for all drugs.

There are still three vague pseudocode components in this design. Let's look at the one inside the loop first. What needs to be done for each drug in the input? Input the drug number and dose rate, calculate and sum the dose, and output the calculated dose:

```
        ( Get the patient weight. )              ( SECOND DESIGN )

count = 0.0;
while ( count < 6.0)
{ drug_num = IO.readDouble ("enter drug num: ");
  dose_rate = IO.readDouble ("enter dose rate: ");

      ( calculate, sum, and then output the dose. )

  count = count + 1.0;
}
      ( Calculate then output the average for all drugs. )
```

The middle oval again looks like a straight sequence. Outputting the dose is easy, and we can fill in that detail. The details of performing a summing operation are in our experience and can also be filled in. We remember we need to initialize a summing variable to zero above the loop and then add each calculation to this variable within the loop:

```
        ( Get the patient weight. )              ( THIRD DESIGN )

count = 0.0;
sum_dose = 0.0;
while ( count < 6.0)
{ drug_num = IO.readDouble ("enter drug num: ");
  dose_rate = IO.readDouble ("enter dose rate: ");

      ( Calculate the dose. )

  output = "dose for ";
  output = IO.concatenate (output, drug_num);
  output = IO.concatenate (output, " is: ");
  IO.showValue (output, dose);

  sum_dose = sum_dose + dose;
  count = count + 1.0;
}
      ( Calculate then output the average for all drugs. )
```

Again, consider the middle oval: There are two formulas for a drug dose calculation, and the remaining oval is a condition based on whether the patient weight is over 120 lb or not:

> *Get the patient weight.*

> **FOURTH DESIGN**

```
count = 0.0;
sum_dose = 0.0;
while ( count < 6.0)
{ drug_num = IO.readDouble ("enter drug num: ");
  dose_rate = IO.readDouble ("enter dose rate: ");
  if (patient_weight > 120.0)
  {
```

> *calculate dose using formula for heavy patients.*

```
  }
  else
  {
```

> *calculate dose using formula for light patients.*

```
  }
  output = "dose for ";
  output = IO.concatenate (output, drug_num);
  output = IO.concatenate (output, " is: ");
  IO.showValue (output, dose);

  sum_dose = sum_dose + dose;
  count = count + 1.0;
}
```

> *Calculate then output the average for all drugs.*

The two formulas can now be implemented. Let's resolve the top pseudocode oval as well. At the top, you want to output a prompt as well as input the weight:

```
patient_weight = IO.readDouble ("enter  patient weight: ");
count = 0.0;
sum_dose = 0.0;
while ( count < 6.0)
{ drug_num = IO.readDouble ("enter drug num: ");
  dose_rate = IO.readDouble ("enter dose rate: ");
  if (patient_weight > 120.0)
  {
      dose = dose_rate * patient_weight;
  }
  else
  {
      dose = dose_rate * 120.0;
  }
  output = "dose for ";
```

> **FIFTH DESIGN**

```
   output = IO.concatenate (output, drug_num);
   output = IO.concatenate (output, " is: ");
   IO.showValue (output, dose);

   sum_dose = sum_dose + dose;
   count = count + 1.0;
}
```

> *Calculate then output the average for all drugs.*

The last pseudocode oval is to be done after the loop. The remaining responsibility is to calculate and output the average dose. This is obviously a straight sequence. The completed design (still without the required variable declarations, boilerplate, and comments) now needs to be tested and debugged:

```
patient_weight = IO.readDouble ("enter patient weight: ");
count = 0.0;
sum_dose = 0.0;
while ( count < 6.0 )
{  drug_num = IO.readDouble ("enter drug num: ");
   dose_rate = IO.readDouble ("enter dose rate: ");
   if ( patient_weight > 120.0 )
   {    dose = dose_rate * patient_weight;
   }
   else
   {    dose = dose_rate * 120.0;
   }
   sum_dose = sum_dose + dose;
   output = "dose for ";
   output = IO.concatenate (output, drug_num);
   output = IO.concatenate (output, " is: ");
   IO.showValue (output, dose);
   sum_dose = sum_dose + dose;
   count = count + 1.0;
}
average_dose = sum_dose / 6.0;
IO.showValue ("average dose is: ", average_dose);
```

This approach to design ensures that the opening and closing braces are matched, that nested **if** statements each have appropriately placed components, and that each loop is initialized appropriately.

Now, although this example illustrates the concept of logical stepwise decomposition, do not expect that every programming problem can be mechanically designed by following a simple set of rules. This procedure and these questions will help, but some method designs also require a certain degree of flexibility and creativity. This approach will, however, get you off to a good start.

Desk testing

Desk testing can be helpful to verify a design prior to actual coding. You need four pieces of paper. On the first sheet, you have the written method design. On the second sheet, draw a box for each of the variables used in the final design and write the name of the variable above the box. On a third sheet of paper, write an example set of input data that the user might type. The fourth sheet is blank; this is where you will write output during the execution of the class. Now pretend that you are the computer and "execute" your class one step at a time.

Place a check mark beside a statement line each time you execute it. Each time a statement line indicates that data are to be input into variables, cross off the data consumed from the input sheet and copy the data value into the appropriate variable boxes. Be sure to cross off the previous variable value because a variable may only represent the last value stored there. Each time you execute an output line, write the corresponding output on the output sheet.

At each output line, go back and compare your execution answer with the paper-and-pencil solution you produced *before the class solution was designed*. Any differences will help you identify lines in the method design that do not produce the expected results.

Debugging revisited

The final step in class problem solving is to test run your class. Add declarations for all variables used and other necessary boilerplate. Let's review the process of debugging. As you remember from Chapter 1, when you compile your class to prepare for execution, the compiler will find *syntax errors* or typos.

Let's look again at why the compiler will always indicate that a syntax error exists but may not be able to correctly determine where and why. In other words, a compiler will attempt to show you the line that contains the error and give you an explanation of why the line is in error, but the location and explanation may be incorrect. In addition, one syntax error may produce more than one error message as the compiler attempts to cover all the possibilities. Consider the following `main()` method:

```
1.    public static void main(String[] args)
2.    {   a = IO.readDouble ("enter a: ");
3.        b = IO.readDouble ("enter b: ");
4.        if (a > b)
5.        {   IO.showMessage ("a is greater");
6.        }
7.        else
8.        {   IO.showMessage ("b is greater or equal");
9.        IO.showMessage ("class is done");
10.       IO.showMessage ("thank you.");
11.   }
```

BUG!

The programmer forgot the closing **}** below the **else** (between lines 8 and 9). Since the compiler does not consider indentation (which is strictly to make a method more readable to humans), the error isn't detected until the end of the method is reached. The last } on line 11 is matched with the opening { on line 8. At the end, the compiler still hasn't found a remaining } to match the opening { on line 2. This typo by the programmer may produce a variety of error messages (and often more than one), but none of them will accurately indicate that a missing } is needed between lines 8 and 9.

Think of syntax error messages as "best guesses" by the compiler. All you can count on is that the error will be detected at or after where the actual syntax error or typo occurs.

As we discussed in Chapter 1, a method may also contain logic and semantic errors. A good program development environment always comes with a debugger, and there are a variety of Java debuggers available. A debugger is an invaluable tool to allow you to single step through your class and watch as statements change variables or branch in a condition (among other things). Your instructor will have the information you need to use a debugger for execution testing.

KEY TERM
foot printing

The addition of helpful output statements is called *foot printing*. Extra output statements are placed in the class to notify the programmer of computer progress and perhaps the current value of important variables as execution proceeds. These output statements are not part of the problem solution design—they are added to provide additional output to aid in debugging. Regardless of the debugger used, foot printing can be employed to aid in identifying semantic and logic errors.

4.6 The software life cycle

Let's look at the larger picture of how programs are developed in the commercial world. Consider for a moment that you are the manager of a software development group in a large company. Ask yourself the following question: "What is a successful program?" There are many possible answers to this question. You may claim that a good program must *run correctly* and *be efficient*. But these are insufficient because a program may be completely without bugs and run very efficiently and yet do nothing particularly useful. Okay, amend your response to include that a good program must also *perform a useful job*. What about a correct, efficient program that does an important job but is so difficult to use that clients quickly look for other solutions? Now you amend your answer to include that a good program must be *easy to use* (have a good user interface). In addition, you might expect to upgrade or modify a program. If a program is not *easily maintained*, initial usefulness will fade.

All five of these concepts are important to a *good* program, but insufficient for a *successful* program. The graveyards of business are full of software companies that have gone broke with programs that were good—correct, efficient, useful, as well as easy to use and maintain! On the other hand, there are some highly successful programs that still contain annoying bugs, that are disappointingly slow, or that are only moderately useful or perhaps difficult to use. Can you see where we're headed?

A successful program is one that makes money! Now, not all programs are written to be sold to outside customers. Many companies employ a software staff to produce programs for the company's own use. This may include engineering, military or scientific research firms, or even government and public-service institutions. Nevertheless, the analogy is still true. These organizations operate effectively by saving money on the cost of operations (including software). If the cost of developing programs is more than the savings realized when these programs are used or implemented in company operations, the programs are not successful.

CONCEPT
a class must be cost-effective

This may seem a little hard-nosed and capitalistic, but it is the way the free-market world works. We can be a bit more specific: A successful program costs less to produce and maintain than the sales or savings it generates. Naturally, to have the best chance of generating savings or sales, a program should have the five qualifications you initially proposed: be correct, efficient, useful, maintainable, and easy to use. To these five qualifications, we will now add one more: *A program must be cost-effective*. It also follows that a good programmer must be cost-effective. If one programmer can produce a good program in fewer salary hours than another, his or her value to the company is greater. A good programmer who cannot produce programs in a cost-effective manner will end up flipping burgers.

The same concept is important for programming students or professionals who program only occasionally. You need to produce good programs as quickly as possible to have time for other important things in your career (and perhaps a social life). In this text, much more than just Java language syntax and rules are presented. The goal is to teach you how to program in a way that will lead to a successful career. Some of these concepts that are introduced are just as important now, while you are still a student (and working on relatively small programs), as they will be when you are a software professional (working on much larger programs). In any case, a lot of study and experience has gone into these proven concepts. Our experience is that when correctly followed, they tend to lead to good cost-effective programs. Cost is a relative term: It might relate to a company paying your salary or might relate to your own invested time.

KEY TERM
software life cycle

Experience has shown that the following five stages of development are part of a successful commercial software product. They are appropriately named the *software life cycle*. You may find slightly different terms in other texts, but the concepts are generally the same.

1. **Analysis.** During this stage, the purpose for the proposed class is analyzed. What are the client's needs and requirements? Does the client have a clear understanding of his or her needs? What are the expected benefits? What are the trade-offs or alternative approaches? What is the expected or potential profit or savings? Near the end of this stage of development, a budget and schedule are generally formed. The goals and objectives of the class are specified.

2. **Design.** Formulas and algorithms are developed or decided on. A programming language is chosen. The user interface is designed and the user's manual is written. This allows both the customer or consumer and the programmer/company to agree on exactly what the class will do and how it will be used. Any misconceptions between the client's expectations and the programmer's goals should be

resolved. Consider this metaphor: It is always cheaper and faster to build a three-lane bridge than to build a two-lane bridge and later add a third lane.

3. **Coding.** During this stage, the actual class and methods are written and debugged.

4. **Testing.** The completed class is rigorously tested to verify that it works correctly and according to the user's manual and the specifications developed during the analysis stage.

5. **Maintenance.** Features are modified, enhanced, or added to meet the evolving needs and requirements of the client.

KEY TERM
software
engineering

The effective management of these stages is called *software engineering*. All active programs are in one of these stages. Many programs cycle through the five stages repeatedly as new revisions and releases are continually being developed from earlier versions. The time and budget allocated to each stage vary with the type and complexity of the software being developed. However, it is almost universally true that the coding and maintenance stages require more time and budget than the other three combined. It is also true that the maintenance stage generally requires more than two or three times as much budget and time as the coding stage.

4.7 Summary

KEY TERMS

Several terms are presented in this chapter on problem solving:

1. *decomposition*—breaking a large problem down into a sequence of smaller and simpler problems.

2. *pseudocode*—expressing code segments in conversational English, leaving details of how these statements are to be expressed in Java until later.

3. *desk testing*—the process of "executing" a design with paper and pencil as if you were the computer.

4. *foot printing*—adding extra output statements to a class to have the computer indicate progress and intermediate values of variables.

5. *software life cycle*—the steps or stages of commercial software development that experience has shown lead to successful programs.

6. *software engineering*—the application and effective management of methods for software development.

CONCEPTS

The concepts of decomposition and applying experience from previously solved problems are very useful in producing good programs.

A simple premise can be used to help design software solutions to problems: All programs can be designed with a sequence of the six components that you have learned from previous chapters. These six design components are:

1. input statements

2. output statements

3. calculation or formula implementation statements

4. indefinite loops

5. counted loops

6. conditions

(Future chapters will demonstrate efficient variations of these components and ways of shortening long programs.) Each of these components has a basic design that you have learned from previous examples and applied in previous projects. Most of the complexity of method design comes from the fact that loops and conditions may contain nested components.

When designing a programming problem solution, it is best to start with recognizing the basic sequence of these components, leaving any details and nested components as pseudocode for later refinement. The basic sequence can be recognized by asking the basic questions outlined in this chapter.

Pseudocode components can be refined or broken down into a more detailed sequence of the basic components by again asking the basic questions for that pseudocode component. Each subsequent refinement replaces pseudocode with a sequence of more refined pseudocode and explicit Java statements. When no more pseudocode remains, the design is ready for desk testing. Finally, variable declarations and other boilerplate are added and the class can be debugged.

4.8 Exercises

Short-answer questions

1. List the five stages of the software life cycle.
2. List and explain the six basic design components.
3. Explain what a professional programmer will attempt to accomplish during the analysis stage of the software life cycle.
4. Explain what a professional programmer will attempt to accomplish during the testing stage of the software life cycle.
5. During which stage of the software life cycle will a method design actually be coded into Java?
6. Explain what a professional programmer will attempt to accomplish during the design stage of the software life cycle.
7. Explain what a professional programmer will attempt to accomplish during the maintenance stage of the software life cycle.
8. Which stage of the software life cycle is likely to require the greatest amount of budget and time?
9. Indicate which of the six basic design components should be used in the refining of the following pseudocode components. You do not need to refine the pseudocode—just indicate which single component would be used in the next design refinement (each of the following represents a single component).

a. Calculate the number of inches associated with variable `feet`.

b. Choose either formula A or formula B to calculate interest on the variable `principal`.

c. Process six sets of mortgage data to produce monthly payment values.

d. The user will input the number of student scores in the class. Following that number, the user will input each individual score. Process these grades to output a letter grade for each score.

e. The user will input a list of student grades followed by a score of −1. Process these grades to output a letter grade for each score.

f. The user will input a list of student grades followed by a score of −1. Process these grades to obtain a total score so that the average score can later be calculated.

10. Consider the class of Listing 2.I. Work backward from this class to produce a first design of this method, leaving all nested components as pseudocode.

11. Consider Listing 2.II. Work backward from this class to produce a first design of this method, leaving all nested components as pseudocode.

12. Expand the first design of the previous problem to produce a second or more refined design.

13. Consider Listing 2.VIII. Work backward from this class to produce a first design of this method, leaving all nested components as pseudocode.

14. Expand the first design of the previous problem to produce a second or more refined design.

15. Consider Listing 2.IX. Work backward from this class to produce a first design of this method, leaving all nested components as pseudocode.

16. Expand the first design of the previous problem to produce a second or more refined design.

17. Consider Listing 2.X. Work backward from this class to produce a first design of this method, leaving all nested components as pseudocode.

18. Produce a first design for the following problem: A buyer needs a class to calculate the total cost of an apple order. The user will input the number of apple boxes and the cost per box. The class should output the total order cost.

19. Produce a first design for the following modification to the previous problem: If an apple order exceeds $1,000.00, the total cost is reduced by 5 percent.

20. Expand the first design for the previous problem to a second refinement.

21. Produce a first design for the following problem: A contractor needs to know the total number of board feet in a stack of 15 wood planks. For each plank, the user will input the length, width, and thickness in inches. Board feet for a plank can be calculated with the following formula:

$$board\ feet = \frac{(length \times width \times thickness)}{144}$$

22. Expand the first design for the previous problem to a second refinement.

23. Produce a first design for the following problem: A bodybuilding clinic would like to know the average weight of all customers over 150 lb. The user will input

a list of body weights followed by −1. The class should output the average weight of all customers over 150 lb.

24. Expand the first design for the previous problem to a second refinement.

25. Produce a first design for the following problem: A dealership needs to estimate the average amount of time for a car repair. The user will input a list of repair times measured for cars seen during the last week. The list will terminate with −1. The class should output the average repair time.

26. Expand the first design for the previous problem to a second refinement.

More Data Types

All of the classes examined and written to this point have used **double** variables for numeric data. You need to understand that these variables are not infinitely accurate but have bounds on accuracy and range. In addition, they make it difficult to enforce the use of whole numbers or allow simple representation of textual data. How would you write a class to calculate the number of quarters in a given amount of money? The class output must reasonably be a whole number. How about text processing? How would you compare two names? This chapter introduces several additional variable types and points out where they are appropriate in programming problems and solutions. In addition, two more relational comparison operators are introduced.

5.1 Floating-point numbers

Up to this point, variables have all been declared using the reserved word **double**. If functions returned a value, these functions were declared with this same **double**. The reserved word **double** is actually the definition of a variable or function *type*. In this case, the type is a decimal number. Before pointing out that there are several other available types in the Java language, you should first better understand the meaning of the type **double**.

Representation

Floating-point values are stored internally using a form of scientific notation. If you will remember back to earlier math classes, scientific notation is a method of expressing very large or very small numbers using a small decimal number and a power of 10. For example, the value 1,234,560,000,000,000,000.0 would be expressed as:

$$0.123456 \times 10^{19}$$

The number 0.000,000,000,000,123456 would be expressed as:

$$0.123456 \times 10^{-12}$$

The advantage of this approach is that fewer digits need to be written *if the number ends or begins in a lot of zeros*. If a very long number does not end or begin with zeros, there is no savings in the number of digits that must be written *unless we decide to round the number to a smaller number of digits*. Suppose you decide you only need six digits of accuracy in your numbers. The value 1,234,567,890,123,456,789.0 would be written as:

$$.123457 \times 10^{19}$$

If you decide on the convention that every number in this form of scientific notation is to be written with the decimal point before the first nonzero digit, then you really only need to write two simple integer numbers: the digits of the decimal number and the digits of the power of 10. The above value could be expressed with a pair of integers as:

$$123457, 19$$

The net result of this notation is that you can express very large or very small numbers with only a few digits—in this case, eight. You need to keep in mind that this representation is only an approximation, however, accurate to the first six digits of the actual number. This means that two very different numbers may have the same notation as long as they are within six digits of accuracy to each other:

123,456,000,000,000,000.0   represented as 123456, 18

123,456,400,000,000,000.0   represented as 123456, 18

Even though these two numbers are 400 billion apart, this notation represents them the same.

Java represents **double** numbers and variables using a form of scientific notation. Each floating-point number is truncated to about 16 significant digits and represented as two integers: the first represents the fractional part with an assumed point to the left of the digits, and the second is the power to which this fraction would need to be multiplied to arrive at the correct value. (Actually, it turns out to be simpler to use powers of 2 instead of powers of 10 in a binary computer, but the principle is the same.) The fractional part (with the implied point) is called the *characteristic*, and the power is called the *mantissa*.

E notation

KEY TERM
E notation

To save some typing keystrokes, floating-point constants can be written using *E notation* in Java. In this form, we use the letter "e" to represent the phrase "× 10," or *times ten*. So, 0.9×10^{25} would be written as 0.9e25 using this notation. Consider the following method segment used to input a **double** value from the keyboard:

```
double x;
x = IO.getDouble("enter a number: ");
```

Suppose the value of 0.00000000054 is to be input. Typing any of the following would result in the correct number being placed into variable x:

```
0.00000000054
5.4e-10
0.54e-9
54.0e-11
```

Precision and range

CONCEPT
truncation

The key point to remember is that to save space and force all **double** numbers to require the same amount of memory, *values are truncated to a predetermined accuracy* of about 16 significant digits. You may be thinking that is close enough for most applications, and you are right. It certainly has been for our programming problems up to this point. This method of representing decimal numbers has some definite limitations, however. In Java systems, the characteristic utilizes enough bits to represent about 16 digits, leaving only enough room for the mantissa to be in the range of about 10^{-308} to 10^{308}.

The reason for not being very definitive here and saying "about 16 digits" and "about −308 to +308" is that **double** values are stored as binary numbers. Binary numbers in this range do not always convert to an exact number of decimal digits. The bottom line is this: There is a limit to accuracy in **double** variables. If you write a constant or input a value in a Java class with more than about 16 digits of accuracy, the system may truncate it to the correct number. If you perform a calculation with two **double** variables, the system may need to truncate the result.

There is another less common floating-point or decimal data type—**float**. Variables of type **float** are about half as precise as **double**, having about eight significant digits. The range is only about 10^{38} to 10^{-38}. The advantage of this data type is that it only requires half as much memory. The disadvantage is that Java does not normally allow you to use a **float** when a **double** is expected, although you will shortly see how to convert between data types. Floating-point constants are automatically type **double**. All Math package helper functions expect **double** variables.

Years ago, memory was much more of an issue in programming, and most floating-point variables were of type **float**. The term **double** actually means "double-precision floating-point."

Overflow, underflow

KEY TERM
overflow, underflow

What if you need to express a number with a characteristic larger than will fit, say, 0.9×10^{400}? The answer is that you can't with the **double** data type. We call this variable *overflow*. The very small number 0.9×10^{-400} will not fit either and would result in *underflow*.

CONCEPT
rules for double
constants

Three important rules to remember when inputting or writing **double** constants are:

1. Always use a decimal point but never use a comma.

2. When using E notation, the mantissa (exponent) must be a whole number.

3. If you write more than about 16 digits in the decimal part, the system may truncate the number.

Truncation errors

To illustrate the importance of understanding that floating-point variables are truncated, consider the following class intended to add the salaries of a few software professionals to the national debt. The national debt is a very large number, and the generous software professional salaries are (individually, of course) quite small in relation. We'll use **float** variables because the problem is much more easily demonstrated due to the fact that they have about half the precision of **double** variables, but the problem exists with either data type (Listing 5.I). Note that we utilize the readFloat() helper method of the **IO** class to input **float** variables.

Listing 5.I

```
// A class to add 6 salaries to the national debt.
public class help_salary
{
 public static void main (String[] args)
 {
   float sal1, sal2, sal3, sal4, sal5, sal6, debt;
   debt = IO.readFloat ("enter national debt: ");

   IO.showValue ("The debt is now: ", debt);
   sal1 = IO.readFloat ("Enter a salary: ");
   sal2 = IO.readFloat ("Enter a salary: ");
   sal3 = IO.readFloat ("Enter a salary: ");
   sal4 = IO.readFloat ("Enter a salary: ");
   sal5 = IO.readFloat ("Enter a salary: ");
   sal6 = IO.readFloat ("Enter a salary: ");

   debt = debt + sal1;
   debt = debt + sal2;
   debt = debt + sal3;
   debt = debt + sal4;
```

WRONG!

```
    debt = debt + sal5;
    debt = debt + sal6;
    IO.showValue ("Thank you, the debt is now only  ", debt);
    System.exit(0);
  }
}
```

Suppose we enter a debt of −5.0e12 (about $5 trillion). The first display box shows the following:

This isn't exactly what we entered, but it is accurate to eight significant digits. Now let's input the following salaries: 40341, 120400, 121000, 37600, 50124, and 124000.

Two important points to notice from this class execution are the following:

1. When a floating-point number is very large (or very small), it may be output using E notation. Notice how `debt` is displayed.

2. After the addition of all six salaries, there was no change in the `debt` value. In other words, when a significantly smaller number is added to a very large number, the result may not be different from the original large number. The sum of `debt` and any one salary was not different from the original value of `debt` within the precision of a **float** variable (the first eight or so digits).

Consider the first assignment statement that adds the first salary to `debt`. The following shows the stages this addition will go through:

$$
\begin{array}{r}
-\,5{,}000{,}000{,}000{,}000.0 \\
+\quad\quad\quad 40{,}341.0 \\
\hline
-\,4{,}999{,}999{,}959{,}659.0
\end{array}
$$

After truncating this number to eight significant digits, we end up back where we started: 49999999 E 12.

KEY TERM
truncation error

When the result of the addition is truncated to eight digits accuracy, the effect of the small salary is lost. We call this a *truncation error*. In other words, it would not matter in this class how many salaries we added into the national debt; as long as each salary is less than the debt by more than the precision of a **float** variable, the national debt would never change! Some may think this adds credence to the thought that we will never be able to pay off the national debt, but the purpose here is to illustrate a situation when the limited accuracy of floating-point variables can cause a significant problem. (The above math demonstration uses decimal numbers. The computer uses binary values, so the exact rounding is somewhat different.) The concept you should understand is that the computer will round to the precision limit of a variable. This same problem occurs with **double** variables, but the effect is less noticeable because the precision extends to about 16 significant digits.

EXPERIMENT

What would happen if the following snippet of code is executed? Why do you think this occurs?

```
double one, first_third, second_third, third_third;
first_third = 1.0 / 3.0;
second_third = 1.0 / 3.0;
third_third = 1.0 / 3.0;
one = first_third + second_third + third_third;
```

Suppose we *first* added all six salaries together to form a much larger composite salary. If this composite salary were then finally added into the national debt, it might be large enough to make a difference. Consider the changes to Listing 5.I presented in Listing 5.II:

Listing 5.II

```
// A class to add 6 salaries to the national debt.
public class help_salary2
{
 public static void main (String[] args)
 {
  float sal1, sal2, sal3, sal4, sal5, sal6, debt;
  debt = IO.readFloat ("enter national debt: ");

  IO.showValue ("The debt is now: ", debt);
  sal1 = IO.readFloat ("Enter a salary: ");
  sal2 = IO.readFloat ("Enter a salary: ");
  sal3 = IO.readFloat ("Enter a salary: ");
```

```
   sal4 = IO.readFloat ("Enter a salary: ");
   sal5 = IO.readFloat ("Enter a salary: ");
   sal6 = IO.readFloat ("Enter a salary: ");

   debt = debt  + (sal1 + sal2 + sal3 + sal4 + sal5 + sal6);
   IO.showValue ("Thank you, the debt is now only  ", debt);
   System.exit(0);
  }
}
```

The execution of this class with the same inputs would now appear as follows:

The answer is not exactly right; it is correct only to eight significant digits. At least we made a difference in the debt. The reason is that the total of the six salaries is greater than $500,000.

This problem of truncation must be appreciated by the Java programmer. It is usually not a problem with scientific or engineering calculations. (Consider for a moment that even the most precise scale or micrometer is usually accurate to only four digits.) In financial calculations, however, no one would tolerate such errors.

5.2 Integers

CONCEPT
int data type

From the previous section, you learned that decimal or floating-point variables have limited precision but an extremely large range. Not all the world's data contain a decimal point, however, and another variable type is provided for values that are always whole numbers or integers: the type **int** (short for integer).

Range

In Java programs, an **int** variable is allocated 32 bits of memory space and is capable of storing a whole number in the range of −2,147,483,648 to +2,147,483,647. (The reason for these particular limits has to do with the binary representation of integers.) Typically, **int** variables are used to represent values from the real world that must be whole numbers, such as the count or size of a list, the number of people in a room, the number of loan payments, and so on. Declaring a variable to be type **int** is a programmer's way of documenting that this variable will only represent whole numbers and ensuring that nonwhole numbers are not used in important calculations.

Integer constants are written without decimal points of course, and users should enter values for **int** variables without decimal points.

```
int a;
a = 256;          // proper
```

It is incorrect to write an integer constant with a leading zero:

```
a = 0256;
```

WRONG!

CONCEPT
avoid leading zeros

This assignment does not produce an error message, but a value very different than 256 will be assigned to variable a. The reason is that Java interprets constants that begin with a leading zero as representing a base-8 number and not a base-10 number like you are accustomed to dealing with.

Variables of type **int** can be input using the readInt() method function of the **IO** class. A method called showValue() can be used to output **int** values in the same way we output **double** values. In the same manner, the concatenate() helper method can be used to concatenate an **int** or **float** as well as a **double** onto the end of a message. This feature of Java, which allows one method name to be used for similar but different operations, is called *method overloading* or *polymorphism*—we'll return to this later.

Mixed-mode expressions

KEY TERM
mixed-mode
expressions

Often, we need to utilize **int** and **double** variables in the same assignment statement or expression. Any expression (mathematical calculation) that uses both **int** and **double** (or **float**) variables or values is called a *mixed-mode expression*. There are three important rules to remember for mixed-mode expressions:

CONCEPT
rules for mixed-mode expressions

1. Java will automatically *promote* an **int** or a **float** to a **double**. This automatic conversion results in no loss of information and is not considered an error.

2. Java will not automatically *demote* a **double** to a **float** or an **int** because information may be lost (due to the loss of precision or range). An attempt to assign a **double** to an **int** variable will result in a compiler error.

3. *Any mathematical operation involving two integers always results in an integer.* This may seem obvious: The product of two integers is an integer, the sum of two integers is an integer, and so on. Where it becomes extremely important is when we *divide* two integers: The result is an integer. Remember, an expression or calculation in an assignment statement must be calculated before the result is assigned to the variable on the left side of the = operator. For example:

```
int a, b, c;
double x;
a = 2;
b = 7;
```

```
c = b / a;                        // 'c' now contains 3, not 3.5
IO.showValue ("c is: ", c);       // will display 3, not 3.5
x = b / a;                        // 'x' will contain 3, not 3.5
x = 1 / a;                        // 'x' will contain 0, not 0.5
```

The corollary to the above statement is that *any mathematical operation involving a floating-point value always results in a floating-point value.* In other words, if at least one of the two operands of a mathematical operation is a floating-point value, the result will be a floating-point value. So, a floating-point value times an integer results in a floating-point value. An integer divided by a floating-point value results in a floating-point value and so on.

```
int a;
double x;
a = 2;
x = 1.0 / a; // 'x' will contain 0.5, the result of the divide
```

CONCEPT
rule of thumb for integer division

These three rules can be condensed into a single rule-of-thumb that many students find easier to remember:

An integer divided by an integer is always an integer.

The reason this simple statement is a nice condensed version of the three rules is that the only time you will get into trouble is when you divide an integer by an integer! Any other operation will result in the correct answer you expect—whether it is an integer or floating-point value won't matter. Assigning an integer to a **double** variable produces a floating-point number, but appending .0 to an integer does not change the value (as long as the range and precision of the **double** variable are appropriate).

KEY TERM
casting

There are times when you may actually wish to use truncation to solve a problem. You may force Java to demote a double or float to an int by placing the desired type in parentheses in front of an expression to be demoted. This is called *casting*. Suppose we need a function to return the number of quarters in a given amount of money. The following function accepts as a parameter a decimal amount of money and returns the integer number of quarters in this amount. For example, if called with the amount 13.45, it should return 53.

Listing 5.III

```
// a method to calculate the number of
// quarters in the money represented by the parameter
//  IN:  amount -- a decimal amount of money
//  RETURNS: the number of quarters
public static int NumQuarters (double money)
{  int quarters, cents;
   cents = (int) (money * 100);        // convert to pennies
   quarters = cents / 25;              // number of whole quarters
   return (quarters);
}
```

This function first converts the **double** money amount into cents by calculating a double value of money*100 and then forcing or casting that value to an integer. Any fractional cents are dropped by truncation. By dividing the number of cents (an integer) by 25 (another integer), the integer number of quarters is determined. Any fractional amount left over is dropped by truncation.

Any numeric data type may be cast to any other—you are responsible for whether this results in a loss of information or not.

Parameters

CONCEPT
method call rules

Now that you are aware of several different variable types, let's clarify the rules for calling a method at this point in your career:

- The number of arguments must match the number of parameters (you know this already).
- The type of each argument must match the type of the corresponding parameter.

In other words, an **int** argument should be used for an **int** parameter, a **double** argument should be used for a **double** parameter, and so on. If this is not the case, you may or may not see a warning message when compiling your class. Java will automatically promote variables to a higher type (as described earlier). Java will generate an error message if it would need to demote a variable to match a parameter.

5.3 More comparison operators

Back in Chapter 2, you learned to use four basic comparison operators in an **if** or **while** statement test: >, <, <=, and >=. These comparison operators are most appropriate for **double** variables and values because they make *relative* comparisons. With **int** variables or values, it is also appropriate to test *exact* relationships. Two additional operators that allow such comparisons are:

==   equal to

!=   not equal to

For example:

```
int a, b, c;
a = IO.readInt ("enter a: ");
b = IO.readInt ("enter b: ");
c = IO.readInt ("enter c: ");
if (a == b)
   IO.showMessage ("the first two numbers are exactly equal");
else ;
if (b != c)
   IO.showMessage ("the last two are not exactly equal");
else ;
```

Tests for exact equality may not be appropriate for **float** or **double** variables because they might be *truncated* to a limited number of digits:

```
float d, e;
d = IO.readFloat ("enter d: ");
e = IO.readFloat ("enter e: ");
if (d == e)
     IO.showMessage (" these numbers are exactly equal");
else ;
```

WRONG!

Suppose for the above segment of code the user entered the two decimal values of 1.000000005 and 1.0. This segment would state that these numbers are exactly equal, which of course would surprise the user.

The exact comparison operators == and != are very useful. Be particularly careful, however, in noting that the test for exact equality (==) is not the same operator used for assignment (=). It is a common mistake to do something similar to the following:

```
if (a = b)
     IO.showMessage (" these are equal";)
else ;
```

WRONG!

CONCEPT
don't confuse
= with ==

This segment is obviously wrong because the = operator was mistakenly used in place of the intended == operator, but it may not produce an error message when compiled. The reason is that Java *allows an assignment statement to be used anywhere an expression is expected*. The value of the expression is simply the value assigned. In other words, the segment first assigns the value of b to a and then tests the value assigned to see if it is true or false to determine whether to execute the showMessage() output operation statement. If a and b are Boolean variables, this makes sense! We'll return later to this concept.

Long and short integers

KEY TERM
primitive

Just as there are several types of decimal representations for variety in precision and range (**float** and **double**), there are also several varieties of integer representations. Variables declared to be of type **short** are half the size of ints but have half the range. Variables of type **long** are integers of twice the range as int values but require twice as much memory. This relationship between range, precision, and memory requirements is summarized in Table 5.1 for the data types so far presented. These are known as the *primitive* data types for a reason that will become clear.

Table 5.1   Primitive Java data types

Type	Number of Bits	Range
byte	8	−128 to 127
short	16	−32,768 to 32,767
int	32	−2,147,483,648 to 2,147,483,647
long	64	−9,223,372,036,854,775,808 to 9,223,372,036,854,775,807
float	32	−3.4029234 E 38 to 3.4029234 E 38
double	64	−1.7976931348623157 E 308 to 1.7976931348623157 E 308
char	16	ISO Unicode character set

5.4 **Characters**

Suppose you were asked to write a class to manipulate nonnumeric data: You have a paper list of students letter grades and would like this class to read this grade data and output a summary table with the number of As, Bs, and so on. Having only **double** or **int** variables in your bag of skills, about the only approach to this problem is to *code* the letter grades in some way—that is, convert them to some numeric form so they could be stored in **numeric** variables. Consider the following attempt at a solution (Listing 5.IV):

Listing 5.IV

```
// A class to compile a table of student grades
public class stud_grades
{
 public static void main (String[] args)
 { int a=0, b=0, c=0, d=0, f=0, grade;
   String output;
   grade = IO.readInt ("Enter grades (0 for F, 1 for D, 2 for C, 3 for B, and 4 for A (-1 to end)");
   while (grade >= 0)                       // sum each grade
   { if (grade >= 4) a = a+1;               // category. . .
     else if (grade >= 3)  b = b+1;
     else if (grade >= 2)  c = c+1;
     else if (grade >= 1)  d = d+1;
     else          f = f+1;
     grade = IO.readInt ("enter next grade: ");
   }
   output = "summary of grades: \na:";
   output = IO.concatenate (output, a);
   output = IO.concatenate (output, "\nb:");
   output = IO.concatenate (output, b);
   output = IO.concatenate (output, "\nc:");
   output = IO.concatenate (output, c);
   output = IO.concatenate (output, "\nd:");
   output = IO.concatenate (output, d);
   output = IO.concatenate (output, "\nf:");
   output = IO.concatenate (output, f);
   IO.showMessage (output);
   System.exit(0);
 }
}
```

CONCEPT

char data type

This is a very clumsy solution because it forces the user to perform a mental conversion for each grade on the list. Entry mistakes would be quite likely if the list was very long. A more appropriate solution would be to represent the grades exactly as they are: as letters. Java provides the variable type **char** (short for character) that can be used to store a single letter. Character constants in a class are written using single quotes.

Now, go back and read the last line of the previous paragraph again. In other words, the following are not the same:

```
'A'      this is a character

"A"      this is a literal
```

There is a readChar() method in the **IO** class, just as you would expect. This method will accept and return the first letter of the line entered in the dialog box. Any leading whitespace characters are ignored. A whitespace is a character that doesn't have a printable representation (e.g., a blank or control character such as the Enter key). You may utilize the showValue() method to output characters, as you have with other data types. A more appropriate solution to the above problem follows (Listing 5.V):

Listing 5.V

```
// A class to compile a table of student grades (using char variables)
public class stud_grades2
{
 public static void main (String[] args)
 {  int a=0, b=0, c=0, d=0, f=0;
    char grade;
    String output;
    grade = IO.readChar ("Enter grades as capital letters(ending with the letter X): ");
    while (grade != 'X')                       // sum each grade
    {   if (grade == 'A')      a = a+1;         // category. . .
        else if (grade == 'B')  b = b+1;
        else if (grade >= 'C')  c = c+1;
        else if (grade >= 'D')  d = d+1;
        else          f = f+1;
        grade = IO.readChar ("enter next grade: ");
    }
    output = "summary of grades: \n a:";
    output = IO.concatenate (output, a);
    output = IO.concatenate (output, "\n b:");
    output = IO.concatenate (output, b);
    output = IO.concatenate (output, "\n c:");
    output = IO.concatenate (output, c);
    output = IO.concatenate (output, "\n d:");
    output = IO.concatenate (output, d);
    output = IO.concatenate (output, "\n f:");
    output = IO.concatenate (output, f);
    IO.showMessage (output);
    System.exit(0);
 }
}
```

EXPERIMENT

What would happen if you enter lowercase letters for grades in Listing 5.V? Why do you think this occurs?

Since **char** variables are exact, the == and != operators are appropriate for comparisons. Typically, a class will use **char** variables for input, output, testing, and assignment. They are not usually appropriate for arithmetic operations such as * or /. (You will see later, however, when such arithmetic manipulation of **char** values is occasionally useful.)

Representation

You might ask how letters are actually stored in the memory reserved for a **char** variable. Well, they're not actually. Memory cells are simply collections of bits that allow representation of numbers. To store a letter, the character is represented by a number code. For example, assigning the letter A to variable grade in the following statement

```
grade = 'A';
```

CONCEPT

**character
representation
is by ISO Unicode
numbers**

is interpreted by the compiler as assigning the *code* for the letter A to the variable grade. Character constants (or actual letters) are always expressed within single quotes.

When a **char** variable is output or input, you might think of the IO.showValue() method as essentially using a table to look up the appropriate letter display. There are several different tables of character codes in use today. The one utilized by Java systems is called the ISO Unicode character set (see Appendix C).

In the ISO Unicode set, there are codes assigned for a wide variety of different characters: uppercase letters, lowercase letters, numeric digits, punctuation, and so on. Many of these characters are printable, and some are not. It is helpful to remember that the codes for letters follow the alphabet. In other words, the code for the letter A is less than the code for the letter B and so on. This means that it is quite appropriate to compare **char** variables for alphabetical order:

```
char grade1, grade2;
grade1 = IO.readChar("enter a grade: ");
grade2 = IO.readChar ("enter a grade: ");
if (grade1 < grade2)
    IO.showMessage (" the first grade is better than the second");
else ;
```

In this class segment, the code in grade1 is compared to the code in grade2. If grade1 contains the code for a B and grade2 contains the code for a D, then the **if** statement will be true—the first grade is less than (alphabetically before) the second grade. Just as you might suspect, however, Java is still case sensitive. In other words, a comparison like the following

```
char grade1 = 'A';
char grade2 = 'a';
if (grade 1 == grade2)
    IO.showMessage ("these are the same grades!");
```

will not be true—these are completely different characters. Actually, all the upper-case letters come before any of the lowercase letters.

EXPERIMENT

What would happen if you add an integer to a **char** variable? Try the following:

```
char c;
c='A';
c=c+2;
IO.showValue(c);
```

Character class static functions

It would be quite difficult to memorize the ISO Unicode set table and remember the codes used to represent characters. Often, however, we may need a good understanding of such information. For example, consider the problem of determining if a character is a lowercase letter. You might know that the codes for all lowercase letters are between the code for lowercase a and lowercase z (inclusive). Let's write a method that could be used to make such a test. The following method *islower()* returns the integer 1 if the character argument is a lowercase letter; otherwise it returns the integer 0 (Listing 5.VI):

Listing 5.VI

```
// islower()  Return 1 if the char. argument is a lower-
// case letter, otherwise return 0.
public static int isLower (char c)
{if (c >= 'a')
    if (c <= 'z') return (1);
    else return (0);
 else return (0);
}
```

This function might be invoked in a main() method in the following manner:

```
char x;
x = IO.readChar ("enter a character: ");
if (isLower(x) == 1)
    IO.showMessage ("this is a lower-case letter");
else ;
```

CONCEPT

true means nonzero

Actually, we do not need to compare the value returned by the `islower()` function with the constant 1. Anytime an expression is found within a test (e.g., an `if` or `while` statement) without a comparison being made, the expression itself is assumed to be true if nonzero and false if zero. In other words, the following segment is equivalent to the previous one:

```
char x;
x = IO.readChar ("enter a character: ");
if (islower(x))
    IO.showMessage ("this is a lower-case letter");
else ;
```

There is an existing class of useful **static** methods as a part of the Java language library (in the `java.lang` package) called the **Character** helper class (Table 5.2). For reasons that will become clearer in Chapter 7, this is more commonly called a *wrapper* class. Some are listed in Table 5.2. Note that this list also includes a similar *isLowerCase()* function. They are used just like other helper methods. We'll present more of the capabilities of wrapper classes in the future.

Table 5.2   Some `static` character class methods

Function	Returns
isLowerCase (c)	true if c is a lowercase letter, otherwise zero
isUpperCase(c)	true if c is an uppercase letter, otherwise zero
isLetter(c)	true if c is an upper- or lowercase letter, otherwise zero
isDigit(c)	true if c is a digit character, otherwise zero
isLetterOrDigit(c)	true if c is a letter or digit character, otherwise zero
toUpperCase(c)	the uppercase equivalent character of c
toLowerCase(c)	the lowercase equivalent character of c

Look again at the grading class of Listing 5.V. If we add the following statement, whatever letter grade is entered by the user will be converted to uppercase:

```
grade = IO.readChar ("Enter grades as letters (ending with the letter X): ");
while (grade != 'X')
{   grade = Character.toUpperCase (grade);
   . . .
```

What happens when the user enters something that isn't a grade at all, such as the letter G? We could expand this class to check the input and verify that the letter is a valid grade and, if not, return to the user for another try. Suppose we write a helper method called `isNotValidGrade()`. Now, the complete class with user error-checking for improper input could be defined as in Listing 5.VII:

Listing 5.VII

```
// A class to compile a table of student grades (with user error checking)
public class stud_grades3
{
    // Returns false if the parameter 'grade' is not an upper or lower-case grade
    // IN:  grade -- a character
    private static int isNotValidGrade (char grade)
    {   char c;
        c = Character.toUpperCase (grade);
        if (c == 'A')     return 0;
        else if (c == 'B') return 0;
        else if (c == 'C') return 0;
        else if (c == 'D') return 0;
        else if (c == 'F') return 0;
        else return 1;
    }

    public static void main (String[] args)
    { int a=0, b=0, c=0, d=0, f=0;
      char grade;
      String output;

      grade = IO.readChar ("Enter grades as letters (ending with the letter X): ");
      while (isNotValidGrade(grade))
          grade = IO.readChar ("*INVALID GRADE, re-enter: ");

      while (grade != 'X')                         // sum each grade
      {   grade = Character.toUpperCase (grade);
          if (grade == 'A')       a = a+1;         // category . . .
          else if (grade == 'B')  b = b+1;
          else if (grade >= 'C')  c = c+1;
          else if (grade >= 'D')  d = d+1;
          else    f = f+1;

          grade = IO.readChar ("enter next grade: ");
          while (isNotValidGrade(grade))
              grade = IO.readChar ("*INVALID GRADE, re-enter: ");
      }
      output = "summary of grades: \n a:";
      output = IO.concatenate (output, a);
      output = IO.concatenate (output, "\n b:");
      output = IO.concatenate (output, b);
      output = IO.concatenate (output, "\n c:");
      output = IO.concatenate (output, c);
      output = IO.concatenate (output, "\n d:");
      output = IO.concatenate (output, d);
      output = IO.concatenate (output, "\n f:");
      output = IO.concatenate (output, f);
      IO.showMessage (output);
      System.exit(0);
    }
}
```

5.5 **Strings**

You have already been exposed to some limited use of **String** variables. Although **String** variables are not primitive data types like the others covered in this chapter, this distinction is not important at this point in your career. We'll get to the difference in Chapter 7. Let's review what you know to this point: **String** variables are declared just as other data types and may be initialized with a literal:

```
String name, location, address = "123 Oak Street";
```

String variables may also be assigned literals during the execution of a method or assigned the values of other **String** variables:

```
name = "John Smith";
location = address;
```

KEY TERM
string

Let's get a bit technical here with our terms. Between programmers, a literal is often refered to as a *string*. (Remember, a literal is a text message between two quotation marks.) Notice the case difference: A **String** is a variable type while *string* is another term for a literal or a sequence of text. This is very similar to saying that **int** is a variable type while integer is another term for a whole number. An **int** variable can hold an integer; a **String** variable can hold a string.

Just as there are methods in the IO class for the other data types learned, there is a method for reading in a string (a sequence of text) to a **String** variable:

```
name = IO.readString("enter a name: ");
```

In this situation, everything the user types in the display box prior to clicking OK or pressing the Enter key will be assigned to the String variable. For example:

In this case, when the user clicks OK, this full string will be assigned to the name variable, just as if we had used a literal. In other words, it has the same effect as:

```
name = "John C. Smithers";
```

Naturally, it does not make sense to try to multiply two strings or apply other mathmatical operations because **String** variables contain text. Even if the textual contents of a String variable are digit characters, it is still text:

```
String textnumber = "1234";
int value;
value = textnumber * 2;
```

In this example, the **String** variable textnumber contains the textual string "1234" or, in other words, the codes for each of these characters. That is quite different from the number 1234. Don't confuse numbers with strings.

Having said that, the + symbol may be used to concatenate two strings. Remember, this means to "join together." For example:

```
String first = "Fred", last = " Jones", fullname;
fullname = "Mr. " + first + last;
```

The + symbol means concatenation when placed between two strings. This concept of having an operator symbol mean more than one thing, or having the meaning of an operator symbol depend on the context in which it is used, is called *operator overloading*.

The concatenation operator (+) means we never really did need the concatenation method of the **IO** class after all! In fact, here is the complete method itself; it just applies the concatenation operator and returns the result:

```
public static String concatenate (String s1, String s2)
{   return (s1 + s2);
}
```

What happens when you wish to concatenate a string with a number? You will remember that numeric values or variables can automatically be promoted if you wish to apply an operator between them. If you attempt to multiply a **double** by an **int**, Java will automatically promote the **int** to a **double** prior to the multiplication. If you wish to assign a **float** to a **double**, Java will promote the **float** to a **double** to allow the assignment. (Java does not automatically demote because this may cause a loss of information—you may not assign a **double** to an **int** variable.)

A **String** is considered a higher data type than any of the numeric types. As such, a numeric type will be automatically promoted to a String if you wish to concatenate. For example:

```
String address = " Oak Street";
int number = 456;
address = number + address;
```

This last statement promotes number to a **String**, concatenates to produce "456 Oak Street" and assigns this to address. Be very careful that one of the arguments in a concatenation is a string. The following

```
String funnyname = 123 + 456 + "Fred";
```

will produce

```
579Fred
```

because the first + operator is addition.

Now you are thinking, "Hey, we don't really need IO.showValue() either!." That is correct. Here is the complete method itself; it just uses the + concatenation operator and invokes showMessage():

```
public static void showValue (String s, int i)
  { IO.showMessageDialog (s+i);
  }
```

CONCEPT

Java does not promote arguments

Be careful! Java does not promote arguments to parameters! When a method is invoked, the arguments must match the parameters in the intended method. What about displaying characters and floating-point values? You cannot call the above method with a **double** because the second parameter must be an **int**. The **IO** class actually has a showValue() method for each of the data types. In other words, there is another method of the same name:

```
public static void showValue (String s, double d)
  { IO.showMessageDialog (s+d);
  }
```

KEY TERM

polymorphism

Allowing more than one method to have the same name is a feature called *polymorphism*. When Java finds a statement invoking a method, it searches for the method (in the appropriate class) by finding a matching method signature. A signature consists of

1. the method name
2. the number and type of parameters
3. the method return value

No two methods in the same class may have the same signature, but they may have the same name. If Java cannot find a matching method signature, it won't give up yet—it searches for a signature close enough to allow promotion to fit the required signature. Remember, promotion implies that a type can be changed as long as there is no potential for loss of information.

The + operator is the only symbol used with **String** variables. Do not use the other numeric or relational operators (*, /, -, <, >, ==, !=, etc.). There is a way of alphabetically comparing two strings, but we'll leave that topic for Chapter 9.

5.6 Boolean variables

KEY TERM

boolean type

Often, we need to express a condition that can only be true or false. We've done this in the **if** and **while** statements. The results of a true/false expression can also be saved in a **boolean** variable. There are only two possible constants for **boolean** variables: the constant **true** and the constant **false**.

```
boolean passing;
if (grade > 75.0)
     passing = true;
else
     passing = false;
```

This variable can then later be used by another conditional statement:

```
if (passing)
    . . .
```

Notice that in this expression, the variable `passing` is **true** or **false** all by itself. It is the result of a previous assignment statement and does not need to be compared with anything. No other values except **true**, **false**, or the value in another **boolean** variable should be assigned. Arithmetic operators may not be used in a **boolean** expression. The relational operators (<, >=, etc.) all produce **boolean** results. When output, a **boolean** variable will display the word "true" or the word "false."

5.7 Example project

Let's write a class that could be used to make change at a checkout counter. The user will enter the price to be paid and the amount tendered. The class will then output the correct change—in dollars, quarters, dimes, nickels, and pennies. We'll use the truncation feature of integer division to produce the correct whole number of each denomination, just as we did early in this chapter. We'll also do this project without the **IO** class methods `showValue()` and `concatenate()`. We start with **int** variables for each denomination and **double** variables for the *cost* and *tendered* amounts:

```
int dollars, quarters, nickels, dimes, pennies;
double cost, tendered;
```

The number of dollars is the *tendered* amount minus the *cost*, with the fractional part thrown away caused by converting:

```
dollars = (int) (tendered - cost);
```

Notice that this is very different mathematically from the following:

```
dollars = (int) (tendered) - (int) (cost);
```

Now, the number of each denomination can be determined in turn, and the following class is produced (Listing 5.VIII):

Listing 5.VIII

```
// A class to calculate change for a given cost and amount tendered
public class make_change
{
 public static void main(String[] args)
   {
   double cost, tendered, change;
   int dollars, quarters, dimes, nickels, pennies;
   String output;
   cost = IO.readDouble("enter cost: ");
   tendered = IO.readDouble ("enter amount tendered: ");
   change = tendered - cost;                  // remaining change
   dollars = (int) (change);
   change = change - dollars;
   quarters = (int) (change / 0.25);
   change = change - (quarters * 0.25);   // remaining change
   dimes = (int) (change / 0.10);
   change = change - (dimes * 0.10);      // remaining change
   nickels = (int) (change / 0.05);
   change = change - (nickels * 0.05);    // remaining change
   pennies = (int) (change / 0.01);
   output = "change is dollars: " + dollars +"\n quarters: " + quarters
    + "\n dimes: " + dimes + "\ nickels: " + nickels + "\n pennies: " + pennies;
   IO.showMessage (output);
   System.exit(0);
 }
}
```

WRONG!

When this is executed with a cost of \$14.94 and an amount tendered of \$20.00, the following is displayed:

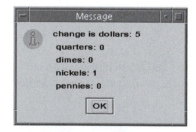

What happened? Go through this calculation in your head. The answer is correct except for the number of pennies. The last calculation

```
pennies = (int) (change / 0.01);
```

should have been performed when `change` was 0.01, resulting in an integer of 1, not 0. Well, one of these two double values (or both) might be accurate to only 16 decimal places. Suppose change was 0.00999999999999999. Now when we divide by 0.01, the result isn't 1.0, but 0.9999999999999999. When this is truncated, the answer is zero.

What we wanted was to *round* the final calculation to the nearest whole number, not simply truncate. How do you round a decimal value? Add 0.5 before truncation! Here is a simple method to round a double:

```
private static int round (double d)
{   return ((int) (d+0.5));
}
```

The final class (producing the correct answers) is Listing 5.IX:

Listing 5.IX

```
// A class to calculate change for a given cost and amount tendered
public class make_change
{ private static int round (double d)
    {       return ((int) (d+0.5));
    }
  public static void main(String[] args)
    {    double cost, tendered, change;
         int dollars, quarters, dimes, nickels, pennies;
         String output;
         cost = IO.readDouble("enter cost: ");
         tendered = IO.readDouble ("enter amount tendered: ");
         change = tendered - cost;              // remaining change
         dollars = (int) (change);
         change = change - dollars;
         quarters = (int) (change / 0.25);
         change = change - (quarters * 0.25); // remaining change
         dimes = (int) (change / 0.10);
         change = change - (dimes * 0.10);     // remaining change
         nickels = (int) (change / 0.05);
         change = change - (nickels * 0.05);   // remaining change
         pennies = round (change / 0.01);      // round the last calculation
         output = "change is dollars: " + dollars +"\n quarters: " + quarters
             + "\n dimes: " + dimes + "\ nickels: " + nickels + "\n pennies: " + pennies;
         IO.showMessage (output);
         System.exit(0);
    }
}
```

5.8 Summary

We have actually covered a great deal in this chapter. Some topics have only been introduced, and more will be seen in later chapters. Nevertheless, we have added quite a few new capabilities to your bag of programming skills.

KEY TERMS   Several new terms were introduced in this chapter:

1. *characteristic, mantissa*—the fraction and power or exponent of a number stored in scientific or E-notation.

2. *E notation*—representation of a very large or very small number using a characteristic and mantissa.

3. *overflow, underflow*—the error that occurs when an attempt is made to store a value too large or too small for a particular variable type.

4. *truncation error*—the error that results when a floating-point number is truncated to a limited number of precision digits.

5. *mixed-mode expression*—an arithmetic expression involving both floating-point and integer variables or values.

6. *casting*—forcing Java to convert from one data type to another, even though a loss of information may occur.

7. *primitive*—data types that are native to Java (examples are in Table 5.1).

8. *string*—a literal or **String** variable value.

9. *operator overloading*—using an operator symbol to mean more than one operation, depending on the context in which it is found.

10. *polymorphism*—having more than one method with the same name.

11. boolean—a variable that may only take on the values of true or false.

CONCEPTS   In addition to the **double** variable type previously used, several additional variable types were introduced: **float**, **int**, **short**, **long**, **char**, **String,** and **boolean**. Two additional comparison operators were also introduced for exact comparisons: **==** (equal to) and **!=** (not equal to). Input methods in the IO class are available for each of these data types. **String** variables are not appropriate for the numeric and relational operators. The + symbol implies concatenation when used with strings.

Java allows an assignment statement to be used anywhere a simple expression is expected.

Double values are rounded to a predetermined number of digits, usually about 16. **Int** variables are exact but have a more limited range than **double**. Neither floating-point nor integer constants are written with a comma. **Long** integers have more range than **int** but require much more memory. **Short** variables require less space than **int** but have a much smaller range. Integer values should not normally be written with a leading zero, as this implies a base-8 number.

Char variables are used to store codes for characters using the ISO Unicode standard. Character constants are written inside of single quotes. Both **int** and **char** variables and constants are appropriately compared using the **==** and **!=** exact comparison operators. Exact comparisons with floating-point values may not be appropriate because they represent rounded accuracy.

It is important that the types of function arguments match the corresponding function parameter types. Also, a function call must pass the correct number of arguments.

The rules for mixed-mode expressions are:

1. Java will automatically *promote* an **int** or a **float** to a **double**. This automatic conversion results in no loss of information and is not considered an error.

2. Java will not automatically *demote* a **double** to a **float** or an **int** because information may be lost (due to the loss of precision or range). An attempt to assign a **double** to an **int** variable will result in a compiler error. Demotion can be forced by casting.

3. Any mathematical operation involving two integers always results in an integer.

The most important concept to remember about these three rules is that *an integer divided by an integer always results in an integer.*

The assignment statement may be used anywhere the compiler expects to find an expression. This may lead to inadvertent errors because the following two if statements may appear similar, but they have very different meanings:

```
if (x == y) . . . // test for exact equality
if (x = y) . . .  // test of the value assigned to x (zero or non-zero)
```

String variables and strings may be concatenated with the + operator. If one of the arguments in a concatenation is numeric, Java will promote the number to its textual representation as a string prior to concatenation.

Table 5.3   Example segments

`double x, y;`	x and y are to be double-precision real variables
`x = 5.3E-5;`	x is to be assigned 0.000053.
`char c;`	c is to be assigned the question mark character
`c = '?';`	(code).
`if (c < 'z')` `    IO.showMessage("yes");`	Output `"yes"` if the character assigned to c is less than the letter z.
`int a;` `a = 5 + 3 / 2;`	Since 3/2 is an integer calculation, the 5 is added to 1 (1.5 truncated). a is then assigned 6.
`if (done) . . .`	True if done is not zero.
`int a;` `a =(int) (6.3 / 2.9);`	The division results in 2.17. This is demoted (truncated) to 2 for assignment.

5.9 Exercises

Short-answer questions

1. Which type of variable in Java has a more limited range—**int** or **float**?
2. Which type of variable in Java may only approximately represent the following decimal input number: 1.2345678
3. The following number is in scientific notation. Identify the characteristic.
   3×10^5
4. Identify the mantissa in the above scientific notation number.
5. What is wrong with the following assignment statement?

   ```
   cost = 1,234;
   ```

6. Briefly explain truncation error.
7. The arguments in a function call must match function parameters in both
   _____ and _____.
8. When **double** variables are assigned, the representation is accurate to approximately _____ significant digits.
9. When inputting characters into **char** variables, the readChar() method operation will skip over _____ _____.
10. Briefly explain what a *whitespace* character is.
11. What values would be assigned to the **int** variable x in each case:
    a. x = 5 + (int) 7.6;
    b. x = (int) (5 / 7.6);
    c. x = 7 / 5;
    d. x = (int) 7.6 / (int) 5.5;
12. What values would be assigned to the **float** variable y in each case:
    a. y = 5 + 7.6;
    b. y = 5 / (int) 7.6;
    c. y = 5 / 7;
    d. y = (int) (5.5 / 7.6);
13. Express each value in E notation:
    a. 0.00000576
    b. 576000000000.0
14. Write a segment of a method to appropriately add the following five variables to the value in sum. Assume each of these variables contains a relatively small number, but sum contains a relatively large number:

    ```
    float small1, small2, small3, small4, small5, sum;
    ```

15. Briefly explain a situation where variable overflow could occur.
16. Briefly explain why it may not be appropriate to compare two **double** variables with the exact comparison operator ==.
17. Propose a small segment of a method that could be used to test whether the **double** variable x contains a whole number.

18. Explain briefly why the variable type **double** guarantees a decimal representation with more precision and more range than a **float** variable in any given Java system.

19. Determine the possible character values for c for which the following **if** statements would output "yes":

```
char thischar;
if (thischar > 'a')
     if (c <= 'f') IO.showMessage ("yes");
     else ;
else ;
```

20. What would be stored in variable name as a result of the following?

```
String name;
int age = 21;
double weight = 175.4;
name = "Fred Smith " + (age + weight);
```

Projects

1. Write a class to calculate and output the integer number of ounces in a given weight expressed as a floating-point number of pounds.

2. Write a method named IsOdd() to return 1 or true if an integer parameter is odd. The function should return zero or false otherwise.

3. Write a method named IsDivisibleBy5() to return 1 or true if an integer parameter is evenly divisible by 5 and return false or 0 otherwise.

4. A researcher has a list of weights for two different rats in a nutrition study. These rats are named X and Y. Each line in the list contains a rat name and a weight for a different study day. Each rat has five weights, but the list is in no particular order. Write a class to input such a list and output the average weight for each of the two rats.

5. Write a method to input a character and then output the equivalent uppercase letter.

6. Modify the class of Project 5 so that the input character is converted to lowercase if it is entered in uppercase and to uppercase if it is entered in lowercase.

7. Write a method to determine if two double values are very close—in this case, within 0.0001. Tip: Compare the absolute value of the difference of the two numbers using the Math.abs() method.

8. Write a class to input text characters from the keyboard and output the equivalent Morse code. The translation table is as follows:

```
A   .-          B   -...        C   -.-.

D   -..         E   .           F   ..-.

G   --.         H   ....        I   ..

J   .---        K   -.-         L   .-..
```

M	--	N	-.	O	---
P	.--.	Q	--.-	R	.-.
S	...	T	-	U	..-
V	...-	W	.--	X	-..-
Y	-.--	Z	--..		

9. Creative Challenge: Write a class to input a paragraph ending with a Return keystroke and then output the same paragraph with the first word of each sentence capitalized.

10. Creative Challenge: Write a function to input a paragraph and then count and return the number of times a spelling mistake is made because this rule was not followed: *i before e except after c*. (Yes, there is more to the rule, but this is enough of a challenge as it is!)

More Control Structures

Your programs are becoming sufficiently complex that you need to learn more of the control structures and operators available in Java. These extra capabilities will not necessarily enable you to write classes that you could not have written before, but they will allow you to write them more concisely, express your ideas more clearly, and develop classes and methods faster. They will also lower the probability for mistakes in complex programs and allow such classes to be more easily maintained.

6.1 The single-choice `if`

CONCEPT
a variation of the
`if` statement

Up to now, we have used an `if` statement form that provided both a true and a false alternative for each choice. There is a second form of the `if` statement that is best used when there is only a single choice to be made (without an alternative). In this form, the `else` clause is simply omitted. In other words, if the expression within the parentheses is true, the statement associated with the `if` is executed, and control is then passed to the following statement. If the expression is false, control is passed to the following statement. Naturally, the statement associated with the `if` can be a

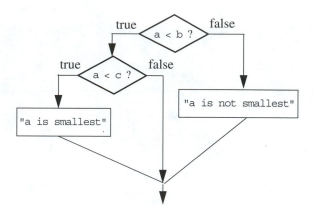

Figure 6.1 Symbolic diagram of a desired nested **if**

compound statement enclosed within { } braces. The general form of this statement is given in the following syntax diagram:

> **if** (*expression*) *statement*   **Syntax form**

Here is a simple statement that outputs a warning message if the variable age is less than zero:

```
if (age < 0)
    IO.showMessage (" Warning, age is negative");
```

This may seem like a very simple statement to learn, after having learned the **if** statement with two choices, but there is a subtlety here when we nest the single-choice form inside the two-choice form. Consider Figure 6.1. According to this diagram, the message "a is smallest" should be output when a is less than both b and c. The message "a is not smallest" should be output when a is not less than b. If a is less than b but not less than c, no message should be output at all. The first condition appears to be the familiar two-choice **if** because something needs to be done for both a true and a false choice. The second condition appears to be a single-choice **if** because there is nothing to be done when false. Your first attempt at coding this diagram in a top-down fashion might be the following:

```
if (a < b)

    statements if true
```

```
else
```

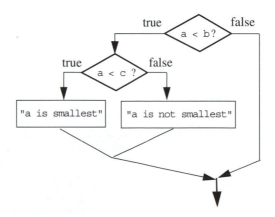

The oval here contains: statements if false

Here the two ovals represent the true and false sides of the outer two-choice **if**: The false side is the output for the message "a is not smallest". The true side is the single-choice **if**. Now, when you fill these ovals in, you come up with something like the following:

```
if (a < b)
      if (a < c)
            IO.showMessage ("a is smallest";)
else
      IO.showMessage ("a is not smallest");
```

WRONG!

CONCEPT
associating an
else with an if

When this code is run, you find that when a is not less than b, nothing is output even though you expected the second message to appear! The reason has to do with which **if** the **else** belongs to. Look again at Figure 6.1. Even though you have written the code with the proper indentation to show that the **else** belongs to the top **if**, the compiler doesn't consider indentation or spacing. *An **else** will always be associated with the closest **if** possible.* Notice that when you tab the bottom two lines over a bit, you can see what the compiler is assuming:

```
if (a < b)
      if (a < c)
            IO.showMessage ("a is smallest");
      else
            IO.showMessage ("a is not smallest");
```

Figure 6.2 shows what logic is really being expressed by this nested **if** segment.

Figure 6.2   Symbolic diagram of nested
if as written

You can see why the results were not as expected. How can such errors in logic be avoided so that an **else** is always associated with the **if** you intend? There are several methods. A good rule of thumb here is to *always place* **{ }** *braces around both choices* of a two-choice **if** as follows:

```
if (a < b)
{      if (a < c)
              IO.showMessage ("a is smallest");
}
else
{   IO.showMessage ("a is not smallest");
}
```

Notice that now the **else** can only be associated with the top **if**—which is what you originally had in mind.

6.2 Compound comparisons

Suppose you would like to display an error message if the user inputs a value for a variable age that you consider to be outside expected limits. The purpose is to warn the user that an entry error may have occurred. Let's say that an age value should lie between the values of 0 and 100. With what you have learned so far, this is probably going to require two **if** statements and two output statements:

```
age = IO.readInt ("enter age: ");
if (age > 100)
    IO.showMessage (" ERROR; age is outside expected limits");
if (age < 0)
    IO.showMessage (" ERROR; age is outside expected limits");
```

Actually, Java allows you to combine these two tests in a single **if** through use of the operators || and **&&**. The || operator represents the logical OR of two expressions: If *either* expression is true, the entire test is true. The **&&** operator represents the logical AND of two expressions: If *both* expressions are true, the entire test is true. Both of these operators have a precedence lower than any of the comparison or arithmetic operators. The **&&** operator has a precedence greater than the || operator. (Of course, anytime you are not sure in what order the operators of a particular expression will be evaluated, simply use parentheses to indicate your desires.) The above segment of code could be expressed much more simply with a single **if**:

```
age = IO.readInt ("enter age: ");
if ((age > 100) || (age < 0))
    IO.showMessage (" ERROR; age is outside expected limits");
```

Table 6.1   `boolean` `&&` and `||` **operators**

a	b	a && b	a || b
true	true	true	true
true	false	false	true
false	true	false	true
false	false	false	false

KEY TERM
boolean
operators

These two operators are called **boolean** operators because they compare two expressions that are true or false themselves to determine whether an entire test is true or false. A **boolean** expression or value can only take on the values true or false. It should be obvious now that an **if** or **while** statement treats the expression inside the parentheses as a **boolean** value even if the expression is arithmetic. (Remember that any arithmetic expression or variable is considered true if nonzero and false if zero.) Table 6.1 summarizes the use of these operators.

Now, suppose you wish to test if the variable a is smaller than both b and c:

```
if (a < b && a < c)
    IO.showMessage ("a is smallest");
else
    IO.showMessage ("a is not smallest");
```

CONCEPT
be careful with
English statements

Be sure to use these operators correctly; a single `&` or `|` means something quite different, just as a single `=` is quite different than the `==` operator. (The `|` and `&` operators are used for bitwise manipulation and testing). Another common error is to try and translate an English statement of a test into Java directly. For example, in English, you might express a test by saying "a is less than b or c." Coding this directly into Java produces:

```
if (a < b || c) . . .
```
(WRONG!)

The **boolean** operators `&&` and `||` are used to combine two expressions or tests that are already true or false. In other words, the operands on either side of a **boolean** operator are assumed to represent true or false themselves. The English statement just given implies that we are testing that "a is less than b and a is also less than c." The correct coding is:

```
if (a < b && a < c) . . .
```

Always make sure that you intend both sides of a `&&` or `||` operator to be true/false comparisons or tests themselves. Remember, both sides of a **boolean** operator are considered as **boolean** expressions. The **if** statement marked WRONG! above does not produce an error message. If you think about it, this statement tests whether a is less than b OR whether c is true or nonzero.

CONCEPT
boolean operator precedence

In this example, the less than operator has precedence over the || operator. In general, all comparison or relational operators have precedence over **&&**, which in turn has precedence over ||. Rather than memorize these rules, the simple strategy of always using sufficient parentheses will ensure that operators will be performed in the order you intend.

CONCEPT
NOT operator

There is one more **boolean** operator: the **!** or NOT operator. This is a unary operator in that it is placed just before a single operand. The effect is to *complement* the operand or take its opposite. The **!** operator has precedence over the relational or comparison operators and the other **boolean** operators. For example:

!a	true if a is not true
!(a<b)	true if a is not less than b (a is greater than or equal to b)
!(a==b)	true if a is not equal to b
!(a>=b)	true if a is not greater than or equal to b (a is less than b)

Remember, the opposite or complement of less than is not greater than, but greater than or equal to. Expressions involving the **!** operator become a bit more complex when used in compound expressions with **&&** and ||. For example, consider the following expression:

!((a<b) && (b>=c))   same as   (a>=b) || (b<c)

You can convince yourself this is the case with Table 6.2, which examines all the possibilities.

CONCEPT
comparison conversions

In general, any **boolean** expression with a **!** operator in front of it can be converted to an equivalent **boolean** expression without the preceding **!** by first complementing every operator within the expression. In the expression, the < is changed to >=, the **&&** is changed to ||, the >= is changed to <, and so on. Next, if any subexpressions are themselves **boolean** (with && or || operators), you complement each operand.

KEY TERM
DeMorgan's theorem

A **boolean** expression or result may of course, be stored or assigned into a **boolean** variable (refer to Chapter 5). This is known as *DeMorgan's theorem*. Here are some simple examples of equivalent **boolean** expressions generated with this theorem:

!(!a)	same as	a
!(a == b)	same as	(a != b)

Table 6.2 Comparison of ! ((a<b) && (b>=c) and (a>=b) || (b<c)

a<b	b>=c	a>=b	b<c	!((a<b)&&(b>=c))	(a>=b)||(b<c)
true	true	false	false	false	false
true	false	false	true	true	true
false	true	true	false	true	true
false	false	true	true	true	true

`!(a || b)`	same as	`(!a && !b)`
`!(a && b)`	same as	`(!a || !b)`
`!(a < b)`	same as	`(a >= b)`

When there are `!` operators inside the expression, it is best to convert these sub-expressions first and and then convert the entire expression. For example:

`!((a>b) && !(c<d))`	same as	`!((a>b) && (c>=d))`
	same as	`(a<=b) || (c < d)`

6.3 The `for` loop

The definite or *counted loop* is very common in programming. If you remember, this is a loop where the number of iterations is known beforehand—for example, when you need a method to input exactly *N* decimal values and then return the average to the calling class. With your current knowledge and skills, you would use a **while** statement. Your counted loop would probably consist of segments that perform three operations—initialize, test, and update:

1. Initialize a counting variable to 0 prior to the loop.

2. At the beginning or top of the loop, test the counting variable against the limit *N* for each loop iteration.

> *loop body*

3. At the bottom of the loop, update (increment) the counting variable.

Your method might look like Listing 6.I:

Listing 6.I

```
// AverageInput1 ()  Input N values and return average.
//  IN:  N -- the number of values to input and average.
//  ASSUMPTION: at least one value is entered.
private static double AverageInput1 (int N)
  { double sum = 0.0, value;

    int count = 0;                              // 1. initialize counter to 0
    while (count < N)                           // 2. test count against limit
    {value = IO.readInt ("enter value: ");
     sum = sum + value;
     count = count + 1;                         // 3. update counter
    }
    return (sum / count);
  }
```

There is a Java statement that combines all three operations of the counted loop—the **for** statement:

> **for** (*expr₁*; *expr₂*; *expr₃*) *statement*

Syntax form

CONCEPT

the for statement

As you can see, the **for** statement contains three expressions within parentheses. The statement following the parentheses is the body of the loop. Naturally, this statement body can be a single statement or a compound statement within { } braces. There are three rules governing the execution of a **for** statement:

1. The first expression is evaluated *prior* to the loop.

2. The second expression is tested at the *beginning of each loop iteration* to determine if the statement body should again be executed.

3. The last expression is evaluated *after* each loop iteration.

Remember that an assignment statement can be used where an arithmetic expression is expected. Consider the following segment:

```
for (count=0; count < N; count=count+1)
      statement;
```

The statement (or compound statement inside { } braces) will be repeatedly executed in a counted-loop fashion. First, count is initialized to 0. Next, count<N is tested. If true, the loop is entered and the *statement* body of the loop is executed. At the bottom of the loop, count=count+1 is executed, and control returns to the top of the loop to retest count<N. The loop continues to execute until the test is false. At this point, control is passed to the next statement. Suppose N is 3. This **for** loop is shorthand for the following intended operations (in English):

set count to zero	*(first expression)*
is count < N? yes, so do:	*(second expression)*
statement;	
set count to count+1	*(third expression) [1]*
is count < N? yes, so do:	*(second expression)*
statement;	

set count to count+1   *(third expression) [2]*

is count < N? yes, so do: *(second expression)*
    statement;

set count to count+1   *(third expression) [3]*

is count < N? no,   *(second expression)*
    continue with rest of class . . .

So, if N is 3, the statement body of the loop is executed three times. If N is 5, the statement body is executed five times. At this point, you could rewrite the method of Listing 6.II:

Listing 6.II

```
// AverageInput2 ()  Input N values and return average.
//  IN:  N -- the number of values to input and average.
//  ASSUMPTION: at least one value is entered.
private static double AverageInput2 (int N)
 {  double sum = 0.0, value;

    for (count=0; value > N; count=count+1)
    {  value = IO.readInt ("enter value: ");
       sum = sum + value;
    }
    return (sum / count);
 }
```

The **for** statement is not limited, however, only to counted loops. Any type of loop can be implemented as long as the three rules are considered. For example, here is a variation of Listing 6.II with a *sentinel loop* using the **for** statement. The purpose of the method is to input and average an indeterminate number of positive values ending with a negative number as the sentinel value (Listing 6.III):

Listing 6.III

```
// AverageInput3 ()  Input positive values until a negative sentinel value is
// encountered. Return the average.
//  ASSUMPTION: at least one value is entered.
private static double AverageInput3 ()
 {  double sum = 0.0, value;
    int count;
    value = IO.readInt ("enter a value (-1 to end): ");
    for (count=0; value > 0.0; count=count+1)
    {     sum = sum + value;
         value = IO.readInt ("enter value: ");
    }
    return (sum / count);
 }
```

It could be argued that this version of a sentinel loop is no less complex than what would have been written using a **while** statement. Generally, a good programmer will use a **for** statement for a definite loop (e.g., a counted loop) and a·**while** statement for an indefinite loop (e.g., a sentinel loop).

To help ensure that you understand the three rules for evaluating **for** statements, consider the following code segment in which two **for** statements are nested:

```
for (n=0; n<3; n=n+1)
    for (k=n; k<3; k=k+1)
        IO.showMessage (n + "   " + k);
```

First, let's represent the segment in a top-down fashion and look at the top loop:

```
for (n=0; n<3; n=n+1)
```

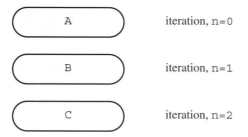

The oval now represents the statement body of this top or outer loop. By examining this **for** statement, you can see that the statement body will be executed three times, once for each value of n (0, 1, and 2). The following diagram represents these three iterations as three ovals labeled A, B, and C:

A	iteration, n=0
B	iteration, n=1
C	iteration, n=2

Let's now look at the first iteration of the oval A when n = 0. The statement inside this oval is the second **for** loop. During this oval, n is 0:

```
for (k=(0);  k<3;  k=k+1)
    IO.showMessage ( (0) + "   " + k);
```

This is just a simple **for** loop that will execute the output statement three times with k having values of 0, then 1, and then 2. For each output statement, the values of n (0) and k are output in three separate display boxes (represented with the following three lines):

0   0

0   1

0   2

Now look at the second iteration, or oval B, when n = 1:

```
for (k=(1); k<3;  k=k+1)
    IO.showMessage ( (1) << "   " + k);
```

This loop will execute the output statement two times with k having values 1 and then 2:

1   1

1   2

Next look at the last iteration, or oval C, when n = 2:

```
for (k=(2);  k<3;  k=k+1)
    IO.showMessage ( (2) + " " + k);
```

This loop will execute the output statement one time with k as 2:

2   2

Finally, just put all the oval results or outputs together in order (each line represents a display box):

0   0

0   1

0   2

1   1

1   2

2   2

To illustrate this concept of loops within loops, let's write a method that could be used to graph the cosine from 0 radians to 2π radians. We begin using a top-down design approach. We decide that our graph should have 20 plot points, which means angle steps of $\pi/20$. Recognizing that display output goes from top to bottom and left to right, we choose to orient the output graph vertically. The `main()` method can now be written (Listing 6.IV):

EXPERIMENT

What would happen if you initialized the counter to a value that is greater than the limits of the test? Try:

```
for (n=5; n<4; n=n+1)
    IO.showValue ("n: ",  n);
```

Listing 6.IV

```
// DrawCos --  Plot the cosine method horizontally on the
// screen for angles from 0 to 2π.
public class Drawcos
{private PlotYAxis ()
  {                                         // to be done . . .
  }

 private PlotPoint (double angle)
  {                                         // to be done . . .
  }
public static void main (String[] args)
  { double angle, anglestep, limit;
    String output;
    limit = 2 * Math.PI;
    anglestep = limit / 20.0;                       // angle for each plot point

    output = PlotYAxis ();
// draw the Y axis and
// plot a point for each angle from 0 to 2PI in steps of 2PI/20

    for (angle=0.0; angle < limit; angle = angle+anglestep)
      output = output + PlotPoint (angle);

    IO.showMessage (output);
    System.exit(0);
  }
```

We've left the two helper methods blank—using our "top-down" design approach. Let's look at the requirements for the method `PlotYAxis()`. This draws the `Y` axis (now horizontal) and scale marks into a `String` to be returned. The following would work:

```
// Returns:  A String text line containing the Y axis and scale marks
 private static String PlotYAxis ()
  { String s;
    s = " -1.0                              0.0                              1.0 \n";
    s = s + "---------------------------------|-------------------------------- \n";
    return s;
  }
```

At this point, you might stub in the method `PlotPoint()` to output the parameters and ensure that the class was working to that stage. In any case, let's now approach the `PlotPoint()` method. It must accept an angle as a parameter and draw a horizontal line with a plot point in the appropriate position for that angle. In other words, each plot point becomes a line on the screen. Suppose you choose to use the capital `X` as a plotting symbol.

First, walk through the problem with an example angle value, say, 0.786 radians. Your calculator will indicate the cosine is 0.707. You know the cosine goes from a maximum of 1.0 to a minimum of −1.0, and these must fit within your line; the 1.0 should be on the far right of the screen with the −1.0 on the far left. Let's say we want a horizontal line to be 40 characters wide. So a cosine of 0.707 should correspond to about position 28. The only trick now is to generate 27 blanks, and then an `X`!

To scale any cosine value to fit in the appropriate proportional position along these 40 character lines, you might use the following calculation:

```
position = (int) (Math.cos(angle) * 20 + 20);
```

Now your method becomes similar to the following:

```
// Plot the cosine of the angle parameter
// on a line across the screen
//  IN:  angle -- the angle in radians to be plotted
//  OUT:  a String text line containing the plot point.
  private static String PlotPoint (double angle)
 { String s = "";
   int blanks, position;
   position = (int) (Math.cos(angle) * 20 + 20);
   for (blanks=0; blanks<position; blanks=blanks+1)
   s = s + "  ";
   s = s + "X \n";
   return s;
}
```

When you run the class project developed using these listings (with the private helper methods fleshed out as shown), you will see a plot similar to Figure 6.3 on your screen.

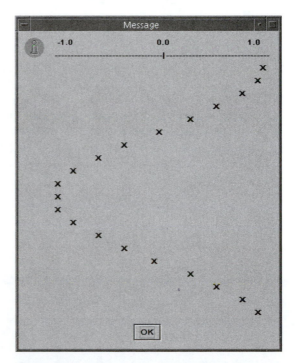

Figure 6.3 Plot of cosine from 0 to 2π using the **DrawCos** class

6.4 **Shorthand operators**

Now is a good time to introduce an interesting concept that you haven't seen before: Java generally allows the use of an assignment, input, or output statement anywhere an arithmetic expression is expected. This feature has a number of useful applications. For example, consider Listing 5.V. It required five assignment statements to initialize the five variables all to zero. Look at the following statement:

```
a = (b = 0);
```

This may appear quite strange at first glance. Actually, it is just an example of the feature just mentioned: The variable a is being assigned the value of the expression within the parentheses. This expression is the result of the enclosed assignment statement. In other words, zero is assigned to b, and then the value of that expression (the value assigned or zero) is copied into a. The net effect is to assign zero to both a and b in one simple statement.

An assignment operator to the right has precedence over any to the left. As such, the parentheses in the above example are actually not needed. We could now combine all five assignment statements from Listing 5.V with the following:

```
a = b = c = d = f = 0;              // initialize all to zero
```

This shorthand notation can easily be abused, however. The following statement is quite valid but in very poor style:

```
a = (b = c+2) * (d = 5);           // POOR STYLE!
```

CONCEPT
avoid nesting
nontrivial
assignments

Here, the value of c+2 is assigned to b, then the value of 5 is assigned to d, and then the two values assigned (c+2 and 5) are multiplied and assigned to a. This is poor style for several reasons. First, this statement is difficult to read at first glance. It must be examined carefully to determine the intended effect. Second, it is more difficult to debug because it is more difficult to examine the intermediate operation results. Be careful with nesting assignment statements as a shorthand method. You are undoubtedly learning by now that it may take a bit more typing to be clear and simple when writing a class, but it tends to *save a lot of time in the debugging stage* of class development.

CONCEPT
shorthand
operators

Several other shorthand notations or operators are allowed in Java:

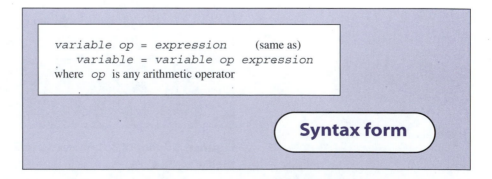

```
variable op = expression      (same as)
    variable = variable op expression
where  op  is any arithmetic operator
```

Syntax form

This syntax form indicates that the following pairs of assignment statements have exactly the same meaning; one is just a shorthand notation for the other.

```
a *= b;          same as      a = a * b;

x += y+z;        same as      x = x  + (y+z);

z += 1;          same as      z = z + 1;
```

CONCEPT

++ and -- operators

The last statement simply increments or adds 1 to a variable. This operation is very common, and there is another shorthand notation to do just that:

```
variable ++      increment the variable after use
++ variable      increment the variable before use
variable --      decrement the variable after use
-- variable      decrement the variable before use
```

Syntax form

This syntax form indicates that the following line represents three different ways of saying exactly the same thing—add 1 to the current value of a:

```
a++;      a += 1;      a = a + 1;
```

KEY TERM

pre-, postincrement

When the increment operator follows a variable, it is called a *postincrement*. When the operator precedes the variable, it is a *preincrement*. When the increment (or decrement) operator is used by itself, it doesn't really matter which of the two forms is used. The difference between pre- and postincrementing (or decrementing) is important, however, when the operator is used within another statement, such as is illustrated by the following segments:

```
b = a++;    // 'a' is assigned to 'b', then 'a' is incremented
```

Assume a initially to contain 5; b would be assigned 5, and a would be incremented to 6. In other words, a is incremented after it is used in the assignment. If you used the other form instead

```
b = ++a;    // 'a' is incremented, then assigned to 'b'
```

then a would first be incremented to 6 and then used in the assignment; b would be assigned 6. In both cases, a changes to 6. The only difference is whether to use the original value of a or the incremented value of a in the assignment. By the same token, the following statement

```
IO.showValue ("a: ", a++);        // output 'a', then increment
```

would output the current value of a and then increment a. If a were to originally contain 5, that value would be output. After the output, however, a would contain 6.

Many good programmers find that time is saved in the long run if the increment and decrement operators are generally used alone rather than within another statement. Breaking a statement such as the previous output into two separate statements may require a few extra keystrokes, but it tends to save debugging time downstream. When this rule of thumb is followed, it really doesn't matter which form of increment (or decrement) is used:

```
IO.showValue ("a: ", a);
a++;
```

EXPERIMENT

What would happen if you attempt this?

```
int a;   ++a = 5;
```

How is this different from the following?

```
a++ = 5;
```

CONCEPT

avoid using =, ++, or -- in a compound test

Be very careful not to embed assignment or increment/decrement operators within an **if** or while test. (Later, you will see there are other operators that can change the value of a variable, and these are to be avoided here too.) The reason is that a compiler will usually attempt to optimize the machine instructions generated from a Java class so that no unnecessary instructions are performed. For example, consider the following **if** statement:

```
if (a<5 && (b>a++)) . . .
```

The intent of this statement is to test whether a is less than 5 AND b is greater than a. After a is referenced on the right side of this compound comparison, it is to be incremented. The compiler, however, may generate instructions such that if the left part of the expression (a<5) is not true, the *rest of the test is skipped* because the entire test is guaranteed to be false. The result is that the right part of the test (b>a++) is never considered, and the value of a is never incremented. This rule of thumb holds for any operation that you expect to be evaluated. If it should always be done, do not place it inside a test.

KEY TERM

optimization

Although a complete discussion of *optimization* is beyond the scope if this text, you should be aware that this may include the abovementioned short-circuiting of compound expressions as well as actual reconstruction of some code segments to make a class faster or require less space. For example, which of the following segments do you think will execute faster (given the same machine and compiler)—segment #1 or segment #2?

```
a = (b * c)  + d / e + 5;                    // segment #1
x = (b * c)  + d / e  + 6;

temp = (b * c) + d / e;                      // segment #2
a = temp + 5;
x = temp + 6;
```

Actually, there will probably be little difference in execution time. Even though the first segment seems to contain more operations, a good compiler will optimize or reconstruct the first segment to be as efficient as the second without further programmer effort.

CONCEPT

the modulo operator

There is another arithmetic operator that has not yet been covered. It isn't really a shorthand operator, but we'll present it here anyway. You know that the / operator results in the dividend of the first or left operand divided by the right operand. The %, or *modulo operator*, results in the remainder of the left operand divided by the right operand. For example:

```
int a=3, b=4, c=5;
IO.showValue ("a%b: ", a%b);  // (3/4) has remainder 3; outputs 3
IO.showValue ("c%a: ", c%a);  // (5/3) has remainder 2; outputs 2
IO.showValue ("27/c ", 27/c); // outputs 5
IO.showValue ("27%c ", 27%c;  // outputs remainder 2
```

In a previous problem, we needed a method of determining whether a given integer was even. The modulo operator provides a simple solution. An **if** statement can be used to check the remainder after a division by 2 for a true (nonzero) or false (zero) value:

```
if (a % 2)
    IO.showMessage ("a is not even");
else
    IO.showMessage ("a is even");
```

Table 6.3 summarizes the precedence and associativity (order of evaluation for equal precedence operations) of many common operators.

Table 6.3   Precedence and associativity of operators

Operators	Associativity
(highest) ++ -- !	right to left
* / %	left to right
+ -	left to right
>> <<	left to right
< <= > >=	left to right
== !=	left to right
&&	left to right
||	left to right
(lowest) = *= += -= &= |=	right to left

6.5 **Multiple choice and the** `switch`

Occasionally, many more than two choices are needed in a class decision. We can accomplish this with many **if** statements, but it is usually much simpler to employ the **switch** statement. For example, look back at Listing 5.V, used to compile a list of grades. It required four nested **if** statements to determine whether an input grade was A, B, C, D, or F. This class becomes much simpler to code using the **switch**. The syntax for this statement is:

```
switch ( expression )
{ case value₁ :   statements₁
  case value₂ :   statements₂
  case value₃ :   statements₃
  . . .
  default:   statements
}
```

Syntax form

CONCEPT
the switch
statement

Although it may appear complex, the interpretation of the **switch** is quite simple: When a **switch** statement is executed, the *expression* is compared to each of the listed **case** *values* from the top down. At the first match, the class begins execution of the *statements* at that entry point (at the *statements* associated with that **case** *value*). For example, if the *value* of the *expression* matched *value*$_2$, then *statements*$_2$ would be executed, followed by *statements*$_3$ and so on down through the list of *statement* groups. The *values* associated with each **case** must be integer or character constants. The *expression* must result in an integer or character *value*. Decimal or **double** values are not allowed. In this syntax form, *statements* can be a single *statement,* a sequence of *statements,* or a compound set of *statements* in { } braces. For example:

```
int x;
x = IO.readInt ("enter x: ", x);
switch (x)
{   case 1:      IO.showMessage ( "first line");
                 IO.showMessage ( "  continued first line" );
    case 2:      IO.showMessage ( "second line");
                 IO.showMessage ( "  continued second line" );
    case 3:      IO.showMessage ( "third line");
    default:     IO.showMessage ( "last line");
}
```

Suppose when this segment is executed, the user enters 2. The output would be as follows:

```
second line continued second line
third line
last line
```

The *statements* associated with a **case** *value* are optional. This allows several **case** *values* to be associated with the same *statement.* In addition, the **default** clause is optional. For example:

```
switch (x)
{   case 0:
    case 1:                IO.showMessage ( "first line");
    case 2:                IO.showMessage ( "second line" );
    case 3:
    case 4:                IO.showMessage ( "third line" );
}
```

In this example, a *value* of 0 or 1 for x would cause all three messages to be displayed. A value of 3 or 4 would cause the "third line" message to be displayed. A user entry of 5 (not in the list) would have no associated **case** *value,* and the **switch** statement would be ignored.

CONCEPT
the break
statement

Frequently, a programmer will desire that the rest of the *statements* in a **switch** not be executed. To accomplish this, we need another Java statement—the **break**.

```
break ;
```

Syntax form

When the class encounters a **break** statement, it will exit the current control statement (in this case, a **switch)** and move to the following statement. Consider the following modification to the above code segment:

```
int x;
x = IO.readInt ("enter X: ");
switch (x)
{   case 1:        IO.showMessage ( "first line" );
                   break;
    case 2:        IO.showMessage ( "second line");
                   break;
    case 3:        IO.showMessage ( "third line");
                   break;
    default:       IO.showMessage ( "last line");
}
```

CONCEPT
use break only for
the switch
statement

Now when the user enters 2, only the "second line" message is displayed. As mentioned, the **break** can be used to exit several control structures, including the **for** and **while**. In practice, however, a good programmer only needs it for the **switch** statement. In the other control structures, the test associated with the statement determines when the statement is finished, just as we have done all along.

Let's rewrite the class of Listing 5.V. If you turn back to Chapter 5, you will remember that this class allowed the user to enter a list of letter grades and then output a summary table containing the number of As, Bs, and so on. The rewrite appears in Listing 6.V.

Listing 6.V

```
// A class to compile a table of student grades (updated from Listing 5.V)
public class stud_grades3
{
 public static void main (String[] args)
 { int a=b=c=d=f=0;
   char grade;
   String output;
   grade = IO.readChar ("Enter grades as capital letters (ending with the letter X): ");
   while (grade != 'X')                    // sum each grade
   {       switch (grade)
           {   case 'A':        a++;  break;
               case 'B':        b++;  break;
               case 'C':        c++;  break;
               case 'D':        d++;  break;
               case 'F':        f++;   break;
               default:         IO.showMessage ("illegal grade");
           }
           grade = IO.readChar ("enter next grade: ");
   }
 }
    output = "summary of grades: \n a:";
    output = IO.concatenate (output, a);
    output = IO.concatenate (output, "\n b:");
    output = IO.concatenate (output, b);
    output = IO.concatenate (output, "\n c:");
    output = IO.concatenate (output, c);
    output = IO.concatenate (output, "\n d:");
    output = IO.concatenate (output, d);
    output = IO.concatenate (output, "\n f:");
    output = IO.concatenate (output, f);
    IO.showMessage (output);
    System.exit(0);
   }
}
```

6.6 The `do-while` loop

CONCEPT

the `do-while` statement

When using the **while** statement for a loop, the test for continuing is always made at the top of the loop. It is possible that the loop body might not be executed at all if the test is initially negative when the loop is reached. Occasionally, it might be desired that a loop execute at least once regardless of the initial value of the test. In these cases, a programmer would use the **do-while** statement.

```
do
   statement
while ( expression );
```

Syntax form

Naturally, the *statement* body of the loop can be a single statement or a block of statements enclosed within **{ }** braces. The **do-while** is just a variant of the **while** statement, the only difference being that the test is made at the bottom of the loop instead of at the top. There are some situations where this type of loop corresponds better to the structure of an algorithm or design. Consider the problem of inputting an uppercase letter. If a character is input that is not an uppercase letter, the class should reject that input and reprompt the user to reenter a correct character. The following method might be utilized (Listing 6.VI):

Listing 6.VI

```
// GetLetter()  Prompt the user for an uppercase letter. Ignore
// all entries that are not valid letters until one is entered.
// Return the first valid uppercase letter entered.
private static char GetLetter()
{   char letter;
    do
       letter = IO.readChar ("Enter an upper-case letter: ");
    while (!Character.isUpperCase(letter));
    return (letter);
}
```

In the **do-while** statement, the loop will always be executed at least once because the test is at the bottom of the statement. The body of the statement is continually executed until the test is false (indicating a valid uppercase letter has been entered).

6.7 Block-local variables

We have declared all method variables at the top of the method definition. As such, these variables, while being local to the method in which they are defined, are available throughout the entire method. Java allows a programmer to declare a variable for only a block (set of nested { } symbols). For example, in the following code snippet, the variable `temp` is only available within the block in which it is declared and then deallocated when that block exits:

```
if (a < b)
{    int temp;
     temp = a * b + c;
     IO.showValue ("temp is: ", temp);
}
```

KEY TERM
dynamic variable

This approach has several nice advantages. For one, it might allow some savings of memory because variables are only allocated or available within the block and then automatically deallocated. This is called a *dynamic variable*. We have only introduced this concept—we'll return to it in the future.

Perhaps a more important advantage is that it allows the programmer to more effectively modularize a statement or block. By having the needed variables declared and used within the block (but nowhere else), the block is more independent of the rest of the code around it. Perhaps the most common use of such local dynamic variables is within a `for` loop. Usually, the index or counter of a `for` loop is only needed for the loop itself. As such, it can be declared dynamically within the `for` statement. For example:

```
for (int count = 0, count < N; N++)
{    . . .      // variable count now is available
}
     . . .           // variable count has been deallocated.
```

A programmer could replace this loop block with another without needing to find and remove or change the declaration of the variable count at the method top.

6.8 Example project

A common problem in scientific research is attempting to classify items based on a set of measurements. For example, a laboratory rat might be measured for weight, age, the number of hours of activity per day, and the number of times the rat feeds each day. It is likely that no two rats in a study will have the same four measurements, but nevertheless, rats can be clustered into similar groups.

Suppose a particular researcher has devised the following set of rules to classify study rats into one of four groups:

Group A	weight <= 5 g
	age < 2 months
	activity <= 4 hours
	feedings <= 5
Group B	weight less than 7 g
	2 <= age < 4 months if activity < 4 hours or
	4 <= age < 6 months if activity >= than 4 hours
Group C	any weight
	6 <= feedings < 10 if age > 6 or less than 3 or
	>10 feedings if age >= 6
Group D	all others

Suppose you decide to write a class to input these four measurements for each of 25 rats and then output the appropriate classification decisions for the researcher. The main() method could be a **for** loop for 25 iterations (Listing 6.VII):

Listing 6.VII

```
// A class to output classifications for rat features
// ASSUMPTION: 25 different rats, 4 measurements per rat
// consisting of age, weight, feedings, and activity
public class RatClass
{ final int NUMRATS = 25;

  // Classify(); returns a char (A, B, C, or D) corresponding to the group for this rat
  // IN: age, wt, feedings, activity (describing a particular rat)
  private static char Classify (double age, double wt, int feedings, double activity)
  {              // to be written
  }

  public static void main (String[] args)
{  double age, weight, activity;
   int feedings;
   char group;
   String output;
   for (int count=0; count<NUMRATS; count++)
   {    output = "enter age for rat " + count + ": ";
        age = IO.readDouble (output);
        weight = IO.readDouble ("enter weight: ");
        feedings = IO.readInt ("enter number of feedings: ");
        activity = IO.readDouble ("enter activity: ");
        group = Classify (age, weight, feedings, activity);
        output = "rat " + count + " belongs to group " + group;
        IO.showMessage (output);
   }
}
```

As usual, the main() class was easy to write. The real work is done in the Classify() method. To begin this method, you realize that these groups should be mutually exclusive—a rat cannot belong to two groups. Next, recognize that the notation used for these rules may make sense in English but not in Java. Look at the first group. By expressing four criteria with one on each line, the researcher is indicating that all four must be true. These individual criteria must then be combined with the && operator. Look at the following expression:

```
(wt <= 5.0) && (age < 2.0) && (activity <= 4.0) && (feedings <= 5)
```

That appears to be near the limit of complexity that a reader can easily follow! Unfortunately, the next group is even more complex. You might decide to evaluate these criteria in two steps. There is no reason why you cannot save the result in a **boolean** variable and then refer to it later. The English statement "a <= b < c" simply implies that "a<=b" and "b < c":

```
boolean class1 = ((2 <= age) && (age < 4)) && (activity < 4);
boolean class2 = ((4 <= age) && (age < 6)) && (activity >= 4);
```

In these criteria, lines 2 and 3 are obviously combined with an OR or || operator. These subexpressions can then be combined into a complete test for Group B as follows:

```
((wt < 7.0) && (class1 || class2))
```

Group C doesn't care about weight. Either of two criteria must be met as represented on lines 2 and 3 of this group of rules. We will combine these with the || operator. Look at the 2nd line criteria. Feedings must be between 6 and 10 but only if the age is greater than 6 or less than 3. Let's form a test for the right age group first:

```
boolean ageclass1 = (age > 6.0) || (age < 3.0);
boolean feedclass = (6 <= feedings) && (feedings < 10);
boolean class3 = (feedings > 10) && (age >= 6.0);
```

The complete test for Group C is then as follows;

```
((ageclass1 && feedclass) || class3)
```

We can visualize the entire method as a single **if** statement. A rat is in Group A or not (which makes it a member of B, C, or D):

```
if ( test for group A )
     class = 'A';
else
{

         check for membership in other 3 groups        1.

}
```

The oval labeled 1 is itself a single `if` statement. A rat is in Group B or not (which makes it a member of C or D):

```
if ( test for group B )
    class = 'B';
else
{
```

check for membership in other 2 groups   **2.**

```
}
```

Oval 2 is another **if** statement to separate the remaining rats into two groups. The complete `Classify()` method now combines these three tests into a cascading **if** statement (Listing 6.VIII):

Listing 6.VIII

```
// Classify(); returns a char (A, B, C, or D) corresponding to the group for this rat
// IN: age, wt, feedings, activity (describing a particular rat)
  private static char Classify (double age, double wt, int feedings, double activity)
{     char group;
      if ((wt<=5.0)&&(age<2.0)&&(activity<=4.0)&&(feedings<=5))
          group = 'A';
      else
      {   boolean class1 = ((2 <= age) && (age < 4)) && (activity < 4);
          boolean class2 = ((4 <= age) && (age < 6)) && (activity >= 4);
          if ((wt < 7.0) && (class1 || class2))
              group = 'B';
          else
          {   boolean ageclass1 = (age > 6.0) || (age < 3.0);
              boolean feedclass = (6 <= feedings) && (feedings < 10);
              boolean class3 = (feedings > 10) && (age >= 6.0);
              if ((ageclass1 && feedclass) || class3)
                  group = 'C';
              else group = 'D';
          }
      }
      return (group);
}
```

6.9 Summary

KEY TERMS   The new terms introduced in this chapter are the following:

1. *boolean operator*—The `&&` and `||` operators produce only a true or false result.

2. *DeMorgan's theorem*—a rule that states that the complement of any expression can be formulated by changing every relational and `boolean` operator to its opposite.

3. *pre-, postincrement*—incrementing a variable before or after it is used in an expression (same for decrement).

4. *optimization*—a compiler's induced changes to a class to make it more efficient or to require less space.

5. *dynamic variable*—a variable may be dynamically declared within a block and remains locally available until that block closes.

CONCEPTS   Several new statements were introduced. First, the single-choice **if** statement:

if (*expression*)   *statement*

The **for** loop is convenient for counted loops:

for (*expression*$_1$ **;** *expression*$_2$ **;** *expression*$_3$)
      statement

In the **for** statement, *expression*$_1$ is evaluated prior to the loop, *expression*$_2$ is the test at the beginning of each iteration, and *expression*$_3$ is evaluated after each loop iteration. If a variable is used in *expression*$_1$, it may declared within the expression.

The **switch** statement provides a simple means to express multiple choices. In this statement, the expression is compared against each **case** value to determine entry into the list of statements:

switch (*expression*)
{   **case** *value*$_1$ **:**   *statements*$_1$
       case *value*$_2$ **:**   *statements*$_2$
       . . .
       default **:**   *statements*$_n$
}

The **break** statement provides a means to exit out of a switch statement without continuing through the entire list of statements:

break **;**

Finally, the **do-while** statement provides a loop with the test at the bottom of each iteration:

do
      statement
while (*expression*)   **;**

Several new operators were introduced. The | | and **&& boolean** operators allow the combination of several simple tests. The expressions on both sides of a **boolean** operator are also considered **boolean** expressions. The **!** operator is used to complement an expression value. DeMorgan's theorem can be used to form the complement of a **boolean** expression.

A shorthand notation was introduced for common arithmetic operations. For example, a+=b is the shorthand for a = a+b. In addition, the increment and decrement operators were introduced for integer variables. When placed prior to a variable (e.g., ++a), preincrement (or decrement) is indicated. When placed after a variable (e.g., a++), postincrement is indicated.

The %, or modulo operator, results in the remainder of an integer division operation.

A few important programming tips were given:

- Avoid nesting ++ or -- operators within other statements and avoid complex nesting of assignment (=) operators.

- Be careful not to confuse the && and || operators with the & and | operators, which have very different meanings.

- To avoid having an **else** matched with the wrong **if** when nested, always enclose the true choice of a two-choice **if** inside { } braces.

- Be sure you intend both sides of a **boolean** && or || operator to be **boolean** (true or false) expressions in themselves.

Table 6.4 Example segments

`if (a<2 || (c==5 && d>3))...`
`{  . . .`
`}`
	True if a is less than 2 or *both* of the following: c is 5 and d is greater than 3.

`for (n=0; n<10; n++)  . . .`
`{  . . .`
`}`
	Repeat this block 10 times as n goes from 0 to 9.

`a++;`	Increment a.
`c = ++b;`	First increment b and then assign to variable c.
`c = b--;`	First assign b to c and then decrement b.
`c *= (b+a);`	The current value of c is multiplied by (b+a) and then stored back into c.

6.10 Exercises

Short-answer questions

1. A good rule of thumb is to always place _____ around both choices of a two-choice **if**.
2. When deciding which **if** is associated with an **else**, the compiler will always choose the _____ **if** possible.
3. A condition in an **if** or **while** statement is considered true if it is _____.
4. When a condition contains both **&&** and || operators (with no additional parentheses), the _____ will be evaluated first.

5. Which boolean operator should be used in a condition to test if either variable a or variable b is true?

6. Which boolean operator should be used in a condition to test if both variable a and variable b are true? Consider the following **for** loop:

```
for ( n=0; n<10; n++ )
    IO.showMessage("hello");
```

7. How many different lines will the loop in question 6 produce?

8. Which section of the **for** loop will be executed once at the top of the loop?

9. Which two sections of the **for** loop will be executed each iteration?

10. Rewrite the following definite loop using a **for** statement:

```
int count;
count = 0;
while (count < 25)
{   IO.showValue ("count is " + count);
    count++;
}
```

11. What would be output as a result of this segment?

```
int n, j;
for (n=0; n<5; n++)
    for (j=n; j<5; j++)
        IO.showMessage ( n + ", " + j);
```

12. What would be output as a result of the execution of this segment?

```
int x, y;
for (x=1; x<=5; x++)
{   IO.showValue ("x is: ",   x);
    for (y=2; y<x; y++)
        IO.showValue ("y is: ", y);
}
```

13. Indicate which of the following expressions are true and which are false:

```
int a=5, b=7; c=0;
```

   a. (a <b || c)
   b. (a && c)
   c. (c && b || a)

14. Determine the equivalent expression using DeMorgan's theorem.
   a. ! (a<b)
   b. ! (a && b)
   c. ! a || ! b

15. Give an example of two different variable types that might be used in a **switch** statement.

16. Propose a **switch** statement using the variable *N* to output messages according to the following table:

N	message
1	"too small"
2	"small"
3	"just right"
4	"large"
5	"too large"

17. Describe what occurs if the expression in a **switch** statement does not match any of the **case** options.

18. Briefly describe the primary use of the **break** statement.

19. Convert the following statements to shorthand notation:
   a. a = a + 1;
   b. b = b * 2;
   c. c = c + (a = a+1);

Projects

1. The ACME Shipping Company uses the following rate schedule:

Weight	Charge	Surcharge for Hazardous Material
0–5 lb	$5/lb	$17
>5–10 lb	$20	
	+ $6/lb for wt over 5 lb	$22
>10 lb	$41	
	+ $7/lb for wt over 10 lb	$27

For example, a package of hazardous material weighing 7 lb would be charged $54–$20 plus 2 × $6 plus the $22 surcharge. A package of nonhazardous material weighing 18 lb would be charged $97, or $41 plus 8 × $7. Write a method to implement this rate schedule and demonstrate your method within a class having a main() method to input package weights and contents and output charges.

2. The GOODHANDS Insurance Agency determines auto insurance rates based on the driver's age, ticket history, and the value of the car. The base rate is 6 percent of the car value. Male drivers under age 25 pay an extra 17 percent; female drivers under age 21 pay an extra 4 percent of the base charge. A driver with more than three tickets pays an extra $100. Write a method to calculate insurance rates based on this information. Test your method within a class having a main() method to input driver information and output rates.

3. Listing 6.V represented a means of compiling a summary table of student grades. Rewrite this method to utilize a **switch** statement to test a letter grade and determine which count should be incremented.

4. Using a **for** loop, write a small method to generate a table of squares and square roots for whole numbers from 1 to 15. For example, your output might begin like the following:

N	Square root	Square
1	1	1
2	1.41421	4
3	1.73205	9

. . .

5. Write a method to generate a table of integer powers for the numbers 1 through 10 in steps of 0.5. On each table line, output the powers from 2 through 5. You may need to use a **long** variable to avoid overflow. The output table should resemble the following:

N	2	3	4	5
1	1	1	1	1
1.5	2.25	3.375	5.0625	7.59375
2	4	8	16	32
2.5	6.25	15.625	39.0625	97.6563

. . .

6. Write a method to calculate N! using a **for** loop. Here is a mathematical definition:

```
N! = 1 if N <= 1, else N! = N * (N-1) * (N-2) * (N-3) * . . . 1
```

Write a main class to allow a user to input a list of positive integers. The list should begin with a count of the size of the list. For each positive integer in the list, output the factorial. For example, the following might be used for input indicating a list size of five elements. The output should consist of five factorials for 7, 3, and so on.

5

7

3

4

2

6

7. Write a method to graph the following method from 0 to 2 in increments of 0.1.

$$y = \frac{1}{1+x}$$

8. The value of the mathematical constant e can be calculated using the following converging series:

$$e = 2 + \frac{1}{2!} + \frac{1}{3!} + \frac{1}{4!} + \dots$$

Each term in this series is smaller in magnitude than the previous term. As a result, the accuracy of the result depends only on the number of terms you calculate. Write a method to calculate the value for e by summing the first 25 terms of this series. Note: The last few terms will have very large numbers in the denominator. You may wish to use **double** variables. You may also wish to consider that 1/4! is (1/4)*(1/3!).

9. The value of the cosine function can be calculated using the following converging series:

$$\cos(x) = 1 - \frac{x^2}{2!} + \frac{x^4}{4!} - \frac{x^6}{6!} + \dots$$

Each term in this series is smaller in magnitude than the previous term. As a result, the accuracy of the result depends only on the number of terms you calculate. Write a method to calculate the cosine of a positive real value (in radians) by summing the first 25 terms of this series. Note: You may want to review Project 8.

10. Creative Challenge: Refer to Project 3. As you develop this class in a stepwise, top-down fashion, you will probably need to repeatedly enter a list of grades as you debug and verify your class. Assume your list (for which you have hand calculated a result) consists of 20 grades. This would be a time-consuming and error-prone process (not to mention boring). Devise a method so that the list of scores does not need to be entered each time during development. In other words, each time you run the class, it should have access to the list without needing the user to enter the values.

Designing
with Classes

Up to this point, we have utilized classes written by others such as those from the Java library (**Math**, **Character**, etc.) or provided with this text (**IO**). We're now ready to start designing our own classes. You will learn that classes can be much more than just a set of related methods. In a more powerful concept, they can also represent objects and data.

7.1 Simple disk I/O

KEY TERM
dynamic

We'll start by doing some simple disk input and output and use that to help you understand how classes can be *dynamic*. The previous helper classes we've utilized have all been static. This implies there is only one copy that is always there. A more powerful mechanism for classes allows more than one copy to exist, and these copies can be created under our control. You were introduced to dynamic or block variables in the previous chapter—we'll now extend this concept to entire classes.

Look again at Creative Challenge Project 10 of Chapter 6. Instead of entering data from the keyboard each time we use a class, wouldn't it be better if the class could read information from a disk file? We could certainly test complicated and involved classes much faster if we didn't need to repeatedly type in the same data each time we executed. You have probably thought that there must be some way to read numbers and strings from disk files in the same way these data were read from the keyboard—and of course, there is.

Refer to Appendix A. Either download the files **DiskInput.class** and **DiskOutput.class** from the given Web site or copy these classes from a disk location provided by your instructor. You could also copy the sources for these classes from the appendix and compile if you are careful. In either case, you will want to have a copy of these classes in the same directory as the class you are currently developing.

Disk files

A disk file can simply be a copy of preentered data. You are familiar with source files (having the extension .java) and compiled files (having the extension .class) for classes. The first contains text, and the second contains binary information needed for execution. All disk files are one of these two types: text or binary. Text files are readable to humans. They can be edited, printed, and displayed. For this reason, we will utilize text files for our preentered data. Since the extension .java is reserved for text files containing Java sources, we need another extension. Most commonly, programmers use .txt to refer to a preentered data file.

Suppose we start by creating a disk file in your working or current directory (containing your Java sources) using the same text editor that you have used for programming. We'll enter the following numbers on separate lines and then save this file under the name data.txt. The first line contains the count of numbers, and subsequent lines contain a set of integers:

4

110

120

130

140

To prepare to read this file during class execution, we can use the open() method of the **DiskInput** class. We first declare a **DiskInput** variable with some new syntax (to be discussed shortly) before using the open() method belonging to that instance:

```
DiskInput instancename = new DiskInput();
instancename.open ( filename );
```

Syntax form

In this case, the *filename* is a string representing the name of the file. The same input methods of the **IO** class are available for input statements:

instancename.**readInt** (*prompt*);
instancename.**readDouble** (*prompt*);
instancename.**readChar** (*prompt*);
instancename.**readFloat** (*prompt*);
instancename.**readString** (*prompt*);

Syntax form

Each of these input statements expects to find one value per line in the disk file to be read. When we have finished reading data, we use the close() method to indicate to Java that the file can be closed:

instancename.**close**();

Syntax form

Here's a complete class that could be used to read the set of integers from this disk file and then output the sum:

Listing 7.1

```
// a class to read the file data.txt and output the sum
// ASSUMPTION: the first integer in the file is the count of numbers
public class FileSum
{
    public static void main (String[] args)
    {   int count, value, sum = 0;
        DiskInput infile = new DiskInput();
        infile.open ("data.txt");
        count = infile.readInt();
        for (int n=0; n<count; n++)
        {   value = infile.readInt();
            sum += value;
        }
        IO.showValue ("sum is: ", sum);
        infile.close();
        System.exit(0);
    }
}
```

Notice that there is something new in this class! The following line is syntax you haven't seen before:

```
DiskInput infile = new DiskInput();
```

KEY TERM
instance

If you think about it for a second, we will probably need the capability of reading from more than one file during a class. If we had only one static **DiskInput** class instance, this would not be possible. For this reason, **DiskInput** is not a static class but rather a dynamic class. An instance must be created during execution. For each *instance* (each copy) of a class to be created, we can use the following syntax:

classname instance_name **=** **new** *classname* **( )** **;**

Syntax form

Suppose we wish to read values from two disk files: `"thisfile.txt"` and `"thatfile.txt"`:

```
DiskInput inputfile1 = new DiskInput();
DiskInput inputfile2 = new DiskInput();
inputfile1.open ("thisfile.txt");
inputfile2.open ("thatfile.txt");
```

A class instance is much like a variable, but in addition to data, the name is associated with a set of methods. The best way to visualize this is to consider that each class instance has its own set of methods. In the above example, `inputfile1` has its own set of `readInt()`, `readDouble()`, and so on methods.

We can write to a disk file using the **DiskOutput** class (after creating an instance):

*instancename***.open** (*filename*)**;**
*instancename***.close();**
*instancename***.println** (*message*)**;**

Syntax form

If the file does not already exist, it will be created in the current directory. If the file exists, it will be emptied (truncated to zero length) and readied for the new output. A `message` is just any string. Each `println()` call produces one new line in the output disk file. Since we understand the `+` concatenation operation, we really don't need a `writeInt()` or `writeDouble()` method—we can generate the appropriate string for the given `println()` method. Here's a version of Listing 7.I that sends output to a disk file named `"results.txt"` rather than to the display. In other words, this class executes without interacting display boxes. The final `"results.txt"` disk file might then be examined with a text editor or copied to a floppy disk to give to a co-worker (Listing 7.II):

Listing 7.II

```
// a class to read the file data.txt and output the sum to a disk file
// ASSUMPTION: the first integer in the file is the count of numbers
public class FileSum2
{
   public static void main (String[] args)
   {  int count, value, sum = 0;
      DiskInput infile = new DiskInput();
      DiskOutput outfile = new DiskOutput();
      infile.open ("data.txt");
      outfile.open ("results.txt");
      count = infile.readInt();
      for (int n=0; n<count; n++)
      {   value = infile.readInt();
          sum += value;
      }
      outfile.println ("sum is: " + sum);
      infile.close();
      outfile.close();
      System.exit(0);
   }
}
```

7.2 Designing your own dynamic classes

First, let's revisit the syntax used to define a class. If your class is to be executed by a human operator or user, it will contain one **public** method named `main()` in addition to other possible **private** methods to be used within the class. If your class is a dynamic helper class to be created and used from other classes, it will not contain a `main()`. Each of the helper methods of this class will be **public** rather than **private**. (As you will recall, **public** implies that a method may be invoked from outside the class.) In this case, methods are invoked by other methods of other classes. In addition, a dynamic helper class will probably contain **private** variables to help it remember what it represents.

KEY TERM
object

A helper class containing variables to represent information and a set of `public` methods used to manipulate that information is most often called an *object*. A `static` class has only one object. A dynamic class uses the class definition as a template to create class objects when needed. We won't bother to bog down in a lot of formal terminology—it all boils down to this anyway. The best way to learn this concept is with a simple example. Suppose you wish to represent three different students in your class. You should first ask yourself: "What is a student?" In other words, what information makes one student different from another?

Suppose we then decide that a student is to be represented by a name (as a `String`), an ID number (as an `int`), and a grade (as a `char`). Initially, our class might look like the following and would reside in a file `Student.java`:

```
public class Student
{   private String name;
    private int ID;
    private char grade;
}
```

To help differentiate between primitive variables and class instances, we usually capitalize the name of a helper class. (If that is the case, what is the difference between **String** and **int**? We'll return to that issue!) Notice that all the variables that contain information about a **Student** are private. In other words, they are not available or visible to anyone using this class. Can this information or attribute variables be public? Well, yes—but that is often not a good idea and may lead to bugs. It is best to encapsulate your class. Provide your own methods to access the information variables. In that way, you will ensure that they will be accessed correctly. Notice also that these **Student** variables are not **static**. In the absence of the keyword **static**, a definition becomes dynamic.

In a class, we could now create several **Student** objects or instances with the following. Each of these students would have his or her own name, ID, and grade:

```
Student fred = new Student(), jane = new Student(), sam = new Student();
```

Now, the second question you must ask yourself is: "What methods might be needed to access or modify a student?" Generally, you will need some way to input data, display data, and update or modify data. Let's create a method to input or read a student's information variables from a disk file. We'll use the **DiskInput** and **DiskOutput** classes you've just learned. Let's also create a method to form a string out of all a student's information that could be displayed. We'll also create a method to change a student's grade and to write a student back onto a disk file (Listing 7.III):

Listing 7.III

```
// a helper class to represent a student (primitive version)
public class Student
{private String name;
 private int ID;
```

```
    private char grade;

    public void diskRead (DiskInput infile)        // read information vars. from a disk file
    { name = infile.readString();
      ID = infile.readInt();
      grade = infile.readChar();
    }

    public String displayStudent ()                // create a String of all information vars
    { return (name + ", " + ID + ", " + grade);
    }

    public void changeGrade (char newgrade)        // update the grade information var.
    {   grade = newgrade;
    }

    public void diskWrite (DiskOutput outfile)     // write information vars. to a disk file
    { outfile.println (name);
      outfile.println (" " + ID);
      outfile.println (" " + grade);
    }
}.
```

At this point, it becomes a simple job to write a class to update the grades for a file of students. Suppose file "CS101.txt" exists and contains student information such as the following:

```
Fred Smith
1234
A
Jane Doe
5678
C
Sara Jones
9012
B
    . . .
```

The following class could be used to allow an instructor to modify student grades and produce a new file (Listing 7.IV):

Listing 7.IV

```
// a class to allow an operator to change the grades of a disk file of students
public class ChangeAllGrades
{
    public static void main (String[] args)
    {   int num_students;                          // declare variables
        char updated_grade;
        String in_filename, out_filename;
        DiskInput infile = new DiskInput();        // declare and create object instances
        DiskOutput outfile = new DiskOutput();
        Student this_student = new Student();
```

```
// open and prepare disk files
        num_students = IO.readInt ("enter number of students in file: ");
        in_filename = IO.readString ("enter input filename: ");
        out_filename = IO.readString ("enter output filename: ");
        infile.open (in_filename);
        outfile.open (out_filename);

// read students in turn: allow user to enter a new grade, then write student to output file
        for (int n=0; n<num_students; n++)
        {   this_student.diskRead (infile);
            updated_grade =
                IO.readChar (this_student.displayStudent() + " \nEnter new grade: ");
            this_student.changeGrade (updated_grade);
            this_student.diskWrite (outfile);
        }

// close disk files
    infile.close();
    outfile.close();
    System.exit(0);
    }
}
```

These two classes would be saved in files `Student.java` and `ChangeGrades.java`. When compiling the `ChangeGrades.java` class, Java will look for the compiled `Student.class` file to utilize for the **Student** objects. Executing this class with the example `CS101.txt` disk file produces the following interactions after inputting the number of students (3) and the two filenames:

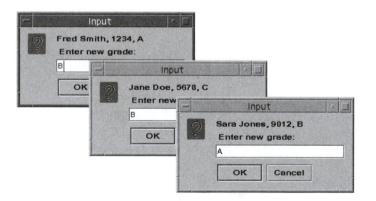

KEY TERM
buffer
You might ask what the purpose is for closing a disk file. Well, you actually don't always need to close an input file because the Java system will do that for you when your class terminates. With output files, it is a different matter, however. When you output to a **DiskOutput** object, Java *buffers* the output in a temporary memory location until a sufficiently large amount of output is available or the file is closed—before actually writing the information to the disk. This is basically because disk

writes are quite slow compared to memory writes. If you output to a disk file and then forget to close the file, you may find that your output has not yet been moved to the disk from the memory buffer. If your class terminates prematurely, the memory buffer can be lost.

7.3 **Object operations**

Let's assume for the following discussion that we have declared two student objects a and b and have read information into them from a disk file (previously defined and opened):

```
Student a = new Student();
Student b = new Student();
a.diskRead (infile);
b.diskRead (infile);
```

Of course, it goes without saying that Java doesn't read English. The names we assign to classes that we design are just words to Java. It has no idea what a **Student** really represents in the real world. We could just as easily have named the class **Jaberwock** as far as Java is concerned. As such, Java has no idea what addition, subtraction, multiplication, division, or concatenation mean between two **Student** objects. (I'm not sure I do either!) In any case, none of the built-in symbol operators are allowed between two class objects.

```
a = a * b; // produces a nasty compiler error!
```
WRONG!

Generally speaking, the only operation that can be performed on class object information variables are those that are defined within the class itself. In other words, the class designer writes all access and operation methods associated with the class—none are built into Java initially.

Having said that, you need to be aware that the Java compiler may not give you an error message if you inadvertently use the assignment (=) or relational operators (<, >=, ==, !=, etc.) for class objects. Dynamic class objects are treated very differently than primitive data types when using these operators. Suppose we did the following:

WRONG!

```
b = a;
b.displayStudent();  // shows the information variables of 'a' as expected.
```

CONCEPT
avoid using symbol operators with class objects

We would see the information variables of a displayed as expected. However, this does not mean that the information variables of a have been copied into b. *It means that b is now another name for a*. Now, if you change the information variables of a, they will also appear to change for b. At this point, there is only one **Student** object, which is a. Confusing! (We'll return to why this is the case in a few pages.) The bottom line is this: *Avoid using symbol operators with class objects*.

Designing helper classes in Java becomes much more straightforward if we define a class method for each and every operation we wish to allow on a class object. For example, suppose in order to allow a comparison between two **Student** objects, you might decide that one student is less than another if the first has a lower grade than the second. You could certainly add a method to the **Student** class with an appropriate name. Consider Listing 7.V. We'll assume for a moment that there is a method in the **Student** class to return the current grade:

Listing 7.V

```
// a method to be added to the Student class
// compares another Student object with this Student
private boolean isLess (Student x)
{    if (grade < x.getGrade())
         return (true);
     else
         return (false);
}
```

Now suppose we have two **Student** objects that have been read from the disk file. They can be compared by grade using this new method:

```
Student a = new Student();
Student b = new Student();
a.diskRead (infile);
b.diskRead (infile);
if (a.isLess(b) )
      IO.showMessage ("the first student has a lower grade");
```

Notice the **if** statement in the snippet of code. Both the **Student** objects a and b are associated with an isLess() method. We are invoking the method that belongs to object a. Object b is being passed to become parameter x in the isLess() method. Now notice the **if** statement in Listing 7.V:

```
if (grade < x.getGrade())
```

The grade variable refers to the grade of the object owning this method—that is, object a. We cannot refer to the grade information of object x because that is, private information available only to the methods of that object. That is why we would need to add the getGrade() method to the **Student** class (Listing 7.VI). Since this method is to be invoked from other objects (even if they are other **Student** objects), it must be a **public** method!

Listing 7.VI

```
// a method to be added to the Student class
// returns the current grade of this student
public boolean getGrade ()
{   return grade;
}
```

This can be a bit confusing. Let's try to simplify with a couple of basic rules:

1. A private object information variable can be referenced within the methods of the object class.

2. Any reference to private object information by methods outside the object class should be done via a **public** method belonging to the class.

You might ask (again) if we couldn't simply make the information variable public:

```
public class Student                    // POOR STYLE!
{   private String name;
    private int ID;
    public char grade;
    . . .
```

In that case, the isLess() method could be simplified to the following:

```
public boolean isLess (Student x)
{   if (grade < x.grade)
        return (true);
    else
        return (false);
```

Well, yes—that would work. Unfortunately, when you make class information variables **public**, experience has shown that you might later introduce bugs. For example, suppose that we later add another information variable to record the date that a **Student** grade was assigned:

```
public class Student
{   private String name;
    private int ID;
    public char grade;
    private String date;
    . . .
```

CONCEPT

keep information variables private

The method changeGrade() that you wrote (the developer of this class) could then be updated to set the date each time the grade was changed. Other programmers and classes currently using your class, however, could probably not all be contacted or trusted to update their code when they changed the public grade. The result is that a **Student** object could contain invalid data. You later begin to get phone calls saying that the **Student** class you developed doesn't seem to work correctly. The best style is to jealously guard any class that you develop. Allow no one to make changes to an information variable of your class without calling one of the members that you control. In other words, allow no one else's code to cause your **Student** object to be incorrect. You do this by making all information variables **private**.

Since we usually want to copy one object to another (the effect of the assignment operation), we usually provide a method to *set* one object to another (Listing 7.VII):

Listing 7.VII

```
// a method to be added to the Student class
// sets the owner Student to have copies of the parameter object information variables
public void set (Student other)
{   name = other.getName();
    grade = other.getGrade();
    ID = other.getID();
}
```

Obviously, we will need a getName() and a getGrade() method added to our class as well (Listing 7.VIII):

Listing 7.VIII

```
// methods to be added to the Student class
// return the ID of this student
public int getID()
{   return ID;
}
public String getName()
{   return name;
}
```

KEY TERM

object-oriented programming

This approach to solving computer problems by designing a helper class (or set of classes) containing (a) the information variables needed to express an object and (b) the operation methods to manipulate those information variables is called object-oriented programming, or OOP. Because Java allows programmers to design their own helper classes, the language is very appropriate for this approach to programming.

7.4 Reference parameters

Up to this point, we have written and used methods that accept the values of parameters but return only a single result. For example, suppose the following method is called with this statement:

```
y = SomeMethod (x);        // pass this method the value of 'x'
```

KEY TERM
value argument

If the method is defined as follows, the method may use the current value of argument x (as parameter a), but any changes to parameter a have no effect on argument x. We say that x is passed by value or that x is a *value argument:*

```
private int SomeMethod (int a)
{   . . .
    IO.showValue ("a is: ", a);    // value of argument 'x'
    a++;                            // changes 'a', but has no effect on 'x'
    IO.showValue ("a is: ", a);    // new value of 'a' is now different from 'x'
}
```

In this method, the variable a is initialized with the value of x. From that point on, however, changes to a have no effect on the value of x. When this method finishes, the local parameter a is discarded.

KEY TERM
reference arguments

All primitive data types and **static** objects are passed as value arguments. By way of review, the primitive data types you have seen are **double**, **float**, **int**, **char**, and **boolean**. One nice advantage of dynamic class objects as method arguments is that they can be modified as a method parameter. All dynamic class object instances are *reference arguments* or passed by reference. When a dynamic **Student** variable is used as a method argument, a reference to the **Student** variable is passed to the method, not the current information variable values of the **Student** object.

KEY TERM
reference

OK, so what is a reference? It is very similar to the concept of a mailing address. Suppose someone wishes to send you a letter. By knowing your name, they look in the phone book to find your address. The mailman doesn't really need your name on the letter; all that's needed to deliver the letter is your address. A class object variable doesn't contain the information variables of a class instance. Rather, it contains a *reference* to, or the address of where, these information variables (and for that matter, the class methods) can be found in memory.

Suppose we wish to swap one student's information with another's. Using the two students previously defined and input from disk, we wish a to be assigned the name, ID, and grade that currently belong to b, and vice versa. We could do this with a simple method call:

```
Swap (a, b);
a.display();       // displays what used to be b's information
b.display();       // displays what used to be a's information
```

The **Student** variable or object a references where this student's information variables are stored. In computer memory, addresses are just numbers (there is only one street!). Consider Figure 7.1, which represents the situation prior to the above Swap() call.

In this example, the object a contains the address 3456. The object b contains the address 7890. At the memory address 3456, Java can find the table of information variables of object a. At memory address 7890, Java can find the table of information variables of object b. Figure 7.1 shows the relationship with dashed arrows. (These address numbers could be anything—these numbers are only examples. As Java programmers, we are usually not concerned with what actual address numbers are.)

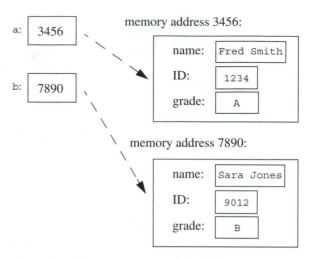

Figure 7.1 A Student reference example situation prior to calling the Swap() method of Listing 7.IX

This Swap() method could be implemented with the following method (Listing 7.IX):

Listing 7.IX

```
// a method to swap the contents of two student objects
public void Swap (Student x, Student y)
{   Student temp = new Student();
    temp.set(x);               // temp is a copy of x
    x.set(y);                  // x is now a copy of y
    y.set(temp);               // y is a copy of temp or x
}
```

The parameter x in Listing 7.IX references the original argument a, and the parameter y references the argument b. Now, watch what happens when the method Swap() is called. Figure 7.2 represents the situation as the Swap() method begins.

Changes that are subsequently made to the information variables of x are actually made to the information variables of a. If you think about it, x is just another name for a.

The first statement of the Swap() method now creates a new **Student** object with the name temp:

```
Student temp = new Student();
```

Remember, temp is actually a reference to a table of **Student** information variables located at some memory address. Suppose temp refers to memory address 1234 (Figure 7.3).

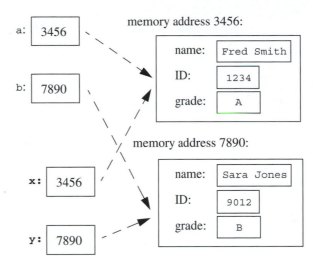

Figure 7.2 Situation as the `Swap()` method begins—method parameters are copies of the references to the original arguments

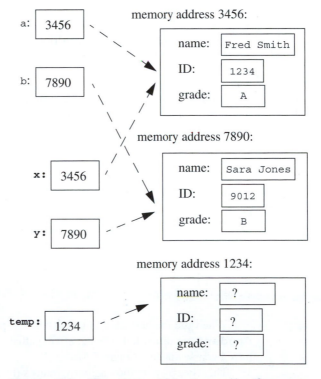

Figure 7.3 Situation within `Swap()` after new `Student` is created

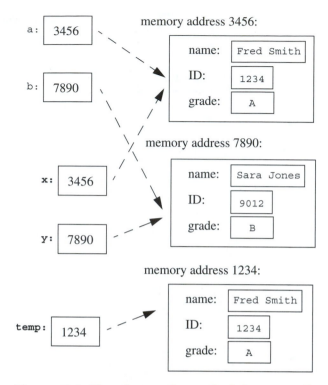

Figure 7.4 Situation at the end of the Swap()
method

Initially, temp is an empty **Student** instance. The next statement now copies
the information variables of the **Student** referenced by x into the empty information variables of **temp**:

```
temp.set(x);    // temp is a copy of x
```

Next, the information variables referenced by y (actually the information variables of b) are copied into the information variables referenced by x (actually a). Finally, the information variables of temp are copied into the information variables
referenced by y.

```
x.set(y);                              // x is now a copy of y
y.set(temp);                           // y is a copy of temp or x
```

When the method Swap() finishes, the parameters x, y, and the local temp
Student are discarded. The net effect is that a and b information variable contents
have been swapped! (Figure 7.5).

This Swap() method actually returns (or changes) two objects. You cannot do
this with primitive variables:

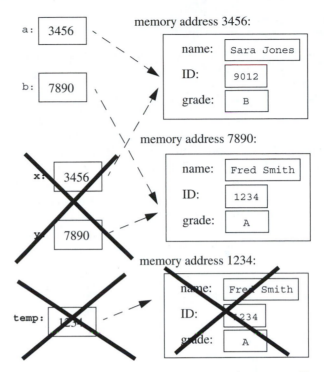

Figure 7.5 The final situation as the Swap() method completes

```
public void Swap (int c, int d)
{   int temp;
    temp = d;
    d = c;
    c = temp;
}
```

WRONG!

Since c and d are just copies of the values of the corresponding arguments, changes to them have no effect on the original arguments when the method was invoked. Now do you see why the assignment (=) operator should not be used (Section 7.C)? If we do the following,

```
a = b;
```

WRONG!

we are copying the reference to b into a. As a result, both a and b reference the same object information table in memory!

Well, the upshot of references and reference parameters is these two issues. If you understand these, you will not have problems with objects:

1. *Changes to reference parameters are reflected back to the corresponding arguments in the calling method.*

2. *Remember not to use the symbol operators you have used for primitive variables.*

7.5 Constructors

We have always been able to initialize a primitive variable in the definition statement. For example:

```
int age = 21;
```

KEY TERM
constructor method

Can we do this with dynamic objects as well? Sure! However, you must implement the feature yourself. Suppose we wish to have all **Student** objects begin with an initial grade by default. Every time a **Student** object is created with the keyword **new**, that particular student begins life with a grade specified. To do this, we add a *constructor method* to the **Student** class. A constructor method is a method automatically invoked each time a **Student** object is created. This is a special method. It must have the name of the class as its name, and it does not return a value nor is it a **void**:

```
public class_name ( parameters )
{ ...
}
```

Syntax form

A constructor for the **Student** class must be named Student(). Here's a constructor to initialize each new **Student** object with a given grade (Listing 7.X):

Listing 7.X

```
// a constructor method to be added to the Student class
public Student ( char given_grade  )
{  grade = given_grade;
}
```

Each time a **Student** is defined or created, the constructor of Listing 7.X will automatically be invoked to set the grade to the specified character. The initial grade is specified within the parentheses of the new Student() statement when the **Student** is created:

```
Student student1 = new Student('F');
```

Look again at this line. After the keyword **new**, it appears that we are invoking a method with the same name as the class. This is when the constructor is invoked! Remember, however, that a constructor will only be invoked following the keyword

new. It may never be invoked as a regular method. (Some Java programmers may argue that we are not actually invoking the constructor—but that is just a question of semantics that isn't important at this point in your career.)

Suppose we would like some **Student** objects to be initialized differently when created. We could overload the Student () constructor method with another constructor to allow a different set of parameters to be specified (Listing 7.XI):

Listing 7.XI

```
// another constructor method to be added to the Student class
public Student (String thisname, int thisID, char thisgrade)
{   name = thisname;
    ID = thisID;
    grade = thisgrade;
}
```

Now, a **Student** object can be initialized by providing arguments when the object is created or defined. For example:

```
Student person1 = new Student ('F');
Student person2 = new Student ("Fred", 999, 'B');
```

CONCEPT
always provide a
default constructor

In this case, person1 is created using the constructor that has only a grade, and person2 is created using the second constructor with arguments. We can overload the constructor with as many different versions as we like—as long as each version is different in the number and type of parameters. Each class you design will be considered by Java to have a default constructor that does nothing. When you add the first constructor to your class, this default constructor is no longer assumed. Since there will always be times when a new object should not necessarily be initialized, we always define a default, or "do nothing," constructor along with the overloaded set of constructors that do specific initialization (Listing 7.XII):

Listing 7.XII

```
// a default constructor method to be added to the Student class
public Student ()
{ }
```

7.6 An introduction to inheritance

Suppose we need a class called **HonorStudent**. What is an **HonorStudent**? Everything a **Student** is—plus a scholarship amount! In other words, an **HonorStudent** class should have all the methods and information variables of a Student plus perhaps a few more. Do we need to copy all the methods and information variables of the `Student.java` file into the `HonorStudent.java` file and then modify that code to produce what we need? What if we don't have the `Student.java` file but only the `Student.class` compiled file?

Java allows us to reuse an existing class to construct a more powerful class. We call the existing class the *base class*. We say the new class can *inherit* methods and information variables from the base class. The syntax is simple. We add the keyword **extends** and the name of the base class to the new class definition. This can be a very powerful tool and is the foundation of the great flexibility of Java. We will only introduce this concept here, but if you continue studying and using Java, you will see much more of this issue.

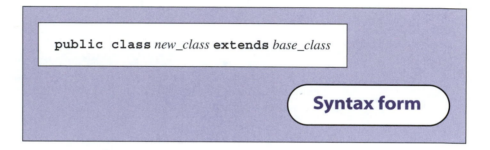

```
public class new_class extends base_class
```

Syntax form

Now, all the developer needs to do to define an **HonorStudent** is take care of the new stuff. All the methods and information variables of the base **Student** are automatically present (Listing 7.XIII):

Listing 7.XIII

```
// an HonorStudent inherits methods and information variables from Student
public class HonorStudent extends Student
{   private double scholarship;

    public double getScholarship ()
    {   return scholarship;
    }

    public void setScholarship(double amount)
    {   scholarship = amount;
    }
}
```

7.7 Static versus dynamic

By now, you are beginning to realize the difference between classes defined as **static** and those that are not. The keyword **static** implies that there is only one such object in an application. It is created automatically by Java when your program is executed. This is generally useful when only one object is needed because all it contains are constants and methods.

When an object is associated with information (other than constants and methods), we leave the **static** off, and our class becomes dynamic. This means that it is our responsibility to create each and every instance with a **new** that returns a reference to the created object. In this manner, we can have several different instances.

For example, the **Math** class is just constants and methods—only one copy is needed, and it is defined as **static**. The **IO** class is also **static**. The DiskInput and DiskOutput classes, however, are dynamic. They are associated with information (disk buffers), and we may need more than one file open at a time.

The bottom line is this: If your class contains only methods and constants, make it **static**. If it contains information and more than one copy might be needed at the same time, make it dynamic.

7.8 Example project

A natural example of a helper class would be a **Fraction** that would allow a programmer to represent simple numeric fractions. Suppose you decide to develop such a class. You might begin by writing a user's manual to describe how **Fraction** objects might be utilized. This manual might be written as follows:

Fraction class user's manual

Fraction objects can be utilized to represent simple arithmetic fractions ($\frac{1}{2}$, $\frac{1}{5}$, etc.). Using these objects, numeric fractions can be input, symbolically or arithmetically manipulated, and then output in the form natural to a mathematician. For example, the **Fraction** of $\frac{1}{2}$ times the **Fraction** of $\frac{1}{3}$ produces the output $\frac{1}{6}$.

Fraction objects are defined using the keyword **new**. A **Fraction** may be initialized with a numerator, a numerator and denominator, or left to a default initialization of $\frac{1}{1}$:

```
Fraction x = new Fraction (1, 2);        // initialized to 1/2
Fraction y = new Fraction ();            // initialized (default) to 1/1
Fraction z = new Fraction (7);           // initialized to 7/1
```

To input a **Fraction** value from the keyboard, use the member method input(). This method will prompt the user for the numerator and denominator integers. To output a **Fraction** value in a display box, use the member method output(). For example:

```
x.input();           // input a fraction from the keyboard
y.output(message);   // display a fraction value with this message
```

To set the value of an existing **Fraction** object, use the set() method, providing a numerator, a numerator and denominator, or another **Fraction**:

```
z.set (8);                // sets this fraction to 8/1
x.set (5/7);              // sets this fraction to 5/7
```

The numerator and denominator of a **Fraction** object can be retrieved with the numerator() and denominator() methods:

```
IO.showValue ("numerator is: ", x.numerator());
```

A **Fraction** object can be compared to another **Fraction** object in a Boolean condition using the isLess() method:

```
if (x.isLess(y))
    IO.showMessage ("fraction x is less than fraction y");
```

Fraction objects can be added to an existing **Fraction** object using the add() method. A similar method of mult() is also available:

```
x.add(y);                 // x is now the sum of x + y
```

Here's an example class using **Fraction** that allows an user to input a **Fraction** and then outputs the sum and product of this value with $\frac{2}{3}$ as a new **Fraction** (Listing 7.XIV):

Listing 7.XIV

```
// a demonstration of the use of the Fraction class
public class TestFraction
{
    public static void main (String[] args)
    {   Fraction two_thirds = new Fraction (2, 3);    // initial value of 2/3
        Fraction x = new Fraction();
        Fraction result = new Fraction();
        x.input();                              // read in a new fraction
        result.set(x);                          // copy to x
        result.add(two_thirds);                 // result is the sum of 2/3 and input
        result.output("The sum is: ");
        result.set(x);
        result.mult(two_thirds);                // result is the prod of 2/3 and input
        result.output("The product is: ");
        if (x.isLess(two_thirds))               // compare input to 2/3
            IO.showMessage ("less than 2/3");
        else
            IO.showMessage ("greater or equal to 2/3");
        System.exit(0);
    }
}
```

Suppose we were to run Listing 7.XIV and input the fraction $\frac{3}{4}$. The outputs would be the following:

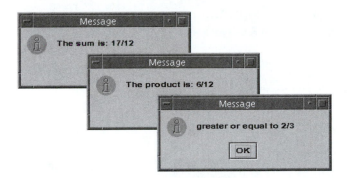

Fraction class definition

Now that you have a good user's guide, you can design a class to fit the description. All the operations are pretty simple, but there are quite a few methods (Listing 7.XV). Let's do a quick review of how to do fraction addition and subtraction. The trick back in grade school was to convert each fraction to a common denominator. The product of the two denominators always works (although that may not be the lowest common denominator). For multiplication, we apply a formula:

$$\frac{\alpha}{\beta} \times \frac{\delta}{\varepsilon} = \frac{\alpha\delta}{\beta\varepsilon}$$

Listing 7.XV

```
// a helper class for symbolic fractions
public class Fraction
{private int num, denom;

public Fraction ()                      // a default constructor
{   num = 1; denom = 1;
}

public Fraction (int a, int b)          // a constructor for both num. and denom.
{   num = a; denom = b;
}

public Fraction (int a)                 // a constructor for just the num.
{   num = a; denom = 1;
}
```

```
public void input ()                // a method to input a fraction
{  num = IO.readInt ("enter the numerator: ");
   denom = IO.readInt ("enter the denominator: ");
}

public void output (String message)// a method to symbolically output a fraction
{  IO.showMessage (message + num + "/" + denom);
}

public void set (int a)             // sets a fraction to a whole number constant
{  num = a; denom = 1;
}

public void set (int a, int b)      // sets a fraction (both num. and denom.)
{  num = a; denom = b;
}

public void set (Fraction f)        // sets a fraction to be a copy of another fraction
{  num = f.numerator();
   denom = f.denominator();
}

public boolean isLess (Fraction f) // returns true if this fraction is less than another
{  double temp1, temp2;
   temp1 = ((double) num) / denom;
   temp2 = ((double) f.numerator()) / f.denominator();
   if (temp1 < temp2)
      return true;
   else
      return false;
}

public int numerator ()            // returns the numerator
{  return num;
}

public int denominator ()          // returns the denominator
{  return denom;
}

public void add (Fraction f)       // sets a fraction to be the sum of itself
{  int newdenom;                    // and another fraction
   newdenom = denom * f.denominator();
   num = num * f.denominator() + f.numerator() * denom;
   denom = newdenom;
}

public void mult (Fraction f)      // sets a fraction to be the product of itself
{  denom = denom * f.denominator();// and another fraction
   num = num * f.numerator();
}
}
```

7.9 **Summary**

KEY TERMS   The terms introduced in this chapter are the following:

1. *dynamic*—a class is dynamic if more than one object instance of a class can be created as needed.
2. *instance*—each dynamically created object of a class is called an instance of that class.
3. *object*—the methods and information variables of a class instance.
4. *buffer*—a temporary memory location used by Java to hold disk file information until needed by the class (input buffer) or until sufficient information is available to warrant writing to disk (output buffer).
5. *object-oriented programming*—an approach to solving computer problems by designing a helper class (or set of classes) containing (a) the information variables needed to express an object and (b) the operation methods to manipulate those information variables.
6. *value argument*—when a copy of a value is passed to a method parameter, the original value argument cannot by changed by changing the method parameter.
7. *reference argument*—when a reference to a value or object is passed to a method parameter, the original value can be changed by changing the method parameter.
8. *reference*—a memory address of where actual information is being held.
9. *constructor method*—a method in a helper class that is automatically invoked when an instance of the class is created.
10. *base class*—a helper class of methods and information variables from which a new class with additional variables or methods is created.
11. *inheritance*—designing a new helper class using an existing base class.

CONCEPTS   Several new concepts were introduced in this chapter. First, you learned that disk files could be used for input and output (in addition to our use of message dialog boxes on the display). The helper classes **DiskInput** and **DiskOutput** provided with the text gave you a useful set of helper methods to accomplish disk operations.

You also recognized that a method may wish to read from (or write to) more than one disk file at a time. This introduced the concept of dynamic helper classes where each needed instance can be created with the keyword **new**.

In designing your own helper classes, you learned that it is helpful to choose a name for the class and then ask "What is a . . .?" to help you determine what information variables will be needed. It is best to make all information variables **private** to avoid complications caused by incorrect modifications by users of the class. You can then ask "What helper methods might be needed to access or modify a . . .?" to help you choose the methods to belong to the class.

Generally, most helper classes will need methods for the following operations:

1. a constructor (or constructors) to initialize an object's information variables with known values,

Table 7.1   Example segments

`DiskInput infile = new DiskInput();`	Create a new disk file instance
`infile.open ("thisfile.txt";`	Prepare `thisfile.txt` to be read.
`infile.readInt ();`	Read an integer from `thisfile.txt`.
`Student thisstudent = new Student();`	Create an instance of `Student`.
`Student x = new Student ('A');`	Create a `Student` and initialize the grade to A.
`Fraction f1 = new Fraction (2,3);`	Initialize a new `Fraction` to $\frac{2}{3}$.
`Fraction f2 = new Fraction();`	Default initialization to $\frac{1}{1}$.
`f1 = f2.add(f1);`	Sum two fractions.

2. a default constructor to provide a default initialization when no arguments are given,

3. a method to display the values of information variables,

4. methods for a user to set information variables,

5. a method to compare two instances of a class (if applicable),

6. methods to retrieve useful information variable values.

Finally, you learned that more complex and capable classes can be readily created by using existing or base classes. The keyword `extends` allows all the capabilities (information variables and methods) of a base class to be automatically inherited by the new class. This concept was only introduced and will be expanded upon in later chapters.

7.10 Exercises

Short-answer questions

1. The acronym OOP stands for _____ _____ _____.
2. Primitive data types are always passed by _____ to a method.
3. Class object instances are always passed by _____ to a method.
4. The term used to note that a method can be used for a variety of similar types and variables is _____.
5. An output disk file should always be closed because data written to the associated _____ may not yet have been physically written to the disk.
6. The combination of a method name and the count and types of parameters of the method are called the _____ _____.
7. An appropriate constructor is automatically invoked by the system when a class object is _____.
8. Suppose the following line is observed in a method:

   `person.GetName ();`

   Which word is the object? Which word is a `public` member method?

9. Explain why using the = assignment operator will not produce a copy of a dynamic object.

10. Can the < operator be utilized to compare two **Fraction** objects? If not, why not?

11. Which information variable may a user access within a **SomeClass** object without invoking a member method?

```
class SomeClass
{    public int some_int;
     private int another_int;
```

12. May helper class information variables by declared as **public**? Should they be declared as **public**?

13. Under what circumstances must a default constructor be provided?

14. In what aspects is a constructor a special member method of a class?

15. Define a class to represent a **Course** object. Each **Course** should be associated with a teacher name, an integer classroom location code, and a count of students. Declare what you think would be the appropriate methods for this class without actually writing the code for these methods.

16. Declare a class to represent a **Vector** object for possible applications programs dealing with graphics. Each **Vector** should be associated with an X,Y starting position on a graph, a direction angle, and a length or magnitude. Declare what you think would be the appropriate methods for this class without actually writing the code for these methods.

17. For the **Fraction** class specified in this chapter, write an Abs () method that would return the absolute value of the object.

18. Design a more capable class called **MixedNumber** by inheriting the **Fraction** class. A **MixedNumber** object should consist of a fraction and a whole number, such as $17\frac{1}{2}$. You do not need to write or declare methods for this class.

19. For the **Fraction** class specified in this chapter, declare (overload) the set () member method to allow a **double** to be assigned to a **Fraction** object—for example, **Fraction x new Fraction( )**; **x.set(0.5)**. This should result in the **Fraction** value of ($\frac{1}{2}$) being assigned to x.

20. How can a nonmember method or user be allowed to access private attribute variables of a class?

Projects

1. Design and implement several overloaded helper methods named Power () to allow the calculation of powers of both **integer** and **float** values. For example:

```
x = Power (5, 3);          // 'x' is assigned 5 cubed
y = Power (6.3, 2);        // 'y' is assigned 5.3 squared
```

2. Define and implement a class named **Cylinder** that has information variable members to represent the radius and length of a cylindrical object. Provide application programs with access methods to:

   a. assign a radius and length to an object,

   b. return the volume of an object of this class, and

   c. return the surface area of an object of this class.

   Write an application class to demonstrate the class.

3. Declare a class to represent a **Complex** class. If you will remember from algebra, each **Complex** object should be associated with a **double** real and imaginary component. Write an application class to demonstrate the class.

   a. Allow initialization of **Complex** declarations as **Complex x(3, 4);**. This should initialize x to a real component of 3 and an imaginary component of 4.

   b. Allow output of **Complex** variables in proper notation such as **x.output();**. This should produce "(3, 4i)".

4. Return to Project 3. Add the following access methods to the class. Update the application class to demonstrate these additional features.

```
public int Numerator ()    // return the object numerator
public int Denominator ()  // return the object denominator
```

5. Develop a **Cash** helper class to accurately represent an amount of money as an integer dollar and integer cents amount.

6. Return to the **Cash** helper class of Project 5. Suppose a user of this class needed to make change from a **Cash** amount. Add a public method that would return the number of quarters in a given **Cash** object. In other words, if the amount were $1.83, the number of quarters should be 7.

7. Return to Project 3. Add member methods to add and multiply two **Complex** objects. (To add complex numbers, add the real components together and add the imaginary components together. For example, $(5, 6i) + (7, 8i) = (12, 14i)$. To multiply, use the following formula:

$$(a, bi) \times (c, di) = (ac - bd), (ad + bc)i$$

8. A business decides to computerize customer information. The same customer records are to be used for billing and generating mailing lists. Develop a class that has information variables to represent an account balance, last name, first name, address, city, state, and zip code. The application class should be able to access an object instance of this class to (a) print a mailing label, (b) update a balance, (c) test if a customer is within a given zip code, and (d) access the current balance.

9. Return to the Short-Answer Question 16. Fully implement the **Vector** class and provide access functions that would allow an application class to:

   a. perform I/O,

   b. update any of the components of a vector, and

   c. test whether two vectors intersect.

   Write an application class to demonstrate this helper class.

10. Creative Challenge: The relational operators allow a simple comparison between two **String** objects. Suppose, however, that a file of 10 different words needed to be examined and a new file created *with these words in alphabetical order*. Write and demonstrate such a class. Tip: One approach would make use of repeated passes through the file, each time finding and outputting just one word.

8

Simple Arrays

A simple variable is one that is associated with a single primitive value or object instance. Unfortunately, some problems are clumsy or even quite difficult to solve using simple variables. For example, how would you write a class to sort a long list of values or names? In this chapter, you will learn that general-purpose programming languages such as Java allow more than one value to be associated with a variable name. Such a variable is called an array. The individual values of an array are stored in adjacent memory locations and are indexed just as one might a table. Arrays are very common and are found in nearly all useful or meaningful programs.

8.1 Array declaration and referencing

KEY TERM
`dimension`

An array variable might best be thought of as a table. For example, consider the following paper table of shirt costs for seven different styles. Such a table might be taped next to the cash register at the local boutique (Figure 8.1).

If the cashier knows the style number of a particular shirt, he can quickly look up or find the cost by referring to the appropriate cell. Since there is only one index (the shirt style number), this is a "one-dimensional" table or array. (Tables can of course, have more than one dimension—we'll return to that later.) Notice that the table begins with an index of zero rather than with one as might be expected. One-dimensional arrays are very common. In fact, it is rare to find a meaningful application without at least one such array.

Shirt Cost Table

3.39	4.52	6.25	7.59	6.49	8.29	9.19
0	1	2	3	4	5	6

(style index)

Figure 8.1   A simple one-dimensional table

One-dimensional array variables are declared in Java in a manner similar to simple or scalar variables. For arrays, the name is followed with a set of brackets to specify the number of cells to be associated with the variable:

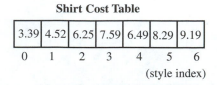

type [ ] *name* = **new type** [*size*] ;

Syntax form

The array variable *type* can be any available data type such as **int**, **float**, **double**, **String**, **boolean**, or **char**. It may also be any available class. (We'll return to arrays of class objects later in the chapter. For now, let's just consider arrays of the primitive data types just mentioned.) The above table of shirt costs might be declared as:

```
double[] shirt_cost = new double [7];
```

CONCEPT
indexes start at 0

This declaration is just like declaring seven new instances of a **double** named `shirt_cost[0]`, `shirt_cost[1]`, up to `shirt_cost[6]`. In other words, we now have a table of seven different cells named `shirt_cost`. Just as the table in Figure 8.1 has an index that begins with zero, all *Java arrays have indexes that begin with zero*. All index values must be ordinal. At this point, the most useful ordinal data types you are familiar with are **int** and **char** or any expression that results in an **int** or **char** value. If an array has N cells, the last cell for an array will always be numbered $N - 1$. This is an important rule to remember and is the cause of many an error in a beginning student's class. Now, you might ask, "Why not start at one?" It turns out that executable programs can be made slightly more efficient if indexes begin at zero. Some historical figure decided that the trade-off was worth the inconvenience to the beginning programmer.

Within a class, a specific `shirt_cost` cell is referred to by following the array variable name with brackets containing the specific cell index. The following examples show some possible uses of this array in a class:

```
shirt_cost[0] = IO.readDouble();           // input a cost into cell 0
sum += shirt_cost[4];                      // add cell 4 into 'sum'
IO.showValue ("cost is: ", shirt_cost[3]); // output the third cell
shirt_cost[4] = 15.75;                     // set cell 4 to 15.75
```

So, the first cell has index [0], the next cell has index [1], and so on. A good way to remember this is to refer to the index as the number of cells beyond the initial cell of the array. For example,

```
shirt_cost[4]
```

CONCEPT
array length

refers to the cell four beyond the initial cell of the array. Don't be confused: *The integer in brackets in the declaration of the array variable specifies the total number of cells in the array. The integer in brackets in an executable statement refers to a specific cell in that array.*

When using an array in an assignment, condition, input, or output statement, always add the brackets and index at the end of the variable name to indicate which cell of the array you are referencing. Normally, you will not use an array name in an assignment, condition, input, or output statement by itself without the brackets and index. For example, the following statements are not appropriate:

```
shirt_cost = 5.6;     // which cell??
IO.showValue ("cost: ", shirt_cost);   // which cell??
```

The index need not be an integer constant. It is often useful to use an integer variable or even a small integer expression. The only requirement is that whatever you place within the brackets evaluates to a valid ordinal index. The following are also valid references to the array. In this fragment, the costs associated with cell 0, cell 3, and cell 5 are added together:

```
int a=0, b=3, c=6;
sum = shirt_cost[a] + shirt_cost[b] + shirt_cost[c-1];
```

As was mentioned earlier, any valid data type can be used for an array variable. Consider a class that needs to keep a table of correct test question answers for a five-question true/false quiz and a table of the number of students who got a particular question correct (Figure 8.2):

```
char[] answer = new char [5];
int[] number_right = new int [5];
```

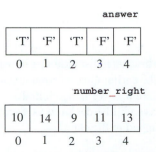

Figure 8.2   Example of parallel arrays

KEY TERM
parallel arrays

In this example, the character ('T' or 'F') in cell *N* of the `answer` array is the correct answer for a particular quiz question—provided the questions are numbered 0 to 4. The integer in cell *N* of the `number_right` array is the number of students who got this question correct. Since *N* relates to the same question in both arrays, we sometimes refer to these as *parallel* arrays. The correct answer to question 2 is 'T' and 9 students answered correctly.

The actual quiz questions themselves might even be stored in a **String** array:

```
string[] question = new String[5];
```

KEY TERM
subscript variable

In this array, `question` can hold 5 different strings. Another name for an array is a *subscripted variable*. We often refer to the index of an array variable cell as the *subscript*. For example, when verbally discussing class code, `answer[3]` may be referred to as "answer subscript 3" or an even more shortened form "answer sub 3."

The syntax for declaring an array variable probably looks somewhat familiar to you. What about the line in a Java class declaring the `main()` method?

```
public static void main (String[] args)
```

Apparently, `args` is an array of type **String**. We'll return to this in a moment.

8.2 Array initialization

If you recall, a simple variable can be initialized when declared. In addition, variables can be declared to be **final** or read-only. There is an alternative form of array declaration that specifies the initial values for each array cell as noted in the following syntax box:

type **[ ]** *name* = **{** *initialization_list* **}** ;

Syntax form

Notice that the keyword `new` is implied in this form, and the number of values in the bracketed list indicates how many cells are to be created. For example, let's return to the earlier quiz information and initialize the arrays to hold the values indicated in Figure 8.2. We'll also initialize the `question` array. The `answer` and `question` arrays will be declared as **final** or read-only so that they cannot be inadvertently changed in the class:

```
final char[] answer = { 'T', 'F', 'T', 'F', 'F' };
   int[] summary = { 10, 14, 9, 11, 13 };
   final string[] question = { "Kennedy was a democrat", "Nixon was a
```

democrat", "Clinton was a democrat", "Reagan was a democrat",
"Ford was a democrat"};

The initialization list is a list of appropriate values separated by commas. If you do not explicitly initialize an array, simple numeric cell types (**int**, **double**, etc.) will be initialized to zero. **String** array cells will be initialized to an empty string. Class object array cells will each be initialized using the default constructor for that class.

EXPERIMENT

What do the cells of an **int** array contain after a declaration if they are not initialized?

8.3 Array processing with loops

Ask yourself how you would fill a very large array or how you would initialize an array at run time. Often, the values of an array are not known when the class is written. Suppose there are two disk files. The file key.txt contains a list of the correct answers to a quiz. The file students.txt contains a list of student answer segments. Each segment in the answers consists of a line containing a student ID number followed by lines containing the answers to the quiz from that student. For example:

```
students.txt:    1234
                 T
                 F
                 T
                 T
                 F
                 5678
                 T
                 F
                 T
                 F
                 F
                 9012
                 T
                 F
                 F
                 T
                 T
                 3456
                 F
                 T
                 T
                 T
                 T
```

In this example file, four students are represented. The student with ID 1234 gave answers T, F, T, T, F, the student with ID 5678 gave answers T, F, T, F, F, and so on.

Our goal is to write a class to initialize the 'answer' array from the correct answers in the `key.txt` disk file. Next the class is to input student data segments, grade the students' answers against the correct key answers, and output a score for each student. The class is also to tabulate the number of students who get each question correct into the `summary` array. Let's call the application the `gradetest` class.

Now suppose the disk file `key.txt` contains the following characters to represent the correct answers to the quiz:

```
key.txt:    T
            F
            T
            F
            F
```

The output of the proposed class should look like the following:

```
student: 1234   score 4
student: 5678   score 5
student: 9012   score 2
student: 3456   score 1
correct answers summary for each question; 3 3 3 1 2
```

This is a reusable class. By simply changing the contents of the two disk files, one could grade subsequent quizzes. Using top-down design methods, this class really consists of three parts (Figure 8.3).

Consider oval a first. In this problem, we need to process or fill the `answer` array cells in sequence from the `key.txt` disk file. The first character read goes into cell 0, the next character into cell 1, and so on. The simplest approach is to use a **for** loop variable as the index of an array. This is a very common construction or mechanism in high-level programs, and you will use it again and again. We'll again need a

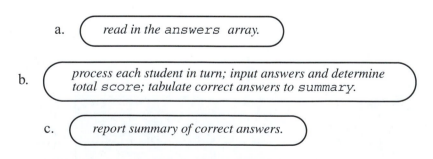

a.   *read in the* `answers` *array.*

b.   *process each student in turn; input answers and determine total* `score`; *tabulate correct answers to* `summary`.

c.   *report summary of correct answers.*

Figure 8.3   Master design chart of `gradtest.cpp`

Table 8.1   Example execution of array loop

value of n	Effective Loop Statement	Effect on answers	Remaining chars in File
0	`answers[0] = keyfile_in.readChar();`	T, , , ,	FTFF
1	`answers[1] = keyfile_in.readChar();`	T, F, , ,	TFF
2	`answers[2] = keyfile_in.readChar();`	T, F, T, ,	FF
3	`answers[3] = keyfile_in.readChar();`	T, F, T, F,	F
4	`answers[4] = keyfile_in.readChar();`	T, F, T, F, F	

char array of five cells named `answer` into which we read the correct quiz answers. The disk file could be opened to file variable `keyfile_in`. Oval a might become:

```
char[] answer = new char[5];
DiskInput keyfile_in = new DiskFile ();
keyfile_in.open("key.txt");
for (int n=0; n<5; n++)
    answer[n] = keyfile_in.readChar();
```

Table 8.1 illustrates the steps that would be executed as the loop variable n goes from 0 to 4.

Now let's look at oval b. This is obviously a loop structure because we need to consider each student in turn. Again, we'll use a `for` loop and process four student segments. We'll use an array called `summary` to hold the number of correct answers for each question (Figure 8.4):

```
DiskInput studentfile_in = new DiskInput ();
studentfile_in.open ("students.txt");
int score;
int[] summary = {0, 0, 0, 0, 0};
for (int n=0; n<4; n++)
{   score = 0;
```

b.1.   *process one student; for each answer, sum correct answers and store in `score`. Tabulate in `summary`.*

```
}
IO.showMessage ("student " + id + "  score: " + score);
```

Figure 8.4   Further decomposition of oval b

Here we are assuming the variable `score` now contains the sum of correct responses for the current student. Oval b.1 represents the grading of one student to place the correct count into `score`. We don't need all student answers in the class to grade one student, just one student's answers. In fact, we only need one student answer at a time. In that way, the processing of one student represents the processing of five answers—which again involves a **for** loop. We could decompose oval b.1 in the following manner:

```
char thisanswer;
int id;
id = studentfile_in.readInt();
for (int ans=0; ans<5; ans++)            // loop over 5 answers . . .
{    thisanswer = studentfile_in.readChar();  // get next answer
     if (thisanswer == answer[ans])      // is it right?
     {    score++;                        // if so, increase grade
          summary[ans]++;                 // and tabulate in summary
     }
}
```

After grading all students, the array `summary` now contains the number of correct answers for each of the five quiz questions.

Oval c is to report the number of correct scores in the `summary` table. Since there are five scores, we will output them sequentially, again using a **for** loop—this time to build the output message:

```
String message;
message = "question summary of\n correct answers: ";
for (int n=0; n<5; n++)
    message += (" " + summary[n] );
IO.showMessage (message);
```

Consider the class of Listing 8.I that puts the whole problem together into a complete class with appropriate declarations. Notice that the number 5 has been removed from the `main()` method and defined as a global **final** constant. Notice also that the various declarations have been grouped together for easier reading and reference.

Listing 8.I

```
// Grade student quiz answers in file 'students.txt' against the key in disk file 'key.txt'.
// Report each student's score and a class  summary of the number correct for each question.
public class GradeTest
{   final int SIZE = 5;

    public static void main (String[] args)
    {   String message;
        char thisanswer;
        int id, score;
        char[] answer = new char[5];
```

```
DiskInput studentfile_in = new DiskInput();
studentfile_in.open ("students.txt");
int[] summary = {0, 0, 0, 0, 0};
DiskInput keyfile_in = new DiskInput();
keyfile_in.open ("key.txt");

for (int n=0; n<5; n++)
  answer[n] = keyfile_in.readChar();

for (int n=0; n<4; n++)
{   score = 0;
    id = studentfile_in.readInt();
    for (int k=0; k<5; k++)                      // loop over 5 answers . . .
    {   thisanswer = studentfile_in.readChar();  // get next answer
        if (thisanswer == answer[k])             // is it right?
        {   score++;                             // if so, increase grade
            summary[k]++;                        // and tabulate in summary
        }
    }
    IO.showMessage ("student " + id + "  score: " + score);
}

message = "question summary of\n correct answers: ";
for (int n=0; n<5; n++)
  message += (" " + summary[n] );
IO.showMessage (message);
System.exit(0);
}
}
```

When this class is executed, we see output display boxes like the following, as we expected:

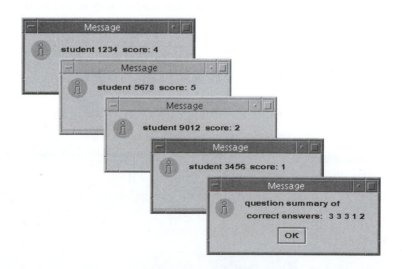

8.4 **Common errors**

Keep in mind that a Java expression should still refer to array variable cells individually. If you need to store a constant in all five cells of an array, you will need five assignment statements or a loop that causes one assignment statement to be executed five times. If you need to output the contents of an array, you will need multiple output statements or a loop. The following, for example, will not output all five cells of the cost array:

```
int cost[5] = { 11, 22, 33, 44, 55 };
IO.showValue ("cost: ", cost);
```

Unfortunately, it may not produce an error message when compiled or a runtime error when executed in some situations. You will just see garbage for output. Using an array name without a subscript is not invalid; it just has a much different (but useful) meaning that will be examined later.

Take another look at the last **for** loop of the class in Listing 8.I. Since the indexes range from 0 to 4 (a total of five cells), the following would be inappropriate:

```
for (ans=0; ans<=5; ans++)
    IO.showValue ("val: ", summary[ans]);
```

CONCEPT
**out-of-bounds
indexes**

This **for** statement attempts to output a value from a cell of the array that does not exist—summary[5], or the sixth cell! This section will compile without an error message and execute just fine—until the method attempts to access the sixth cell. At this point, you will see a system error message similar to the following:

```
Exception in thread "main" java.lang.ArrayIndexOutOfBoundsException: 5
```

The key phrase here is ArrayIndexOutOfBounds. In other words, Java noticed that your statement attempted to access a cell that did not exist, and the class aborted with this error message.

8.5 **Arrays as arguments and parameters**

Passing entire arrays

Arrays can also be used as method parameters as well. To specify an array as a method parameter, the array is declared inside the method parameter list, but no array size is placed within the brackets.

type **[ ]** *arrayname* **;**

Syntax form

CONCEPT
arrays as
parameters

Within the method, the parameter array is referenced in the normal manner. For example, consider this simple method intended to return the sum of the cells in the parameter array (Listing 8.II):

Listing 8.II

```
// SumArray ()  Returns the sum of the integer parameter array
//  IN:  thisarray is a one-dimensional array of 100 integers

int SumArray (int[] thisarray)
{   int sum=0;
    for (int n=0; n<100; n++)      // loop over each array cell
        sum += thisarray[n];        // keep a running sum
    return (sum);
}
```

Notice that the size of the array is expected to be 100 in this method. Without knowing this, the **for** loop could not be correctly set to sum the correct number of cells.

To call a method and pass an array argument, *only the name of the array is placed into the method argument list*. For now, this is the one time you will use an array name without an accompanying subscript. Consider the following three arrays and accompanying method calls:

```
int[] weights = new int [100];
int [] ages = new int [100];
int sumweights, sumages
 . . .
sumweights = SumArray (weights);
 . . .
sumages = SumArray (ages);
```

Obviously, the name of the argument array and the name of the parameter array do not need to be the same (just as with other parameters). The bad news is that the method of Listing 8.II cannot be used for any other sized array. The good news is that there is a way to overcome this limitation.

An array is actually a special kind of object in Java. That means an array instance may have other information variables in addition to the cells of the array itself. There is a public information variable named length associated with every array instance. This variable is automatically set to the current size of the array when the array is created:

arrayname.**length** ;   **Syntax form**

Be careful! This is not the same as the number of characters in a single **String** variable using the " .length() " member method. A **String** is not an array! It is a single object that just happens to have a member *method* to calculate the size of the string. An array uses a member information *variable* length to hold the number of cells in the array.

Let's go back to Listing 8.II and make this method general enough to sum an array of any size (Listing 8.III):

Listing 8.III

```
// SumArray ()  Returns the sum of the integer parameter array
// IN:  thisarray is a one-dimensional array of any size

int SumArray (int[] thisarray)
{    int sum=0;
     for (int n=0; n<thisarray.length; n++)          // loop over each array cell
         sum += thisarray[n];                          // keep a running sum
     return (sum);
}
```

Now, if this method is called with different sized arrays, the correct sum is still returned:

```
int[] weights = new int [256];
int[] ages = new int [25];
int sumweights, sumages
. . .
sumweights = SumArray (weights);       // sum of 256 weights
. . .
sumages = SumArray (ages);             // sum of 25 ages
```

Let's return to the test-grading class designed in Figure 8.3 and implemented in Listing 8.I. This class has become somewhat complex and is reaching the level where it may be difficult for another to read and understand. If we use modular methods, however, the implementation of the design chart of Figure 8.3 becomes quite simple (Listing 8.IV):

Listing 8.IV

```
// Grade student quiz answers in file 'students.txt' against the key in disk file 'key.txt'.
// Report each student's score and a class summary of the number correct for each question.
public class GradeTest2
{  final int QUIZSIZE = 5;
   final int NUMSTUDENTS = 4;
```

```
final String keyfile = "key.txt";
final String studentfile = "students.txt";

private static void InputAnswerKey (String filename, int[] answers);
{        // to be completed!
}
private static void GradeStudents (String filename, int[] answers, int[] summary)
{        // to be completed!
}
private static String ReportSummary (int[] summary)
{        // to be completed!
}


public static void main (String[] args)
{   char[] answers = new char [QUIZSIZE];
    int[] summary = new int [QUIZSIZE];

    InputAnswerKey (keyfile, answers);
    GradeStudents (studentfile, answers, summary, NUMSTUDENTS);
    ReportSummary (summary);
}
}
```

This class is very general. If we wish to use this class for another quiz and a different set of students, we only need to change the **final** constants at the top of the class—specifying the number of quiz questions, the number of students, and the filenames.

The only task now is to write the three functions that the main() method references. As you can see, this is actually a way of performing top-down design without the need for temporary ovals. The three functions represent ovals a, b, and c. The first method is being passed a string and a character array of five cells (Listing 8.V):

Listing 8.V

```
// InputAnswerKey()   Reads a disk file for a quiz answer key and
// sets the correct answers in the array 'answers'.
// ASSUMPTION; input file exists and contains enough answers for the given array
// IN:  filename is a string for the input file name
// OUT: answers is an array for the correct quiz answers

private static void InputAnswerKey (String filename, char ans[ ])
{   DiskInput infile = new DiskInput();
    infile.open (filename);
    for (int n=0; n<ans.length; n++)
        ans[n] = infile.readChar();
}
```

The second method is responsible for grading each student record from the student.txt file using the test answer key array (Listing 8.VI):

___

Listing 8.VI

```
// GradeStudents ()  Using the 'answers' test key, grade
// each student quiz in file STUDENTFILE. Print score.
// ASSUMPTION: file STUDENTFILE exists and contains
//  one record per student.
// IN:  filename is a string file name
//       answers contains test key answers
//       numstudents contains the number of students to be graded
// OUT: summary will be a count table of correct answers.

private static void GradeStudents
        (String filename, char[] answers, int[] summary, int numstudents)
{  DiskInput infile = new DiskInput();
   infile.open (filename);
   int id, score;
   char thisanswer;
   for (int n = 0; n< numstudents; n++)        // loop over students
   {   score = 0;                              // assume a zero score
       id = infile.readInt();                  // read student id for this segment
       for (int k=0; k<answers.length; k++)    // loop over answers
       {   thisanswer = infile.readChar();     // get next answer
           if (thisanswer == answers[k])       // is it right?
           {   score++;                        // if so, update grade
               summary[k]++;                   // and tabulate
           }
       }                                       // end of loop over answers (k)
       IO.showMessage ("student: "+id+"  score: " +score);
   }                                           // end of loop over students
}
```

The last method has the simple responsibility of generating the output report from the summary array (Listing 8.VII):

___

Listing 8.VII

```
// ReportSummary() Generate output report from 'summary'
// IN:  summary, a table of correct answer counts

private static void    ReportSummary (int[] summary)
{   String message = "question summary of\n correct answers: ";
    for (int n=0; n<5; n++)
      message += (" " + summary[n] );
    IO.showMessage (message);
}
```

As you are continually seeing, using helper methods to implement design ovals allows the programmer to neatly compartmentalize each task. Debugging is made simpler by allowing the programmer to check ASSUMPTIONS, IN, and OUT conditions at the top and bottom of each method.

CONCEPT
arrays are passed
by reference

Notice that changes to the parameter arrays in the above helper methods are also reflected in the original argument arrays when these methods are invoked from the main() method. It is important to note that *array parameters are automatically reference parameters*.

E X P E R I M E N T

Since the main() method apparently has a String array parameter, output the contents of this array and see what's there:

```
for (int n=0; n<args.length; n++)
    IO.showMessage (args[n]);
```

Passing individual cells

Entire arrays are used as arguments and declared as parameters. What if only a single cell of an array is to be passed? In this case, a single array cell is just like any other simple variable, and the same approach used back in Chapter 3 applies. That is, the matching parameter is declared as a simple variable. If parameter and corresponding argument are a primitive type, the argument is passed by value, and no changes in the parameter are reflected back in the single cell argument. If the argument and parameter are an object, the object is passed as a reference—allowing changes to the argument through the parameter.

Consider the following method that calculates the cube of a given **int** parameter:

```
private static int cube (int x)
{   return (x * x * x);
}
```

This method can be called with individual **int** arguments or with individual cells of an **int** array. The only requirement is that the arguments must represent individual integers:

```
int[] cost = new int[10];
int age, weight, answer;
. . .
answer = cube (age);                        // valid call
answer = cube (weight);                      // valid call
answer = cube (cost[5]);                     // valid call
answer = cube (cost[0]);                     // valid call
```

If an argument does not represent a single **int** variable, an error will occur:

```
answer = cube (cost);
```

8.6 Array searching

A phone book is used to look up a number given a name. Suppose we would like to look up a name or address given a phone number. (This is sort of a "reverse" phone book that might be handy when your caller ID doesn't show the name of a telemarketer!) Let's design a class to do exactly that. Suppose we have a phone book file that contains two lines for every person. The first line is the person's name and address, and the second line contains the phone number. For simplicity, let's assume the phone number is a string. For example, one entry might look like the following:

```
Fred Smith, 123 Oak Street
567-8901
```

If we develop a class for this problem, we would probably want to interact with the user by (a) asking for the phone number and (b) displaying the associated name and address similar to the following:

```
Enter a phone number:  567-8901
The name is: Fred Smith, 123 Oak Street
```

The class would simply need to accomplish the following three steps:

a. read the phone book file into a set of two arrays.

b. prompt the user to enter a phone number.

c. look up and output the name for that number.

Let's start with the `main()` method of the class (Listing 8.VIII). Again, for simplicity, let's assume we live in a small town of 1000 people. We'll declare two parallel arrays for this problem. The first array is called `phone_number` with enough cells to hold all the phone numbers from the phone book file. The second array is called `name` with enough cells to hold all the name-and-address strings from the phone book file. When we read in the phone book file, we'll be sure to place a phone number in the same corresponding cell as a name. For example, if we read the phone number for Fred into cell 234 of `phone_number`, we will read the name and address of Fred into cell 234 of the `name` array. In that manner, if we find a phone number match in cell X of the `phone_number` array, we'll know that the corresponding name can be found in cell X of the `name` array.

Listing 8.VIII

```
// allow a user to enter a phone number, then display the name and address
public class ReversePhoneBook
{   final static int NUM_ENTRIES = 1000;
    final static String filename = "phone_book.txt";
```

```
private static void InputPhoneBook
            (String filename, String[] phone_number, String[] name)
{   // to be completed
}
private static int LookupName (String[] phone_number, String this_number)
{   // to be completed
}
public static void main (String[] args)
{   String[] phone_number = new String[NUM_ENTRIES];
    String this_number;
    String[] name = new String[NUM_ENTRIES];
    int index;
    InputPhoneBook (filename, phone_number, name);          // oval a)
    this_number = IO.readString ("enter phone number: ");   // oval b)
    index = LookupName (phone_number, this_number);         // this line and next are
    IO.showMessage ("the name is: " + name[index]);         //    oval c)
}
}
```

The first helper method is straightforward (Listing 8.IX). We simply read in entries from the disk file as we have done in previous methods. The first entry for a person is the name and address; the second entry is the phone number (Listing 8.IX):

Listing 8.IX

```
// input a phone book file array into two parallel arrays -- name and number
// OUT:  the  array read from disk
// ASSUMPTIONS: the arrays are the correct size for the disk file information
private static void InputPhoneBook (String filename, String[] number, String[] name)
{   DiskInput infile = new DiskInput ();
    infile.open (filename);
    for (int n=0; n<number.length; n++)
    {   name[n] = infile.readString ();
        number[n] = infile.readString ();
    }
}
```

The next helper method represents a new problem: searching the number array for the correct phone number. The simplest approach is to again use a loop and examine cells in sequence until a match is found. Since we don't know how many cells need to be examined, this is an indefinite loop, and we'll use a **while** statement. This is the first time we've needed to compare two **String** variables. Since a **String** is not a primitive data type, we can't simply use the == (or any other symbol comparison operator). Fortunately, there is a helper method in the **String** class to do just this:

string_var.**equals** (*string_var*);   **Syntax form**

This method returns a **boolean** value that can readily be used in an **if** or **while** statement. The two String values we wish to compare are the phone number input by the user (`this_number`) and cell n of the array `phone_number`. We'll simply have n go from 0 (the first cell index) up until a match is found or the end of the array is reached (Listing 8.X):

Listing 8.X

```
// Search the array phone_number for a match to this_number.
// IN: The phone_number array has been filled with phone numbers from the disk
// OUT:  The index of a match in the phone_number array with this_number or -1
private static int LookupName (String[] phone_number, String this_number)
{    boolean notfound = true;                  // indefinte loop completion flag;
     int n = 0;                                // search position index, starts at 0
     while (notfound && (n < 1000))
     {    if (this_number.equals(phone_number[n]))
              notfound = false;
          else n++;
     }
     if (notfound)
     {    IO.showMessage ("NAME NOT FOUND!");
          System.exit(0);
     }
     return n;
}
```

8.7 Sorting an array

Look again at the Creative Challenge projects at the end of the previous chapter. One task was to input 10 words and then output them in alphabetical order. Using arrays, this project is significantly simpler to solve than it probably was for you at that time. Ordering the elements of an array is called sorting. For simplicity in this next example, we'll use **int** values instead of words. (We'll return to sorting String values later.) The design chart for this class solution is quite simple.

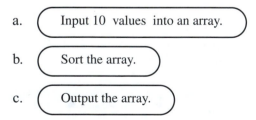

Figure 8.5 Design chart for the word-sorting project

The top and bottom ovals of Figure 8.5 are easy enough to directly implement (Listing 8.XI). We will set the problem of oval (b) into a method and come back to it later:

Listing 8.XI

```
// Sort and output a list of 10 numbers from a disk file provided by the user.
public class SortNumbers
{ final static int SIZE = 10;

   private static void Sort (int[] values)
   {       // to be completed
   }

   public static void main (String[] args)
   {       int[] values = new int[SIZE];
           DiskInput infile = new DiskInput();
           int n;
           String filename, message;
           filename = IO.readString ("Enter filename: ");
           infile.open (filename);
           for (n=0; n<SIZE; n++)                          // input the list of words (oval a)
               values[n] = infile.readInt();
           Sort (values);                                  // sort the list (oval b)
           message = "The sorted numbers are: \n";         // output the list (oval c)
           for (n=0; n<SIZE; n++)
               message += (values[n] + "\n");
           IO.showMessage (message);
           System.exit(0);
   }
}
```

Let's test this incomplete class with a file of 10 values. This will allow us to verify that the `main()` method correctly reads and displays the list of numbers (ovals a and b). The `Sort()` method will do nothing; in other words, the `Sort()` method is just a stub. Here's the file with the original 10 values:

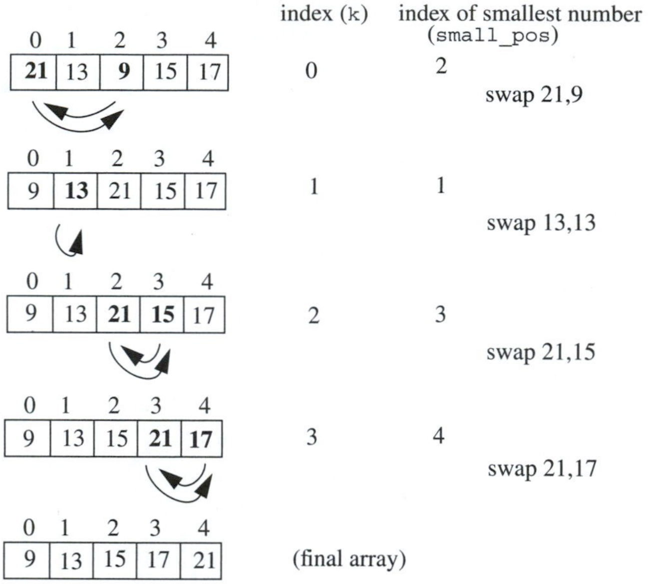

			index (k)	index of smallest number (small_pos)

Figure 8.6 Selection sort of an array of five int cells

Now it is time to figure out how to order the array values. There are numerous methods to solve this problem, and some more efficient than others. The approach or algorithm we will apply is known as a *selection sort*. The approach is not particularly fast or efficient, but it is easy to program. Repeat the following steps as index k goes from 0 to the array size −2;

1. Find the smallest array value in the index range k to the array size −1. Assume it is found at index small_pos.

2. Swap the old value at position k with the value at position small_pos.

In essence, we are considering each cell in sequence. For each cell, we search the remaining array to find the smallest value (from this cell to the end) and then exchange or swap values with the smallest found. (Actually, we do not need to consider the last cell—that is why the index k only reaches the size of the array −2. By the time the last cell is reached, the array is already in order.) Figure 8.6 diagrams how this might proceed for a given array of five integers.

Having the index k go from 0 to the size of the array −2 is just a **for** loop. Searching for the smallest value from k to the size of the array −1 is another **for** loop that is nested within the first loop. The example in Figure 8.6 deals with only five integer values; however, the same algorithm would of course work for any sized array as long as the final SIZE constant is updated (Listing 8.XII):

Listing 8.XII

```
// Sort()  Order the values in the array
//  IN:  words is a String array of size values
private static void Sort (int[] nums)
{   int n, k, small_pos=0, smallest, temp;
    for (k=0; k<nums.length-1; k++)              // repeat; each cell but last.
    {   smallest = nums[k];                       // assume this is smallest
        for (n=k; n<nums.length; n++)             // compare with other values . . .
        if (nums[n] <= smallest)                  // if smaller, save position
        {   small_pos = n;                        //    and value . . .
            smallest = nums[n];
        }
        temp = nums[k];                           // swap these cells
        nums[k]  = nums[small_pos];
        nums[small_pos]  = temp;
    }
}
```

Now when we execute the class, the same 10 values are displayed, but this time they are in ascending order:

8.8 Review of references

Although it is not important to understand how arrays are physically represented in the computer in order to use them (as we have in the examples of this chapter), it will help you understand later topics. Keep in mind that what is presented in this section does not in any way change how you have learned to use arrays in classes and methods in the first part of this chapter.

A reference is just an address; these are interchangeable terms. Although each different computer architecture may utilize a different address form, these addresses are just integer numbers (or occasionally, pairs of numbers). Each cell in computer memory has two attributes: a value (stored or held inside the cell) and an address (specifying where the cell is located). Every memory cell has its own unique address. A physical memory address really has little meaning outside of the execution of a class. In fact, it may change each time a class is run as the operating system allocates different areas of memory for variables. We often represent references in diagrams using arrows.

Consider the following assignment statement in the `main()` method:

```
float[] x = new float[10];
float[] y;
```

The first line produces a reference x initialized to point to 10 **float** cells. The second line produces a reference y that is not initialized. In other words, cell y doesn't yet point to an array. We might later place a valid reference into y to point to an array with the following:

```
y = new float[20];
```

Remember how we pass arrays as arguments by using the name of the array. What we are really passing to the method is the reference. Consider the following method:

```
public static void SomeMethod (float[] z)
{   z[5] = 99.9;
}
```

The method argument declares z to be a reference to a sequence of floating-point cells and initializes it to be a copy of the corresponding argument reference. If this method were invoked with the following from the `main()` method,

```
SomeMethod (x);
```

then z and x would both reference the same array. This is why array parameters are automatically reference parameters. Since z and x are actually both pointing to the same array, assigning a value to a cell 5 in z to 99.9 changes cell 5 in x (Figure 8.7).

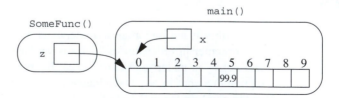

Figure 8.7   Passing array pointers

To solidify this discussion, let's do something out of the ordinary by changing `SomeMethod()`:

```
public static void SomeMethod (float[] z)
{    z = new float[20];
     z[5] = 99.9;
}
```

The first line of this modified method resets reference z to point to a completely new array of 20 cells. The previous value of z (a copy of reference x) *is lost*. Subsequently, any changes to cells referenced by z *have no effect* on array x. When `SomeMethod()` finishes, the 20 cells referenced only by z are deallocated and are no longer available.

A method may return a reference to an array. For example, the following method allocates an array, fills it from a disk file, and then returns the array to the calling method. Let's assume the first integer in the disk file indicates the number of remaining integers that are to be placed into the array:

```
private int[] getArray (String filename)
{   int size;
    DiskInput infile = new DiskInput();
    infile.open(filename);
    size = infile.readInt();              // read the array size
    int[] array = new int[size];          // create an array
    for (int n=0; n<size; n++)
        array[n] = infile.readInt();      // read the array from disk
    return (array);
}
```

Since this method is returning a reference to `array`, you are apparently not through with it, and it will not be deallocated when the method returns. Java keeps track of what methods still contain references to an array and does not deallocate the array until there are no references to it. This is done automatically, and the programmer does not need to be concerned. The above method might be called in the following manner:

```
int[] costs;                    // declare an empty array reference
costs = getArray ("disk.txt")   // create array and read in data
. . .                           // from now on, use array 'costs'
```

8.9 Arrays of objects

Object arrays are really not much different from primitive data arrays. At this point, however, it becomes important to have a better understanding of the difference between **static** and nonstatic (or dynamic) helper classes.

To simplify the discussion, we will assume a class contains all static members or all nonstatic (dynamic) members. A **static** class always exists—it doesn't come into existence and is never deallocated. We say that a `static` class is not associated with an object. As such, it is generally not associated with a reference. We can simply invoke the **static** methods of such a class using the class name. For example, the **Math** class is **static**. We can utilize the **static** members of this class using the class name:

```
IO.showValue ("pi is: ", Math.PI);
IO.showValue ("cos of x is: ", Math.cos(x));
```

It doesn't make sense to allocate or create a **Math** object:

```
Math mathobject = new Math();
```

On the other hand, the **Fraction** class developed in the previous chapter and the **DiskInput** class used for disk I/O are dynamic classes. In other words, when your class application begins to execute, there are no **Fraction** or **DiskInput** objects available. To use one, you must create one with the keyword `new`:

```
Fraction f = new Fraction();
DiskInput infile = new DiskInput();
```

It should now be coming into focus that f and `infile` are references to a **Fraction** and **DiskInput** object that has just been created. Now, we must refer to the object using the reference and not the class name:

```
f.set(2,3);                 // set f to 2/3
infile.open("file.txt");    // open a disk file
```

Can you understand why the following will not work?

```
Fraction f;
f.set (2,3);
```

If you can see that since f is a reference and does not yet refer to any object of type **Fraction**, then you are doing well! The bottom line is this: A helper class of methods and constants (e.g., the **Math** class) can be static. A helper class containing information variables and for which more than one instance might be needed (e.g., having several **DiskInput** objects to use several files in a method) should be non-static. Nonstatic, or dynamic, class objects must be created with the keyword **new**:

OK, what does this have to do with arrays of objects? These are nonstatic! With that said, we can utilize arrays of objects just like we do arrays of primitive data types;

```
Fraction[] table = new Fraction[10];
```

This creates an array of 10 **Fraction** objects. Each of these 10 objects is a complete **Fraction**. Consider the following example statements:

```
table[2].set(3, 4);      // cell 2 is set to 3/4
table[3].set(5);         // cell 3 is set to 5/1
table[3].add(table[2]); // cell 3 is replaced with 3/4 + 5/1
```

One restriction on arrays of objects is that when the **[ ]** notation is used with the keyword **new**, the default constructor is applied (as in the above `table` declaration).

Objects may also contain arrays themselves. Let's define a **StudentGrades** class where each **StudentGrades** has a name and a five-cell array of called grades:

```
public class StudentGrades
{   private String name;
    private double[] grades = new double[5];

    . . .                              // methods need to be added
```

Within the methods of this class, a single grade cell can be referred to just as you would expect. You might also wish to allow each **StudentGrades** object to have a different number of grades. In this case, only the `grades` reference is declared, and it is not initialized with the keyword **new**. Now you could pass the size of the `grades` array to a constructor:

```
public class StudentGrades
{   private String name;
    private double[] grades;

    public StudentGrades (int size)
    { grades = new double[size];
    }
```

Now a **StudentGrades** object can be created, and you have control over how many `grades` cells should be allocated for that object. For example:

```
StudentGrades fred = new StudentGrades(10);   // has 10 grades
StudentGrades sam = new StudentGrades(6);     // has 6 grades
```

8.10 Multidimensional arrays

Let's return to the shirt cost table from the beginning of this chapter. Suppose the company comes out with a new and improved line of shirts where each style comes in four different colors (Figure 8.8).

Improved Shirt Cost Table

	0	3.45	4.59	7.39	9.45	6.78	2.84	4.56
(color	1	3.47	4.63	7.41	9.49	6.83	2.99	4.75
index)	2	3.53	4.66	7.45	9.53	6.89	2.54	4.99
	3	3.69	4.69	7.56	9.65	6.98	3.05	5.76
		0	1	2	3	4	5	6

(style index)

Figure 8.8   A simple two-dimensional table

CONCEPT
avoid physical
visualizations

Now you need to know two indexes to determine the appropriate shirt cost: the style index and the color index. Obviously, this is a two-dimensional table. A word of caution: Some students tend to think of array dimensions as a *physical reality*. As a result, they artificially label these two-dimensional table indexes as the *row* index and the *column* index. In this way of thinking, a three-dimensional table is viewed as a *cube*. Keep in mind that use of the term *dimension* really has little to do with physical diagrams or figures; it is simply a way of specifying how many different indexes there are.

You can easily see that if Figure 8.8 were reorganized so that the color index went from left to right and the style index went from top to bottom, it would still contain the same information. In other words, given a color and style index, the lookup cost would be the same. Another reason this particular labeling should be avoided is that it falls apart when tables have higher dimensions.

For example, consider a collection of books of shirt costs; each volume corresponds to a particular manufacturer, each chapter in a volume corresponds to a particular fabric, each page within a chapter is a particular size, and each size in a chapter contains a two-dimensional table of style and color indexes. This is obviously a five-dimensional table; to look up a shirt cost, you need to know the manufacturer, fabric, size, style, and color. While this analogy is simple to envision, trying to imagine a hypercube of five dimensions as a physical construction could give you a real headache.

You could easily imagine that the publication for the shirt cost volumes could be rearranged in a number different ways. For example, each volume could be organized to contain a particular fabric and each chapter could be a specific manufacturer. Regardless of how publication is organized, *if you know the ordering of indexes*, the look-up cost for a particular shirt will be the same. Suppose the company decides on the first ordering: manufacturer, fabric, size, style, and color. If you were asked to look up the cost of a shirt using the index group (3, 6, 4, 2, 1), you can easily recognize that this refers to a manufacturer index of 3, a fabric index of 6, a size index of 4, a style index of 2, and a color index of 1.

Let's return to Java. Multidimensional array variables are declared by using sets of brackets after the variable name to specify the number of cells for each array index:

```
type [ ] [ ] name = new type [size₁] [size₂];
```

Syntax form

In the syntax box, $size_1$ refers to the number of possible values for the first index, and $size_2$ refers to the number of possible values for the second index. (If there are more indexes or dimensions, simply extend the format for as many indexes as are needed.) The *type* refers to the type of individual cells. The declaration

```
float[][] improved_shirt_cost = new float [4][7];
```

declares a two-dimensional array named `improved_shirt_cost` that is associated with two indexes: The first has four possible values (numbered 0 to 3) and the second index has seven values (numbered 0 to 6) as in Figure 8.8. This is often called a uniform array because all rows are the same size and all columns are the same size. (You will learn later that there are ways of establishing ragged arrays where each row may have a different number of values. There are also ways of establishing arrays where the cells may represent a variety of different types.)

CONCEPT
index associations

Which index is for color and which index is for style? That is the programmer's responsibility to remember and document! Java does not care how you choose to order indexes to represent tables. As far as the computer is concerned, it is just a two-dimensional array of **float** values. The computer has no idea what a shirt is of course.

When a two-dimensional array cell is referenced within a class, the reference needs to use index values in the correct order. Each index is enclosed with brackets. For example, if we associate the first index with color and the second for style,

```
thiscost = improved_shirt_cost [2][4];
```

refers to the cost of the shirt with color number 2 and style number 4. (Remember again that all indexes begin with zero.)

CONCEPT
multidimensional parameters

When passing multi-dimensional arrays as arguments to functions, again only the name of the array is used (which represents a reference to the array). For example, the following method expects a two-dimensional array as a parameter:

```
void SomeFunc (int[][] table);
```

Suppose this information has been stored in the disk file `"shirts.txt"` and we need a class to perform lookups for a user. Assume each line in the file represents a cost for a particular style and color. We'll assume the first entry is for color 0, style 0. The next entry will be for color 0, style 1 and so on until the last line will contain the cost for color 3, style 6.

Consider the following simple implementation in Listing 8.XIII. The first method ReadTable() reads the table information from the disk file. The second method DoLookUps() prompts the user for style and color indexes and then outputs the appropriate cost:

Listing 8.XIII

```
//  Output the cost of a shirt given the color and style indexes.
//  ASSUMPTION: file "shirts.txt" contains the 4x7 cost table
public class ShirtCost
{

// ReadTable() Fill a 2-D cost table from the 'filename' file
// ASSUMPTION: file exists.
// IN:  filename is the correct file name string
// OUT:  table is a 2-D array of costs
private void ReadTable (float[ ][] table, string filename)
{  DiskInput infile = new DiskInput();
   infile.open (filename);
   int color, style;
   for (color=0; color<4; color++)
       for (style=0; style<7; style++)
           table[color][style] = infile.readInt( );
}

// DoLookUps()  Output a cost for a given style and color
// IN: table is the 2-D array of costs.
private void DoLookUps (float[][] table)
{  int color, style;
   style = IO.readInt ("enter style: ");
   color = IO.readInt ("enter color: ");
   IO.showMessage ( " cost  is:  " + table[color][style]);
}

void main ()
{  float[][] cost_table = new float[4][7];    // color is first index, style is second
   ReadTable (cost_table, filename);          // input the table from disk
   DoLookUps (cost_table);                    // perform lookups for user
}
```

OK, now you are ready for the big five-dimensional table example. Suppose you choose the ordering: manufacturer, fabric, size, color, and style. Suppose also there are eight different manufacturers, four fabrics for each manufacturer, two sizes for each fabric, four colors for each size, and seven styles for each color. The following declaration would be appropriate. Notice the importance of documenting the ordering of the indexes:

```
// Table of shirt costs.
// Ordering of indexes; manufacturer, fabric, size, color, style
     float [][][][][]shirt_cost_volumes = new float [8][4][2][4][7];
```

In practical programming, one-dimensional and occasionally two-dimensional arrays are often sufficient for most problems. It is rare that higher dimensioned arrays are used. It is usually much more powerful to declare and use complex tables as arrays of objects with each object in turn having its own subcomponents. For example, it is quite simple to declare a class called **Shirt_Table**, a class called **Color**, and a class called **Style**. Each **Shirt_Table** has four **Color** objects. Each **Color** object has seven **Style** objects. Each **Style** object for a given **Color** object has a cost:

```
public class Style
{   private float cost;
}

public class Color
{   private Style[] style = new Style[7];
    . . .                  // methods need to be added


}

public class Shirt_Table
{   private Color[] color = new Color[4];
    . . .                  // methods need to be added
}
```

Now when a method declares a `Shirt_Table` object, there will be a total of 28 costs—a cost for each of seven styles of each of four colors:

```
Shirt_Table table;
. . .
IO.showValue ("the cost of color 2 and style 4 is: ", table.color[2].style[4]);
```

The best way to read this is backward. Replace the dots in the array reference with the phrase "of the": The 4th style of the 2nd color of the table.

Java actually does not implement multidimensional arrays, although that fact is not often important to the programmer. Java will convert a two-dimensional array declaration into a declaration of an array of arrays. In other words, in the two-dimensional shirt cost table, Java considers the object `improved_shirt_cost` to be a reference to an array of four cells. Each of these four cells is a reference in turn to an array of seven `float` cells. As such, we can use the member length of each array:

```
IO.showValue ("number of colors: ", improved_shirt_cost.length);
IO.showValue ("number of styles per color: ",
            improved_shirt_cost[0].length);
```

The first line displays the number of rows in our table: There are four different colors. The second line shows the number of styles for color 0: There are seven styles. (Since this is a nice rectangular table, the number of styles for *any* color is seven. There are arrays in Java where the number of elements in a subarray may change, but we'll leave that for a later course.)

8.11 Example project

For an example project, let's return to the `StudentGrades` class suggested a couple of pages back and complete the class. Our goal is to have a class to represent a student with a name and an array of grades. The number of grades for each student should be specified when a new student is created (Listing 8.XIV):

Listing 8.XIV

```java
// A class to represent a student with a name and an array of grades
public class StudentGrades
{   private String name;
    private double[] grades;

    public StudentGrades ()              // default constructor
    {
    }
    public StudentGrades (int size)    // constructor defines the size of the grades array
    { grades = new double[size];
    }

    public String getName()            // return the name of this student
    {   return name;
    }

    public void setName(String thisname)
    {   name = thisname;               // set the name of this student
    }

    public double getGrade (int gradenumber)               // return one of the grades
    {   if (gradenumber < 0 || gradenumber > grades.length)
        {   IO.showMessage ("ILLEGAL GRADE NUMBER");
            return 0.0;
        }
        else
            return grades[gradenumber];
    }

    public void setGrade (int gradenumber, double thisgrade)      // set one of the grades
    {   if (gradenumber < 0 || gradenumber > grades.length)
            IO.showMessage ("ILLEGAL GRADE NUMBER");
        else
            grades[gradenumber] = thisgrade;
    }
```

```
public void diskWrite (DiskOutput outfile)              // write this student to disk
{   outfile.writeString (name);
    outfile.writeInt (grades.length);
    for (int n=0; n<grades.length; n++)
        outfile.writeDouble (grades[n]);
}

public void diskRead (DiskInput infile)                 // read this student from disk
{   name = infile.readString();
    int numgrades = infile.readInt();
    grades = new Double[numgrades];
    for (int n=0; n<numgrades; n++)
        grades[n] = infile.readDouble();
}

public void display ()                                  // form a display box with student info
{   String message = name;
    for (int n=0; n<grades.length; n++)
        message += " " + grades[n];
    IO.showMessage (message);
}
}
```

Notice in this example that there are two constructors; one allows a declaration to set the size of the grades array. Notice also that the diskWrite() method writes out the size of the grades array. For example, suppose a student was named Fred and had three grades (98.6, 97.6, and 96.6); this student would be written to disk as:

```
Fred
3
98.6
97.6
96.6
```

Now this student can be read from the disk file at a later time using the following:

```
StudentGrades s = new StudentGrades();
s.diskRead (infile);
s.display();
```

The constructor used in the first line leaves the grades array empty. The diskRead() method first reads the student's name (Fred), then reads the number of grades to be represented (3), and then allocates a new array of three cells to hold these grades prior to reading them in.

8.12 Summary

KEY TERMS   Only a few new terms were introduced in this chapter:

1. *dimension*—the number of indexes needed to reference an array.

2. *parallel arrays*—two (or more) arrays in which cells with corresponding indexes are related.

3. *subscript*—another name for the index of an array.

4. *selection sort*—an algorithm for ordering the cells of an array.

CONCEPTS   A number of new concepts and forms were presented. Arrays must be declared with the size of the array in brackets. Array cells are numbered beginning with zero. When referencing an array in an executable statement, the index is placed within brackets. Arrays may be initialized when declared by assigning an initial-value list within braces. When arrays are thus initialized, the keyword **new** is not needed.

When one-dimensional arrays are passed as arguments to method calls, only the name is placed within the call list. When declaring one-dimensional arrays as method parameters, an empty set of brackets is used. Naturally, the *type* of the argument and parameter array must still be the same. The method being called can determine the number of cells in the parameter array using the .length array member.

Array arguments to method calls are automatically passed by reference. Any changes to the parameter array are reflected in the argument array in the calling method.

Arrays may be declared to consist of any primitive data type or any existing class object. The number of cells in an array can be referenced using the array .length member information variable.

Table 8.2   Example segments

`int[] x = new int[10];`	Declare a 10-cell int array.
`int[] y = {15, -3, 77, 0, 9};`	Declare and initialize.
`for (n=0; n<10; n++)`	Output a 10-cell array.
`    IO.showValue ("val: ",  x[n]);`	
`cost = SumArray(x);`	Pass array x to a method.
`private void SumArray (int[] y)`	Declare an array parameter.
`IO.showValue`	Output the length of an array.
`    ("length is: ", y.length);`	

8.13 Exercises

Short-answer questions

1. Give a declaration statement for each of the following:
   a. an array of 10 **int** cells,
   b. an array of five **float** cells initialized to 5.6, 7.8, 9.1, 2.3 and 4.5,
   c. an array of two **String** cells initialized to the string "hello world".

2. Can one array be copied into another array with a simple assignment statement as in the following? Explain your answer.

```
int [] x = new int [5];
int [] y = new int [5];
. . .
x = y;        // copy array y into array x??
```

3. The ordinal constant or variable within brackets used to reference a particular one-dimensional array cell is called the array _____.

4. The number of different indexes required to reference a single array cell is called the array _____.

5. The index or subscript of an array must be what type of variable or constant?

6. How may the length of a parameter array be determined?

7. What occurs when a statement attempts to assign a value to an array cell using an index that is out-of-bounds?

8. Are arrays passed by reference or passed by value to a helper method?

9. List two common programming errors associated with using one-dimensional arrays.

10. Does the Java system check to verify that an array index is within bounds before executing a statement containing an array reference?

11. Write a simple **for** loop segment to output the following array:

```
int [] values = new int [20];
```

12. Write a simple **for** loop segment to allow the user to input new values in the array of question 11.

13. Write a **for** loop segment to sum the integers in the array of question 11 into the following variable:

```
int sum = 0;
```

14. Show how the array of question 11 should be passed to the method SomeFunc ().

15. If the method SomeFunc () expects a single integer array parameter, show how the declaration of the parameter should be stated.

16. Is it possible to write a method that creates and returns a new array to a calling method?

17. What happens to the original cells of an array if they are replaced with a new set of cells created with the keyword **new**?

18. What is the most common programming error when using arrays?

19. Write a segment of code to declare and fill a two-dimensional array using the following table showing the percentages of ages for males and females of three different heights:

| | | Height | | |
		<5′	5–5.5′	>5.5′
Sex	M	0.13	0.52	0.35
	F	0.26	0.54	0.20

20. Declare a two-dimensional array to hold the powers of integer positive numbers. One index should represent the number itself and have the range 0 to 5. The other index should represent the power and have a range of 0 to 4. For example, the two indexes power = 3 and number = 4 should represent a cell for 4^3. *This question has two equivalent answers.*

Projects

1. Create a text disk file containing 20 integers. Write a class to input this array of 20 integers from the disk file and output the sum and average.

2. Write a class to encrypt a text file by substituting characters using the following parallel arrays. Each input character is to be located in the `plaintext` array and the corresponding character in the `encrypted` array is to be output to a separate file. Input characters not found in the `plaintext` array are to be output as is. Notice `plaintext` begins with a blank.

```
char[] plaintext =
    {" abcdefghijklmnopqrstuvwxyz1234567890,.:;"};
char[] encrypted =
    {"1qaz2wsx3edc4rfv5tgb6yhn7ujm8i k9ol0p!@#$"};
```

3. Write a method to fill a one-dimensional table with the first 100 Fibonacci numbers. A Fibonacci number is simply the sum of the previous two Fibonacci numbers. The first two numbers in the sequence are 1 and 1. Obviously, the next few numbers are 2, 3, 5, 8, and so on. Write a `main()` method to call this method and pass it an array to be filled. When the method returns, the `main()` method should output these Fibonacci numbers *backward*.

4. Create a text disk file containing a list of 50 student segments. Each segment should contain two lines: an integer ID number and a name. Write a class to read this file and allow the user to lookup the ID number for a given name.

5. Create a text disk file containing a list of 50 integer values. Write a class to read this list and issue a warning message to the user for each duplicate found in the list.

6. Using the disk file created for Project 5, write a class to input this file, sort the numbers, and output the resulting array.

7. Using the disk file created for Project 4, write a class to input this file, sort the records by ID number, and output the result to another disk file. This new file should contain the same records as the original (one ID and name per line), but the ID numbers should be in numeric order. Be sure to keep names and ID numbers together.

8. Since Java does not have a built-in power operator, it might be convenient to have a two-dimensional table of integer powers. Declare two-dimensional array for 10 integers (0 through 9), each integer having four different powers (1 through 4). Write a method to fill this table with appropriate values. In the `main()` method, allow the user to enter an integer and a requested power and have the class then look up and display the appropriate answer. If the user enters a request outside the table, display an error message. Notice that the power index is to run 1 through 4.

9. The Game of Life is a traditional computer science program, and you are now ready to give it a try. It is a simple simulation approach to the interaction of primitive life forms such as bacteria colonies. Colonies live out their existence on a two-dimensional matrix. The immediate neighbors of a cell are those eight horizontally, vertically, and diagonally adjacent cells. A cell may contain a colony or be empty. The life of a colony in the next generation is determined according to a set of simple rules:

a. If a colony cell (containing life) has fewer than two neighbor colonies, the colony will die of isolation in the next generation.

b. If a colony cell has more than three neighbor colonies, it will die of overcrowding in the next generation.

c. If an empty cell has exactly three neighbor colonies, a new colony will be born there in the next generation.

The game is played by initializing the matrix with initial colonies and then calculating and outputting the matrices of generations as time passes. For example, the following diagram shows five generations of a given initial matrix:

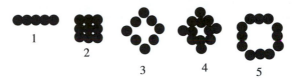

10. Creative Challenge: At this point, you know how to use arrays that have integer indexes beginning with 0. What about tables with indexes that are not even integers? Write a class to read a text file and then output a table of occurrences for each word in the file—the number of times "the" was found, the number of times "in" was found, and so on for each different word in the file.

9

Stream I/O and Text Processing

Many computer programs deal with processing textual data as opposed to strictly numeric data. You encounter such programs in word processors, interactive role-playing games, email programs, and a variety of other applications. In this chapter, you will learn some basic string handling capabilities and Java stream methods for doing more complex I/O with strings.

9.1 String helper methods

Let's start with a simple review of the **String** data type. Although a **String** is technically not a primitive data type, it has many of the features of primitive data types. For example, **String** variables are passed to methods as values—not as object references. The concatenation operation (+) is built-in for strings. **String** variables may be assigned using the = operator. The keyword **new** is not explicitly needed for **String** declarations.

Still, a **String** is not primitive. You need to remember that the relational operators cannot be utilized to compare strings as they can with **int**, **float**, **double**, and the other primitives. A **String** is an object with helper methods. Table 9.1 lists the most useful of these members.

Table 9.1   String class helper methods

Helper method	function
length ()	returns the length of the current string assigned to this object.
equals (*some_string*)	returns true if the owner object equals the *some_string* object; otherwise, returns false. Two strings are equal if they contain the same character sequence.
equalsIgnoreCase (*some_string*)	returns true if the owner object equals the *some_string* object, ignoring the case of characters; otherwise, returns false.
toLowerCase ()	converts (and returns) all characters in the owner object as lowercase.
toUpperCase ()	converts (and returns) all characters in the owner object as uppercase.
trim ()	removes all leading and trailing whitespace characters in the owner object.
charAt (*position*)	returns the single character at the indicated integer position within the owner object.
substring (*start_position*)	returns a substring from the owner object beginning at the indicated integer *start_position* and going to the end.
substring (*start_position*, *end_position*)	returns a substring from the owner object beginning at the indicated integer *start_position* and ending at the character just before *end_position*.
indexOf (*some_string*)	returns the position of *some_string* within the owner object. If *some_string* is not found, returns −1.
compareTo (*some_string*)	compares the owner object string with *some_string* to determine alphabetical ordering. Ignoring case, this method returns (a) a negative number if the owner is alphabetically before, (b) a zero if equal to, or (c) a positive number if the owner object comes after.

We have already seen examples of the length() and equals() helper methods. The equalsIgnoreCase() method is just a variation of the equals() method. In this method, the case of the letters within the object is ignored. The best way to visualize this method is to assume that it first converts all the letters to the same case before making a comparison. Naturally, there is no case for characters that are not letters. For example:

```
String phrase = "hello Fred";
if (phrase.equals ("Hello FRED"))              // this is true!
    IO.showMessage ("yes, they are equal");
```

The equals() and equalsIgnoreCase() methods do not modify the values of the associated **String** variables of course—they simply return a **boolean** value result of a comparison. The toUpperCase() and toLowerCase() methods return a copy of a modified owner string value. For example:

```
String phrase = "hello Fred";
IO.showMessage (phrase.toUpperCase());    // outputs HELLO FRED
IO.showMessage (phrase.toLowerCase());    // outputs hello fred
```

The `trim()` method can be used to make a copy of a string after removing any leading and/or trailing blanks or whitespace characters. For example:

```
String sentence = "     A boy and his dog.     ";
IO.showValue ("length: ", sentence.length());    // outputs a length of 28
String shortened = sentence.trim();
IO.showMessage (shortened);                       // outputs "A boy and his dog"
IO.showValue ("length: ", shortened.length());    // outputs a length of 17
```

CONCEPT

a String object is not an array

The `charAt()` method is useful for examining one of the characters that make up a **String** object. Keep in mind that a **String** object is not an array—you cannot use the [] brackets and an index to reference a **char** cell within a **String** object. The concept is similar, however. You may think of the position argument to `charAt()` as being similar to an index. The first character of the **String** object has position 0, the second character has position 1, and so on. Here is an example of a condition to test whether the first character of a **String** object is an uppercase letter (using the helper method `isUpperCase()` belonging to the **Character** class of static helper methods you have previously learned):

```
if ( Character.isUpperCase (phrase.charAt(0)))
      IO.showMessage ("the first letter is upper case!");
```

If you think about it for a minute, you'll realize that we could write our own method similar in purpose to `equals()` by using the `charAt()` and `length()` methods. Here's a simple method that returns true if the two parameter strings are equal and false otherwise:

```
public static boolean Equals (String s1, String s2)
{   int size1 = s1.length();
    int size2 = s2.length();            // two strings must be equal
    if (size1 != size2)                 // in length to be equal
        return false;
    else
    {    for (int n=0; n<size1; n++)     // now compare each char
            if (s1.charAt(n) != s2.charAt(n))  // in turn
                return false;           // mismatch!
        return true;                    // all are equal, must be true
    }
}
```

In this code, the second **if** statement is comparing two **char** values, and so we can use the `!=` operator. This gives you a pretty good perspective of how two strings can be compared. Of course, this method isn't needed because we already have the `equals()` helper method. If we are really committed to having our own `Equals()` method with two parameters, the above method could be simplified to the following:

```
public boolean Equals (String s1, String s2)
{   return s1.equals(s2);
}
```

KEY TERM
substring

The two `substring()` helper methods are useful for making a copy of *part* of a **String** object. A part or piece of a string is called a *substring*. The `indexOf()` method can be used to find the index of a substring within a **String** object. Suppose we have an individual's name in a **String** with a blank separating the first and last names:

```
String name;
name = IO.readString();
```

In the input dialog box, the user types "Fred Smith." Now suppose we wish to output the name in a more formal format with the last name first:

```
IO.showValue
("name is: ", FormalFormat(name));//should output "Smith, Fred"
```

We could implement the `FormalFormat()` method with the following steps:

1. Find the position of the blank within the name.
2. Make a copy of just the first name and just the last name.
3. Concatenate the last name, a comma, and the first name together.

Consider Listing 9.I:

Listing 9.I

```
// return a name in formal format with the last name first
// IN:  name is a string containing a first name, a blank, and a last name
public static String FormalFormat (String name)
{   String first, last;
    int blank_position  = name.indexOf (" ");        // find a substring of a single blank
    last = name.substring (blank_position + 1);
    first = name.substring (0, blank_position );
    return last + ", " + first;
}
```

Take another look at the sorting problem of the previous chapter (Listings 8.XI and 8.XII). In that class, we input a list of integers and then output them in numeric order. Let's modify that class to input and sort an array of names. Instead of using the

<= operator, we'll utilize the `compareTo()` helper method. Note that when dealing with an array of **String** objects, `length()` method can be used to return the length of any one **String** cell, and `length` returns the number of array cells. Don't confuse these two very different uses (Listing 9.II):

Listing 9.II

```java
// Sort and output a list of 10 names from a disk file provided by the user.
public class SortNames
{  final static int SIZE = 10;

   private static void SortStrings (String[] names)
   { // IN: words is a String array of names
     int n, k, small_pos=0;
     String smallest, temp;
     for (k=0; k<names.length-1; k++)              // repeat; each cell but last.
     {   smallest = names[small_pos = k];          // assume this is smallest
        for (n=k+1; n<names.length; n++)           // compare with other values . . .
           if (names[n].compareTo(smallest) < 0)   // if smaller, save position
           {  small_pos = n;                       //   and value . . .
              smallest = names[n];
           }
         temp = names[k];                          // swap these cells
         names[k] = names[small_pos];
         names[small_pos] = temp;
     }
   }

   public static void main (String[] args)
   {  String[] values = new String[SIZE];
      DiskInput infile = new DiskInput();
      int n;
      String filename, message;
      filename = IO.readString ("Enter filename: ");
      infile.open (filename);
      for (n=0; n<SIZE; n++)                        // input the list of names
        values[n] = infile.readString();

      SortStrings (values);                         // sort the list

      message = "The sorted names are: \n";         // output the list
      for (n=0; n<SIZE; n++)
        message += (values[n] + "\n");
      IO.showMessage (message);
      System.exit(0);
   }
}
```

Let's test this class with a file of 10 names:

names.txt:

Fred
Jane
Juanita
Bill
Ann
Sue
Julio
Dick
Paul
Sam

Here's the output display with the sorted 10 names:

9.2 String parsing

Up to this point, we have input values from input dialog boxes or disk files with one value per line. Haven't you wondered if it is possible to have more than one value per line? It would certainly make data files simpler to display. For example, suppose you needed a disk file containing information for five different **People** objects. Let's assume a **People** object has a name, an address, and a phone number. Wouldn't it be convenient to have a disk file with one complete **People** object per line as in the following example?

people.txt:

Jane Smith, 123 Oak Street, 567-8901
Julio Gonzales, 456 Maple Lane, 234-5678
Bob Jones, 789 Spruce Circle, 345-6789
Rachel Weinstein, 102 Walnut Drive, 456-7890
George Liu, 304 Sycamore Place, 543-2109

We could easily input an entire line into a **String** variable:

```
DiskInput infile = new DiskInput();
infile.open ("people.txt");
String line;
line = infile.readString(); //contains"Jane Smith,123 Oak Street,567-8901"
```

The next step would be to abstract the three components from this line to store into the information variables of a **People** object. In the people.txt file, we have purposely separated the three components of the line with a comma. This should allow us to use the indexOf() helper method to find the position of each comma. Then we could use the substr() helper method to retrieve each component once we know where each component starts and ends within the line.

KEY TERM

parsing

Processing a string to interpret the meaning of the string text is often called *parsing*. Abstracting or retrieving information variables from a line of text is also called parsing or, occasionally, unmarshaling.

Consider the following method to make a helper member of the **People** class. This method is named parse() and accepts a **String** parameter to unmarshal the three information variables of a **People** object by parsing the parameter line (Listing 9.III):

Listing 9.III

```
// a class to represent a People object
public class People
{   private String name;
    private String address;
    private String phone;

    // Set the information variables by parsing the parameter line.
    // ASSUMPTION: line contains a valid person representation
    public void parse (String line)
    {   int comma_pos;
        comma_pos = line.indexOf (",");              // position of 1st comma
        name = line.substring (0, comma_pos);
        line = line.substring (comma_pos+1);
        comma_pos = line.indexOf (",");              // position of 2nd comma
        address = line.substr (comma_pos+1);
        phone = line.substring (comma_pos+1);
    }

    public void display ()
    {   IO.showMessage (name + "\n" + address + "\n" + phone);
    }

. . .       // more methods to be added
}
```

If the following line is read for a **Person** object, the above `parse()` method will find the three associated components of the object and set the appropriate information variables: name is set to Jane Smith, address is set to 123 Oak Street, and phone is set to 567-8901:

```
"Jane Smith, 123 Oak Street, 567-8901"
```

What if a text line to be parsed contains numeric information? Fortunately, the Java library contains static helper classes for each of the numeric primitive data types. Each of these helper classes contains a helper method to parse a string and convert it to the appropriate primitive data:

```
Integer.parseInt ( some_string );
Double.parseDouble ( some_string );
Float.parseFloat ( some_string );
```

Syntax form

In each case, *some_string* must be a string containing a valid textual representation of the associated data type. In other words, the purpose of these methods is to convert a string into a number!

Suppose we wished the user to enter several values in an input box. Let's write a simple application class for a geometry problem: We want to prompt the user for a height and width of a rectangle. The class should then display the area of this rectangle. We'll prompt the user to enter the two **double** numbers separated by a blank. We'll then use the position of the blank to parse the line into two **double** values (Listing 9.IV):

Listing 9.IV

```
// application class to calculate the area of a rectangle
public class CalcArea
{  public static void main (String[] args)
   {  String line, first, second;
      int blank_pos;
      double height, width;
      line = IO.readString ("Enter height and length separated by a blank: ");
      blank_pos = line.indexOf(" ");
      first = line.substring (0, blank_pos);          // parse the line into two doubles:
```

```
    second = line.substring (blank_pos+1);      // second number as text
    height = Double.parseDouble (first);        // first number as a double
    width = Double.parseDouble (second);        // second number as a double
    IO.showValue ("the area is: " height * width);
    System.exit(0);
  }
}
```

If we run Listing 9.IV and enter two numbers separated by a blank, we get the correct answer. Suppose, however, that the user enters the two numbers *with a blank in front of the first number as well*. The following error occurs:

```
Exception in thread "main" java.lang.NumberFormatException: empty String
    at java.lang.Throwable.fillInStackTrace(Native Method)
    at java.lang.Throwable.fillInStackTrace(Compiled Code)
    at java.lang.Throwable.<init>(Compiled Code)
    at java.lang.Exception.<init>(Compiled Code)
    at java.lang.RuntimeException.<init>(RuntimeException.java:47)
    at java.lang.IllegalArgumentException.<init>(IllegalArgumentException.java:43)
    at java.lang.NumberFormatException.<init>(NumberFormatException.java:43)
    at java.lang.FloatingDecimal.readJavaFormatString(Compiled Code)
    at java.lang.Double.parseDouble(Double.java:188)
    at CalcArea.main(CalcArea.java:12)
```

KEY TERM
exception

These messages are cryptic at best! The best way to read Java run-time error messages is from the bottom. That will indicate which method and which line were executing at the time of the error. The next line up indicates that a method being invoked on that line caused the error. Higher up, you can find the message `NumberFormatException`, which shows the real nature of the error. An *exception* is an occurrence or event that is unexpected. If the operator starts the input string with a blank, that will be the blank used to parse the line. In other words, the `first` string will be empty. As a result, when the method calls

```
height = Double.parseDouble (first); // first number as a double
```

an error occurs because `first` doesn't contain a valid text representation of a number. The above block of text error messages is the default result of this entry error exception.

9.3 Exception handing

You can actually specify what you would like done in the event of an exception. Since the Java default for the earlier entry-error example was cryptic, let's do exactly that. We will provide our own exception handling to replace the cryptic block of error messages with our own simple error message. The syntax is the following:

```
try
{      statements
}
catch (Exception e)
{      exception action statements
}
```

Syntax form

KEY TERMS
exception catching
and throwing

The first block (or **try** block) represents the set of statements that you would like Java to try while watching for an exception. The second block (or **catch** block) contains the statements you would like Java to execute if the indicated exception occurs. When an exception occurs during a **try** block, the execution of the **try** block terminates and Java immediately begins to execute the **catch** block. This is often called *catching* the exception. (You'll later see that detecting or generating an exception is called *throwing* an exception. At this point, however, we'll simply use the exceptions generated or thrown by the Java library and run-time code.)

There are a wide variety of exceptions that can occur or be thrown during the execution of a **try** block. Each of these exceptions has a name (e.g., NumberFormatException seen earlier), but we won't try to list them all. The actual name of an exception is probably not very important at this point in your career in any case. The e in the syntax rule above is an object of type **Exception**. The **Exception** class has an information variable of type **String** that is commonly used to store a human-readable message attempting to show the nature or cause of the exception. When an exception is thrown by Java, an **Exception** object is created, and the **String** information variable of that Exception is set to the appropriate message. This object is then copied into e. The message associated with e can be referenced using the getMessage() helper method of the **Exception** class.

Now I know the last paragraph is complicating a fairly simple system, but that's the technical description. What it boils down to can be seen in the following example. Suppose we wish to give the operator a much more friendly and useful message if the data are incorrectly entered in Listing 9.IV. If we provide our own **try-catch** segment, we override the default Java handling of the exception (Listing 9.V):

Listing 9.V

```
// application class to calculate the area of a rectangle -- CATCHES INPUT EXCEPTIONS
public class CalcArea2
{  public static void main (String[] args)
   {  String line, first, second;
      int blank_pos;
      double height, width;
      try
      {  line = IO.readString ("Enter height and length separated by a blank: ");
         blank_pos = line.indexOf (" ");
         first = line.substring (0, blank_pos);          // parse the line into two doubles:
         second = line.substring (blank_pos+1);          // second number as text
         height = Double.parseDouble (first);            // first number as a double
         width = Double.parseDouble (second);            // second number as a double
         IO.showValue ("the area is: " height * width);
      }
      catch (Exception e)
      {  IO.showMessage ("exception: " + e.getMessage() +
            "You probably entered the numbers wrong.");
      }
      System.exit(0);
   }
}
```

Now, if an exception occurs during the `try` block statements, they will be aborted and the `catch` block will be executed. In any case, the class terminates normally with the last statement (`System.exit(0)`). Here is an example in which the operator also enters a comma between the two values instead of just a blank:

You may also decide what conditions constitute an exception and do your own detection. Suppose we specifically want to watch for the entry of a comma in the simple **CalcArea** class input dialog box. In that way, we could specifically notify the operator of the mistake made. Causing an exception to be thrown is done with the **throw** statement:

```
throw new Exception ( message );
```

Syntax form

In this statement, the *message* is a string that you would like associated with the new **Exception** being created. As you can see, an **Exception** will be created and a constructor will be invoked with the given *message* as an argument. Here's the more complete **CalcArea** class (Listing 9.VI):

Listing 9.VI

```
// application class to calculate the area of a rectangle -- CATCHES INPUT EXCEPTIONS
// THROWS AN EXCEPTION IF THE USER ENTERS A COMMA
public class CalcArea3
{   public static void main (String[] args)
    {   String line, first, second;
        int blank_pos;
        double height, width;
        try
        {   line = IO.readString ("Enter height and length separated by a blank: ");
            if (line.indexOf (",") > 0)
                throw new Exception ("DO NOT ENTER A COMMA!");
            blank_pos = line.indexOf (" ");
            first = line.substring (0, blank_pos);        // parse the line into two doubles:
            second = line.substring (blank_pos+1);        // second number as text
            height = Double.parseDouble (first);          // first number as a double
            width = Double.parseDouble (second);          // second number as a double
            IO.showValue ("the area is: " height * width);
        }
        catch (Exception e)
        {   IO.showMessage ("exception: " + e.getMessage() +
                " You probably entered the numbers wrong.");
        }
        System.exit(0);
    }
}
```

Now when the operator enters a comma between two entries, the operator sees a very specific error message:

Java doesn't provide a default way of handling every exception—only the most common. For some exceptions, you are *required* to provide a **try-catch** segment where the exception may occur. Section 9.4 is one such situation.

Now a word of caution: Writing Java programs that throw exceptions allows the programmer to transfer control from one part of a method to another in such a way that makes the class difficult to read and follow. This is quite common. In earlier programming languages, a GOTO statement allowed a similar transfer of execution control. Programming experts later learned that such a statement leads to programs that are very complex and difficult to understand and modify. Later programming languages either did not have a GOTO statement or discouraged its use. All class control was handled by the **if**, **while**, **for**, and method invocations. The Java **throw** statement is actually a way to revert back to the old GOTO style of programming. Exceptions should be used *sparingly*. Before writing a **throw** statement, ask yourself if there isn't a simpler way of handling the problem with an **if**.

9.4 Java streams

KEY TERM
stream

You have learned how to write information to a disk file and how to read information from a disk file using the **DiskInput** and **DiskOutput** classes provided with this text. Java refers to such I/O as a *stream*. A stream is simply an object that is a sequential source of information or a destination for sequential information. Each time you read from a disk file (e.g., using readInt()), you receive the next piece of information available. Each time you write to a disk file, you save information onto the end of the file being constructed.

CONCEPT
text vs. binary files

There are actually two different kinds of stream disk files: *text* and *binary*. Up to this point, we have only used text files. A text file contains information coded using printable strings. As such, you may print the file to a printer or edit the file with a text editor. We say the file is in human-readable form. A binary file, on the other hand, is a memory image of information. In other words, it is a copy of the raw ones and zeros that were in memory for that information item. A binary file is not printable or editable without the help of a special interpretive program of some kind.

A good way to get a feel for these two different kinds of files is to recognize that a .java source file is a text file. The associated .class file produced by the compiler is a binary file. You can edit and print a .java source file. If you attempt to edit or print a `.class` file, you will see undecipherable garbage. So why even have binary files? Well for one thing, information does not need to be converted or parsed from strings when read into memory, and that saves time. Second, binary files are generally smaller than text files of the same information. Consider for a moment the integer number 1234567. The 32-bit binary ones and zeros used internally to represent this value (in an Intel architecture) are the following:

```
00000000000100101101011010000111
```

This is simply the value 1234567 expressed in base 2. To represent this value as a string, however, we would need the Unicode value for the character `1` followed by the Unicode value for the character `2` and so on. Each Unicode character requires 16 ones and zeros for a total of 112 bits.

Since files often need to be in human-readable form and we are not often concerned about saving some disk space, it is quite common in Java programming to use text files.

`PrintWriter` text file streams

To use streams in Java, we almost never need to implement the required functionality ourselves. We almost always rely on a class written by someone else to do the primitive work of stream I/O. Again, consider the **DiskInput** and **DiskOutput** classes that you have utilized so far. You didn't need to understand how the methods of these classes work—you only needed to understand what methods were available and how these methods were to be used.

This is one of the most fundamental advantages of the Java language—the ability to use and enhance classes developed by others. The actual mechanics of accessing a disk file have been solved by others, and we simply reuse their code. Now suppose you need to write to a disk file but don't have the **DiskOutput** class available. Is there a class that is part of the standard Java library that you could utilize? Of course!

The class is called **PrintWriter**. Since the **PrintWriter** class isn't in your current directory (like the **DiskOutput** class file), you need to indicate to the Java compiler that it should search the standard libraries for this class. By way of review, we do this with the following line at the top of a Java source file:

> **import** *directory_path*.*files*;
>
> **Syntax form**

The directory path allows Java to find the correct directory. The files phrase specifies where the correct class may be located. The directory path and files phrase are not specific to any one operating system; they are general. In other words, the phrase used for the **PrintWriter** class is the same on all systems:

```
import java.io.*;
```

KEY TERM
package

Once Java has been installed on your computer, your Java compiler knows physically where the `java` base directory is located. Within the `java` base directory, there is a subdirectory or *package* called io. A package is a collection of related helper classes. Rather than specify one class specifically, we can use a shorthand notation—the `*` simply means "any and all that are needed." The above **import** line gives us access to all the helper classes in the `java.io` package. All the standard Java classes dealing with I/O are in this package.

You create a **PrintWriter** object using the keyword **new** twice:

```
PrintWriter name = new PrintWriter (
    new FileOutputStream (filename));
```

Syntax form

We have two new keywords because we are creating our **PrintWriter** object out of a **File Output Stream** object, which is another class. We are always creating objects out of objects that already exist in Java. Don't worry about the syntax of the above statement at the moment. You simply choose the name of the object and the name of the file. For example, suppose we wish to create and write to the file `"data.txt"`:

```
PrintWriter outflow = new PrintWriter(new FileOutputStream ("data.txt"));
```

CONCEPT
the PrintWriter
constructor may
throw an exception

Notice that the name of the file is a string (or **String** variable). This statement both allocates the `outfile` object and opens the file to prepare it for reading. Remember exceptions? Well, if the file you want to write to cannot be created or the file is not available or some other error condition occurs, one of the constructors being invoked will throw an exception. You must provide a `try-catch` segment for this exception. Here's a more complete segment of Java code that you might try:

```
try
{   PrintWriter outfile
        = new PrintWriter(new FileOutputStream ("data.txt"));
}
catch (Exception e)
{   IO.showMessage (e.getMessage());
    System.exit(0);
}
```

WRONG!

What's wrong? This is a common mistake. Anything declared inside of a block (`{}`) is only alive or available while inside that block. When the block finishes, all declared objects or variables are deleted by the Java system. As a result, if the `outfile` object is correctly opened to the `"data.txt"` file, it is then quickly deleted before it can be used! The following allows `outfile` to be available beyond the **try-catch** segment:

```
PrintWriter outfile = null;
try
{   outfile = new PrintWriter(new FileOutputStream("data.txt"));
}
catch (Exception e)
{   IO.showMessage (e.getMessage());
    System.exit(0);
}
```

We need to initialize the `outfile` object reference to null to keep the Java compiler happy. We then allocate a new **PrintWriter** (and a subsequent **FileInputStream**) within the **try** block in case it throws an exception. Output to a **PrintWriter** object is done with the `print()` and `println()` methods. The first outputs a text message; the second outputs a text message and adds a new line marker (\n).

```
name.print ( string );
name.println ( string );
```
Syntax form

To complete the output and force Java to flush any buffered information to the actual disk file, we perform a `close()` call:

```
name.close ();
```
Syntax form

Here's a complete example to create a disk file `"names.txt"` and write five names to it as provided by the operator (Listing 9.VII):

Listing 9.VII

```
// Create "names.txt" and fill with 5 names provided by the operator
import java.io.*;
public class CreateFile
```

```
{  public static void main (String[] args)
   {  String name;
      PrintWriter outfile = null;
      try
      {   outfile = new PrintWriter(new FileOutputStream ("data.txt"));
      }
      catch (Exception e)
      {   IO.showMessage ("FILE ERROR: " + e.getMessage());
          System.exit(0);
      }
      for (int n = 0; n<5; n++)
      {   name = IO.readString("Enter a name: ");
          outfile.println (name);
      }
      outfile.close();
      System.exit(0);
   }
}
```

In Listing 9.VII, the disk file `"data.txt"` is created anew each time the file is opened. If the file already exists, it would be emptied. However, if you wish to append to the end of an existing disk file, there is an option available in the `FileInputStream()` constructor. Simply add the **boolean** constant **true** as a second parameter to the constructor. For example:

```
outfile = new PrintWriter(new FileInputStream("data.txt", true));
```

If you indicate that you wish to append to an existing file, but the file does not exist, Java creates the file (empty) and then opens it for appending.

KEY TERM
wrapper

Is that a bit more detail to remember than with the **DiskOutput** class? Of course. Take a minute and look in Appendix A at how the **DiskOutput** class is actually implemented. It uses a **PrintWriter** object to do the output but takes care of the associated details to provide a much simpler class to the user. The methods of **DiskOutput** hide the more confusing details and exceptions of **PrintWriter**. You are again seeing how we reuse and modify classes provided by others in Java. When we create a new class to simplify and modify an existing class, we often call the new class a *wrapper*.

BufferedReader text file streams

To input from a disk file, the Java library contains the **BufferedReader** class. (Yes, the **DiskInput** class is a wrapper for **BufferedReader**!) The term *buffered reader* refers to the fact that this class reads a block of information from a disk file into a buffer when the file is opened—when the **BufferedReader** is declared and allocated. From that point on, requests for information from the file actually come from this buffer. When the buffer is exhausted, the **BufferedReader** object will again fill the buffer from the disk. The reason for this approach is speed and efficiency.

Physically reading from a disk file is quite slow (relative to class execution). It is much more efficient to read a few large blocks of data than many smaller ones.

To create a **BufferedReader**, the following syntax is used:

```
BufferedReader name = new BufferedReader (
    new FileReader ( filename ) );
```

Syntax form

Just as with the **PrintWriter** class, the constructor of a **BufferedReader** (and the subsequent **FileReader**) may throw an exception if an error occurs when attempting to prepare the file for input. The new statement must be nested inside a **try-catch** segment. For example, here is a segment that might be used to prepare to read the file of names created earlier:

```
BufferedReader infile = null;
try
{   infile = new BufferedReader (new FileReader ("data.txt"));
}
catch (Exception e)
{   IO.showMessage ("FILE ERROR: " + e.getMessage());
    System.exit(0);
}
```

The method that reads information using a BufferedReader object is the member readLine(). This method reads the next line of text (up to the line terminator) and returns this as a **String**. If there are no more lines of text to be read, this method returns the final constant **null**. The value **null** is a special reference—it indicates that there is no string. If an error occurs when reading a line of text, the method throws an exception.

```
string = name.readLine ();
```

Syntax form

Let's add to the segment of code that declared infile as a **BufferedReader** for "data.txt". Now, we'll read the lines of the file and display them one at a time to the operator:

```
String line;
try
{    line = infile.readLine();
     while (line != null)
     {   IO.showMessage ("LINE: " + line);
         line = infile.readLine();
     }
}
catch (Exception e)
{   IO.showMessage ("READING ERROR: " + e.getMessage());
    System.exit(0);
}
```

Notice that this fragment of code contains a **while** loop. We didn't assume the "data.txt" disk file contained a fixed number of text lines—we simply chose to read until no more lines were available. Reaching the end of a file is not an exception; it simply results in **null** being returned by readLine(). (Trying to read another line after null has been returned is an exception. In other words, don't try to read from a file after the end of the file has been reached.)

Just as with a **PrintWriter** object, the associated disk file can be closed when you are through reading with a close() method. If you neglect to close the file, Java will do it for you when your class terminates.

The StringTokenizer class

A **BufferedReader** doesn't provide much support for disk input. The only method we have reads a line of text. How would you read a **double** or an **int**? How would you read the information if a line contains several **double**s or **int**s? The first question is the easiest. In fact, you have the skills to do this using the parseInt() and parseDouble() methods previously learned. For example, if the input line is a string containing an integer, the following could be used:

```
int value = Double.parseDouble(line);
```

This is exactly what the **DiskInput** class readDouble() method does! The second question is a bit more complex. If an input line contains several numbers, we would need to separate them into individual strings to use the parse.Double() method. You could write a method to do this using the indexOf() method of the **String** class and finding the locations of the separating blanks. Fortunately, as is often the case in Java, someone has already written a class to solve this problem—**StringTokenizer**. You declare a **StringTokenizer** object and give the constructor the string you would like to separate into individual components:

```
StringTokenizer name = new StringTokenizer ( string );
```

Syntax form

Each time the member method `nextToken()` is invoked, it returns a substring consisting of the next token or word in the line. A word just is a substring separated by whitespace or blanks from the rest of the string:

```
string = name .nextToken ();
```

Syntax form

The member method `hasMoreTokens()` tests if there are more words left in the **StringTokenizer** object that have not yet been returned. The member method `countTokens()` returns an integer count of the number of tokens remaining in the object. The **StringTokenizer** class is found in the `"java.util.*"` package, and this must be imported at the top of your source.

```
boolean = name.hasMoreTokens();
int = name.countTokens();
```

Syntax form

As a complete example, suppose the disk file `"numbers.txt"` contains a list of integers to be averaged. We don't know how many lines are in the file, and we don't know how many integers are on each line. The following class is intended to read this file and outputs the average of all the integers:

```java
// a class to input a general file of integers and output the average
import java.io.*;
import java.util.*;
public class GenAve
{  public static void main (String[] args)
    {  String line, thisword;
       int sum=0, count=0, value, numwords;
       BufferedReader infile = null;
       try
       {  infile = new BufferedReader (new FileReader ("num-
bers.txt"));
          line = infile.readLine();
          while (line != null)
          {  StringTokenizer words = new StringTokenizer (line);
             for (int n=0; n<words.countTokens(); n++)
             {  thisword = words.nextToken();
                value = Integer.parseInt(thisword);
                sum += value;
                count++;
             }
             line = infile.readLine();
          }
       }
       catch (Exception e)
       {  IO.showMessage ("ERROR: " + e.getMessage());
          System.exit(0);
       }
       IO.showMessage ("sum is: " + sum + " ave is: " + sum/count);
       System.exit(0);
    }
}
```

WRONG!

Before we discuss what is wrong with this class, let's look at the design. The approach is the following:

1. prepare the `"numbers.txt"` file for reading with a **BufferedReader** object.
2. read a line from the **BufferedReader** object (file).
3. while the line is not null, do the following:
4. create a **StringTokenizer** object for the line.
5. determine the number of words in the **StringTokenizer** object.
6. with a `for` loop,
7. retrieve each word in turn and convert to `int`.
8. sum this integer and increase the count by 1.
9. output the average.

Now, when I first wrote the above class for this book, this is exactly what I wrote—and I was a bit surprised when it didn't produce the correct average. When I went back and added some IO.showMessage() calls to display each word in turn, I found that some words were being missed! Can you see the error? I've even gone back and emphasized the line in bold:

```
for (int n=0; n<words.countTokens(); n++)
```

The problem is that each time the loop executes, the number of available tokens or words in the **StringTokenizer** words object is reduced. The method countTokens() returns the number of remaining tokens—not the number of original tokens. Well, we all make mistakes. The solution was to save the original count of tokens before beginning to remove them from words. Here's the corrected version (Listing 9.VIII):

Listing 9.VIII

```java
// a class to input a general file of integers and output the average
import java.io.*;
import java.util.*;
public class GenAve
{  public static void main (String[] args)
   {  String line, thisword;
      int sum=0, count=0, value, numwords;
      BufferedReader infile = null;
      try
      {  infile = new BufferedReader (new FileReader ("numbers.txt"));
         line = infile.readLine();
         while (line != null)
         {  StringTokenizer words = new StringTokenizer (line);
            numwords = words.countTokens();
            for (int n=0; n<numwords; n++)
            {  thisword = words.nextToken();
               value = Integer.parseInt(thisword);
               sum += value;
               count++;
            }
            line = infile.readLine();
         }
      }
      catch (Exception e)
      {  IO.showMessage ("ERROR: " + e.getMessage());
         System.exit(0);
      }
      IO.showMessage ("sum is: " + sum + " ave is: " + sum/count);
      System.exit(0);
   }
}
```

If the `"numbers.txt"` file contains the following lines

numbers.txt:
3 4 5 6
7 8 9 10 11 12
13
14 15 16 17
18
19 20

then the output of the class is:

9.5 Example project

You've all received what appeared to be a personalized letter informing you that you "may have won one of the following prizes." The mailer certainly didn't type each letter individually. How were they created? Well, it's a simple process for a computer class. Let's start with two files. The first file, `"formletter.txt"`, will contain a template of a form letter with the words NAME, FIRST, and LAST in the place of actual names. We'll assume for simplicity that our form letter has no more than one of these words per line. For example:

`formletter.txt:`

Dear NAME,
Congratulations FIRST! You may have won one of the following
prizes:
a new car
a vacation in Tahiti
a cheezy trinket
Yes, FIRST, you may be one your way to Tahiti! Just send $19.95 to
Suckers Inc., PO Box 123, NY, NY to confirm your prize. Don't delay,
Mr. LAST or this opportunity may be lost . . .

Now, suppose we build a file containing the names of the people we wish to contact. For example:

`listnames.txt:`

Fred Smith
Julio Martinez
Ahmed Laban

For each name in the `listnames.txt` file, we need to substitute the correct word into the form letter for mailing. Sometimes I begin designing complex problem solutions by "wishing" for a helper class. In this case, I would wish for a class called **Letter** that could be used according to the following examples:

```
Letter thisletter = new Letter (10);        // create a letter of 10 lines
thisletter.readLetter ("letter.txt");       // read in a letter from disk
thisletter.writeLetter ("newletter.txt");   // write a letter to disk
thisletter.setLine ("this is a new line", 3);// assign line 3 to this string
```

If I had such a class, the details of reading in and writing back to disk would all be taken care of. I would not need to concern myself with the fact that a letter is made up of many lines and so forth. A **Letter** is only a **Letter**, and what it is made up of is not my problem. It is (was) the problem of the programmer who developed the **Letter** class. Now, I would also wish for the capability of producing a new **Letter** from an old **Letter** with the NAME, FIRST, and LAST words replaced:

```
Letter updated_letter = thisletter.generate ("Fred Smith");
```

In this example, `updated_letter` is a version of `thisletter` with the words NAME, FIRST, and LAST replaced with Fred Smith, Fred, and Smith. In other words, the **Letter** helper method `generate()` produces a new **Letter** object from an existing **Letter**.

With such a **Letter** class, the application becomes fairly easy to write. The design would consist of the following steps (Listing 9.IX):

1. declare a **Letter** `formletter` and read it in from the disk file `formletter.txt`.

2. for each name in the `listnames.txt` file,

3. generate a new **Letter** `thisletter` from `formletter` with the appropriate word replacements.

4. output `thisletter`.

Listing 9.IX

```java
// a class to generate a form letter from existing files
import java.io.*;

public class FormLetter
{
    public static void main (String[] args)
    { String thisname;
      BufferedReader namefile = null;
      String formfilename = IO.readString ("Enter form filename: ");
      String listfilename = IO.readString ("Enter list filename: ");
      Letter formletter = new Letter (10);
      formletter.readLetter (formfilename);

      try
      {   namefile = new BufferedReader (new FileReader (listfilename));
          thisname = namefile.readLine ();
```

```
        while (thisname != null)
        { Letter customerletter = formletter.generate (thisname);
          customerletter.writeLetter ("letters.txt");
          thisname = namefile.readLine ();
        }
    }
    catch (Exception e)
    { IO.showMessage ("LETTER ERROR: " + e.getMessage ());
    }

    System.exit (0);
  }
}
```

The following lines from this class declare `formletter` and read it in from the disk file with the name entered into `formfilename`;

```
Letter formletter = new Letter (10);
formletter.readLetter (formfilename)
```

This line creates a new **Letter** `customerletter` from `formletter` with the name in `thisname` replacing the NAME, FIRST, and LAST words where appropriate:

```
Letter customerletter = formletter.generate (thisname);
```

This line next writes the new **Letter** out to a disk file:

```
customerletter.writeLetter ("letters.txt");
```

The bad news is that there is no such **Letter** class in the Java library. But that's okay; we just write it ourselves. This approach was a technique of top-down design that divides a complex problem into smaller segments that can later be individually solved. The **Letter** class might be implemented as in Listing 9.X:

Listing 9.X

```
// a class to represent a form letter of up to 10 lines
import java.io.*;
import java.util.*;

public class Letter
{   private String[] lines;
    private int maxlines;

  public Letter (int size)
  {     lines = new String[size];
        maxlines = 0;
  }

  private String replace (String a, String b, String c)
```

```java
    {      int loc = a.indexOf (b);
           String before = a.substring(0, loc);
           String after = a.substring(loc+b.length());
           return before + c + after;
    }

  public void readLetter (String filename)
  {    try
       {      BufferedReader in = new BufferedReader (new FileReader (filename));
              int curline = 0;
              lines[curline] = in.readLine();
              while (lines[curline] != null)
              {   curline++;
                  lines[curline] = in.readLine();
              }
              maxlines = curline;
              in.close();
       }
       catch (Exception e)
       {   IO.showMessage ("READ ERROR: " + e.getMessage());
           System.exit(0);
       }
  }

  public void writeLetter (String filename)
  {    try
       {      PrintWriter out = new PrintWriter (new FileOutputStream (filename, true));
              for (int n=0; n<maxlines; n++)
                  out.println (lines[n]);
              out.println ("********** END OF LETTER ****** ");
              out.close();
       }
       catch (Exception e)
       {   IO.showMessage ("WRITE ERROR: " + e.getMessage());
           System.exit(0);
       }
  }

   public void setLine (String newline, int n)
   { lines[n]=newline;
   }

   public Letter generate (String thisname)
   {     Letter thisletter = new Letter(maxlines);
         StringTokenizer nametok = new StringTokenizer (thisname);
         String first = nametok.nextToken();
         String last = nametok.nextToken();
         for (int k=0; k<maxlines; k++)
         {   if (lines[k].indexOf("NAME") > 0)
                   thisletter.setLine(replace (lines[k], "NAME", thisname), k);
             else if (lines[k].indexOf("LAST") > 0)
                   thisletter.setLine(replace (lines[k], "LAST", last), k);
             else if (lines[k].indexOf ("FIRST") > 0)
                   thisletter.setLine(replace (lines[k], "FIRST", first), k);
             else thisletter.setLine(lines[k], k);
         }
         return thisletter;
   }
}
```

A **Letter** is made up of two information variables: lines is an array of **String** to represent the text lines of a letter, and maxline is the number of lines that are currently in a letter, which is initially zero. Let's look at each helper method of the **Letter** class in turn. When a **Letter** is declared, the maximum size (number of lines) is specified for the constructor to use to declare the array lines. For example, in Listing 9.IX,

```
Letter formletter = new Letter (10);
```

declares or creates formletter to have a maximum of 10 lines. The helper method readLetter() accepts a filename and then reads the text lines of this file into the array lines. The method writeLetter() simply appends the array lines onto the named disk file.

The most interesting method is generate(), which is where the text processing is done to replace NAME, FIRST, and LAST with the appropriate name for the new letter. Notice first that this method returns another **Letter** object. In other words, we are creating a new **Letter** from an existing **Letter**:

```
public Letter generate (String thisname)
```

The new **Letter** created is to be the same size as the existing **Letter**:

```
Letter thisletter = new Letter(maxlines);
```

Next this method creates a **StringTokenizer** nametok and uses it to parse thisname into the two words first and last:

```
StringTokenizer nametok = new StringTokenizer (thisname);
String first = nametok.nextToken();
String last = nametok.nextToken();
```

Now the method tests each line of the original **Letter** to see if NAME, FIRST, or LAST is found within the line. If so, that word is replaced with the appropriate thisname, first, or last value using the **private** helper method replace(). For example, here is the test and replacement for FIRST:

```
if (lines[k].indexOf ("FIRST") > 0)
    thisletter.setLine (replace (lines[k], "FIRST", first), k);
```

This line is worth some additional inspection. Notice that when we are referring to lines in the original **Letter**, we simply use lines. However, when referring to a helper method of the newly created **Letter** thisletter, we prepend the name of the object with the dot as in thisletter.setLine().

The interesting work of this class is done in the replace() method. This method uses the substring() member method of **String** to get the line portions before and after the word we wish to substitute. The new line is then the concatenation of these substrings with the actual name in the middle.

Now, if we run Listing 9.X with the **Letter** class of Listing 9.XI using the form letter of `formletter.txt` and the names in `listnames.txt` given earlier we get the following output to file `letters.txt`:

`letters.txt`:

Dear Fred Smith,
Congratulations Fred! You may have won one of the following
prizes:
    a new car
    a vacation in Tahiti
    a cheezy trinket
Yes, Fred, you may be on your way to Tahiti! Just send $19.95 to
Suckers Inc., PO Box 123, NY, NY to confirm your prize. Don't delay,
Mr. Smith or this opportunity may be lost . . .
********** END OF LETTER ******
Dear Julio Martinez,
Congratulations Julio! You may have won one of the following
prizes:
    a new car
    a vacation in Tahiti
    a cheezy trinket
Yes, Julio, you may be on your way to Tahiti! Just send $19.95 to
Suckers Inc., PO Box 123, NY, NY to confirm your prize. Don't delay,
Mr. Martinez or this opportunity may be lost . . .
********** END OF LETTER ******
Dear Ahmed Laban,
Congratulations Ahmed! You may have won one of the following
prizes:
    a new car
    a vacation in Tahiti
    a cheezy trinket
Yes, Ahmed, you may be on your way to Tahiti! Just send $19.95 to
Suckers Inc., PO Box 123, NY, NY to confirm your prize. Don't delay,
Mr. Laban or this opportunity may be lost . . .
********** END OF LETTER ******

9.6 Summary

KEY TERMS   The terms introduced in this chapter are the following:

1. *substring*—a portion of a string, usually indicated with a starting and possibly an ending index.

2. *parsing*—processing text to interpret meaning or perhaps retrieve variable values.

3. *exception*—an unexpected event that should change the way a class continues to execute.

4. *exception catching*—providing a section of code (`catch`) to be executed in the event that Java detects an exception.

5. *exception throwing*—detecting an exception and notifying Java that an associated `catch` section of code should be executed.

6. *stream*—a sequential source or destination for information.

7. *package*—a directory containing a set of related helper classes.

8. *wrapper*—a class that simplifies some of the details of another class.

CONCEPTS
Basically, this chapter first extended your knowledge and skills with the `String` data type. Next, we introduced three object classes available in the Java library: `PrintWriter` (an extension of `FileOutputStream`), `BufferedReader` (an extension of `FileReader`), and `StringTokenizer`.

Several new helper methods available for the `String` data type were explained (Table 9.1). These methods allowed very versatile utility for parsing and text processing:

```
length ()
equals   ( some_string )
equalsIgnoreCase ( some_string )
toLowerCase ()
toUpperCase ()
trim ()
charAt  ( position )
substring  ( start_position )
substring  ( start_position, end_position )
indexOf  ( some_string )
compareTo  ( some_string )
```

The `PrintWriter` class provided two methods to output text lines to a disk file. It was necessary to utilize the `try-catch` block because the constructor for a `PrintWriter` object may throw an exception. The `PrintWriter` helper methods learned were the following:

```
println();
print();
close();
```

The `BufferedReader` class provided a method to input a text line from a disk file. Both the constructor for this class and this helper method may throw an exception and should be used inside a `try-catch` block:

```
readLine();
```

To parse a line of text into numeric variables, we reviewed the following previously covered helper methods:

```
Integer.parseInt ( some_string );
Double.parseDouble ( some_string );
Float.parseFloat ( some_string );
```

9.7 Exercises

Short-answer questions

1. The substring "Java" begins at what index within the larger string "Programming in Java is fun!"?

2. Briefly describe what happens to the remaining statements in a **try** block when an exception is thrown.

3. When an exception occurs and is detected by Java, we say that an exception is _____.

4. When a file is appended, new strings are written to the _____ of the file.

5. A directory containing a set of useful helper classes is called a _____.

6. Which **Integer** helper method could be used to convert a string containing digit characters into an **int** value?

7. The **BufferedReader** class will allow input of what data type?

8. To convert a **String** variable contents into all uppercase letters, the _____ **String** helper method could be used.

9. To remove all leading and trailing blanks from a **String** variable, the _____ **String** helper method could be used.

10. The _____ **PrintWriter** method outputs a line ending with a \n character, but the _____ method does not.

11. What would be the output of the following segment?

```
String line = "this is a short sentence";
IO.showValue ("index is: ", line.charAt(5));
```

12. Give additional statements that could be used to insert the word meaningless in front of sentence in the above line variable.

13. Give a statement that could be used to output the current number of characters in string variable line above.

14. Give additional statements that could be added to the following to output the length or number of characters of the *first word* in the variable sentence.

```
String sentence;
sentence = IO.readString("Enter a sentence: ");
```

15. Give a statement that could be added to the above code to output the length of entire sentence.

16. Give a statement that could be added to the above code to replace the last word in sentence with the word END.

17. Show the correct way to determine if the contents of two **String** variables contain the same word. Assume the variables are named a and b.

18. Give statements that could be used to output the word less if the contents of **String** word1 are less than the contents of **String** word2.

19. Show a **try-catch** block that could be used to prepare the disk file data.txt for input.

20. Show a **try-catch** block that could be used to create the disk file newdata.txt for output.

Projects

1. Briefly explain why the following **if** statement would not alphabetically compare the contents of the these two **String** variables:

```
String a = "hello";
String b = "goodbye";
   . . .
if (a < b) . . .
```

2. Write a simple class to input a line of text and then output this same line with a period added at the end.

3. A word is considered a palindrome if it reads the same forward as backward. For example, "madam" is a palindrome as are "did" and "boob." Write a class to input a word and determine if the word is a palindrome.

4. Refer back to Figure 8.8. Create a simple method to input these data from a disk file with four rows of numbers and seven numbers per row. Test your method with a `main()` method to output the table to the display.

5. Write a simple class to create a disk file representing a table of powers. The output text file should contain 20 lines representing the first 20 integers (1, 2, 3, . . . 20). Each line should contain five columns containing the five successive powers of the integer represented by that line. For example, the fifth line should be the following

```
5   25   125 625 3125
```

representing 5^1, 5^2, 5^3, 5^4, and 5^5.

6. Write an application class to replace single digits in a text file with their appropriate words. You may assume that only single-digit numbers will be found. For example:

```
The box held 7 copies of 2 different books.
```

would be changed to

```
The box held seven copies of two different books.
```

7. Using a **String** variable, read the words of a disk text file and determine if there are any words which violate the following spelling rule:

```
i before e except after c
```

8. Generate an application class to input a list of 10 names and then output these names in alphabetical order.

9. Write a simple spelling-checker application class to determine if the words of a disk file are correctly spelled. One simple approach is to compare each word in turn with the contents of a `dictionary.txt` file. If the word is found, it must be spelled correctly. If not found, it is spelled incorrectly. Create a simple `dictionary.txt` file for testing. For simplicity, you may assume the disk file contains only words—no punctuation or characters other than letters and blanks.

10. The built-in + operator can be used to concatenate the second **String** argument onto the end of the first. Write and demonstrate your own helper method called concatenate() to implement this operation. For example:

```
String a = "hello ";
String b = "my friend";
IO.showMessage (concatenate (a, b));
```

11. Creative Challenge: Refer back to Project 6 which required that single-digit numbers in a text file be replaced with their word equivalents. Expand this problem now to allow multiple-digit numbers. For example:

```
The box held 27 copies of 648 different books.
```

would be changed to become

```
The box held twenty seven copies of six hundred forty eight different books.
```

You may assume that no numbers larger than three digits will be found.

Recursion

Many of the programming problems examined so far in the text have used loops in the problem solution. At this point in your career, you tend to look for obvious ways to apply loops or iteration to help in the design of solutions. There are, however, other very different approaches to program problem solving that generally do not use loops at all. This chapter introduces the concept of recursive solutions and points out the types of problems for which recursion is best suited.

10.1 Recursive definitions

A **Maze** class might be defined with an attribute array representing a two-dimensional character table. Let's suppose walls or filled spaces in this maze table are marked with asterisks and paths or open spaces are marked with the letter p. The goal in the maze is the letter g. All outside cells are walls. For example, consider the following:

```
*********
*p**p**pg*
*pppp*pp**
***pp*ppp*
*ppp****p*
***pppppp*
*ppp******
***p****p*
***pppppp*
*********
```

Now, let's number the rows and columns top to bottom and left to right. That means the cell in the upper left corner is cell 0,0 as in a two-dimensional array. Suppose we are given a starting position of 8,3. If I let a *footprint* on the solution path be represented with an f character, the solution can be easily found with a pencil to be the following:

```
* * * * * * * * * *
*p**p**fg*
*pppp*pf**
***pp*pff*
*ppp****f*
***ffffff*
*ppf******
***f****p*
***fppppp*
* * * * * * * * * *
```

Well, that was easy with a pencil, but suppose you were asked to write an application class to solve any arbitrary **Maze**? In other words, given a **Maze** object, could you write a Java application that would output the path from any p cell to the g cell? Using loops and iteration, this is quite a difficult problem to solve, particularly for a large matrix! Using the technique of recursion, however, the programming is quite simple. By the end of this chapter, we'll write such a maze-solver class using the technique of recursion.

KEY TERM
recursion

Recursion literally means "doing the same thing again." In Java programming, a method that *invokes itself* is a recursive method. A recursive *definition* is one in which the solution or answer to a problem is defined in terms of the same problem. Now, that may sound like a lot of double-talk, but it has very practical implications.

Let's start with a recursive solution to a simple problem. Suppose you are in Los Angeles and want to go to Chicago. You ask someone for directions. Suppose this person doesn't know but can give you directions to a city that is *closer to* Chicago. You go to that city and ask again. Eventually, the person you ask says, "You're here. This is Chicago." As long as each person you ask gives you directions to a city closer to your goal, you will eventually reach it when the only city closer to your goal is the goal city itself. (Cities cannot be subdivided; there is no such thing as half a city in this simple example.)

The algorithm you followed was recursive. Now, not all recursive definitions are helpful. For example, if we change the requirements to allow some people to possibly send you to a city that is *farther* from Chicago, you might never arrive. In general, a *useful* recursive definition is one in which these two characteristics are present:

1. A recursive application of the definition should be applied toward a simpler problem—each step must bring you closer to the goal or solution.

2. At least one application of the definition must be toward a trivial problem—one that is not recursive.

Characteristic 1 is met if each person you ask sends you to a city that is closer to Chicago. Characteristic 2 is met when you ask for directions and the reply is, "You're here." We see the same idea in mathematics. Consider the simple definition of a factorial operation for positive integers N:

$$\text{If } N \leq 1 \text{ then } N! = 1$$
$$\text{otherwise, } N! = N(N-1)!$$

In other words, to apply this definition or rule to calculate the factorial of 5, you must know the factorial of 4 because $5! = 5(4!)$. So, you calculate $5!$ by calculating $4!$. The solution is stated in terms of the original problem. Fortunately, this definition is usable because (a) each successive application of the rule is applied to a smaller problem and (b) the final application is not recursive at all:

$$5! = 5(4!)$$
$$4! = 4(3!)$$
$$3! = 3(2!)$$
$$2! = 2(1!)$$
$$1! = 1$$

If the recursive definition generates a more complex problem, it isn't very helpful. Consider the following rule for calculating some strange value, which we'll call the Cannon of a positive number:

$$\text{If } N = 0 \text{ then } \text{Cannon}(x) = 1$$
$$\text{otherwise, } \text{Cannon}(x) = x * \text{Cannon}(x + 1)$$

This isn't very useful because each application of the rule is toward a problem that is more difficult rather than closer to the simplest problem. No finite number of applications of this defnition would ever lead to a solution to Cannon(5).

Now, many real-world problems can be expressed in useful recursive definitions or rules. For example, consider this almost trivial rule for climbing stairs:

to climb stairs: if you are at the top, stop

                otherwise;   step up one stair,

                        then climb remaining stairs

To climb the remaining stairs, you just reapply the definition. To apply this rule for climbing stairs, you need only be able to perform two simple or primitive operations: *stop* and *step up one stair.*

You are probably thinking that a better rule would instruct the user to *repeat* a primitive operation such as step up one stair *until* the top was reached. That would be an iterative or looping rule. The purpose here is to illustrate that an alternative method of describing a solution or rule is possible—one which does not use iteration or looping. In general, a recursive solution will not contain terms such as "repeat until." We will entirely sidestep the question of which method of stating a rule is better for the moment. Interesting issues on that question will be considered later.

Let's try one more. Remember, the goal is to begin to see recursive rules or solutions. How about a rule for finding a certain name in an ordered (sorted) array of names? Think about how you actually go about finding the right page in a phone book when looking up a friend: The book is opened to some middle location. If your friend is on that page, you are finished. If not, however, you must decide which half of the book to consider next. If the friend is alphabetically prior to the names on that page, you ignore the latter part of the book and consider now only the part of the book prior to your present position. If on the other hand, your friend is after the names on that page, you consider only the pages after your current position. Now what? *You apply the same rule again!* You turn to some middle location in the remaining side of the book.

You could, of course, iteratively page through the book from the start. Which approach do you think is more efficient?

In the above discussion, we were only concerned with finding the right page in a phone book. Suppose you have an ordered array of names and wish to find a specific name. Here is a rule in a pseudo programming language applied with two arguments: a name to be found and an array in which to search:

```
Find (name, array);
a) Find the middle of the array; call this position MIDDLE
b) If name matches the one at position MIDDLE; stop
   Else    i) call the names before MIDDLE the 'priorarray' and the
               names after MIDDLE the 'afterarray'.
          ii) If name is less than the name at MIDDLE
                  Find (name, priorarray)
               else if name is greater than name at MIDDLE
                  Find (name, afterarray)
```

Notice that this rule or method does not contain any commands to repeat anything. The primitive operations that are required are *stop*, *divide the array*, and a couple of comparisons. Are the two features required of a useful recursive definition present? First, each time `Find()` is called within the rule, the array to search is smaller than the original array. Second, there is a nonrecursive solution to the trivial problem approached by the recursive applications: When the name is found, the search stops.

Now, suppose the original array consists of 10 names: `array` = Ann, Bill, Carl, Dan, Eve, Fred, Gary, Hal, Ian, and Julio. We wish to find the index of `"Fred"`. The first application of the rule results in:

```
Find ("Fred", array);
a) MIDDLE = 4,
b) "Eve" is not the name, so
      i)   priorarray = Ann, Bill, Carl, Dan
           afterarray = Fred, Gary, Hal, Ian, Julio
     ii)   "Fred" is greater than "Eve" so
               Find ("Fred", afterarray).
```

Now, the second application of the rule has us searching this `afterarray` of the last five names for `"Fred"`. The argument `array` is now Fred, Gary, Hal, Ian, Julio.

```
Find ("Fred", array);
a) MIDDLE = 2,
b) "Hal" is not the name, so
        i)   priorarray = Fred, Gary
             afterarray = Ian, Julio
        ii) "Fred" is less than "Hal" so
                Find ("Fred", priorarray).
```

The third application of the rule has us searching this `priorarray` for "Fred". The argument `array` is now Fred, Gary.

```
Find ("Fred", array);
a) MIDDLE = 0,
b) "Fred" is found, so stop
```

KEY TERM
binary search

This particular rule for finding something in an ordered array is called a *binary search* and is a very common algorithm in computer science. It is very efficient; each time the rule is recursively applied, the new array is only about half the size of the original array. It is given here simply to help you see that many useful problems have recursive solutions that do not involve iteration. We will return to this algorithm for more detail later in the chapter.

10.2 Recursive methods

KEY TERM
recursive method

A *recursive method* is one that invokes itself. This may happen directly or indirectly. For example, suppose `MethodA()` calls `MethodB()`, which in turn calls `MethodA()` before returning. `MethodA()` would be a recursive method. Suppose `MethodA()` calls `MethodB()`, which calls `MethodA()`, which again calls `MethodB()` before returning. In this case, both methods would be recursive. Anytime a method can be called a second time before the first call effects a return, the method is recursive.

Just like a good recursive definition, a good recursive method must have the same two features:

1. A recursive call of the method should be with arguments that represent a simpler problem.

2. At least one call of the method must be applied toward a trivial problem that will return without another recursive call.

In general, the body of a Java method written for a recursive definition has the simple form of an **if-else** statement:

if (*trivial case*)
    calculate answer;
else
    calculate answer with a recursive call on a simpler problem

Consider now a Java helper method to calculate the factorial of a number (Listing 10.I):

Listing 10.I

```
   // Fact()   Return the factorial of parameter n
 1 //   IN:   n is a positive integer number
 2 public static int Fact (int n)
 3 {   int temp;
 4     if (n <= 1)                          // trivial case
 5          temp = 1;
 6     else
 7          temp = n * Fact(n-1);           // recursive case
 8     return (temp);
 9 }
```

Look carefully at this simple method. Notice that it is *nothing more than a re-stating of the rule* given earlier in the chapter. In a sense, it does not explain how a factorial is to be calculated; it simply states the recursive rule. Listing 10.II is an example application showing how this method might be invoked:

Listing 10.II

```
public class Recursion
{
 public static void main(String[] args)
 {
    int num, answer;
    num = IO.readInt ("Enter an integer: ");
    answer = Fact (num);
    IO.showMessage ("Factorial is: " + answer);
    System.exit(0);
 }

 public static int Fact (int n)
 { int temp;
   if (n <= 1)
        temp = 1;
   else
        temp = n * Fact(n-1);
   return (temp);
 }
}
```

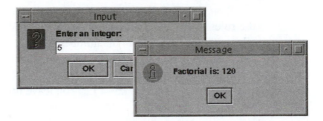

EXPERIMENT

Run the application of Listing 10.II for the factorial of 1000. Consider for a moment why this causes problems.

10.3 Tracing recursion

Let's consider now how the method of Listing 10.I might be used by the computer or executed. We will first do this without the use of a computer as a pencil-and-paper exercise. If you have a reasonable understanding of how such a method might be evaluated or executed by a person, you will have a basic understanding of how it will be executed by the computer.

Suppose you are in a room full of desks. You are sitting at the desk closest to the door, which we will call desk A. The method of Listing 10.I is written on the board. On each desk is a sheet of paper with three labeled boxes:

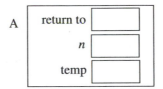

Your boss walks in the door and asks you to calculate the factorial of 5. She does this by writing 5 into the *n* box and Boss into the return to box to tell you to whom the answer is to be returned:

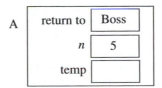

You simply follow the instructions on the board. Each time you need to invoke the rules recursively, you go to a new desk! When you go to a new desk, you must take with you two values: the number for which this rule is to calculate a factorial and the desk to which the answer is to be returned. You begin: 5 is certainly greater than 1, so you must first know the factorial of 4 before you can perform line #7: `temp = n * Fact (n-1);`. You leave this desk and go to desk B and write into the appropriate boxes:

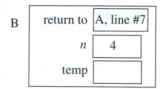

Sitting now at desk B, you begin the instructions (from the top): 4 is greater than 1, and you must perform the instruction of line #7. First you must know the factorial of 3 so you leave this desk and go to desk C, taking with you the arguments indicating you need to return to C, line #7, and the value of 3. Arriving at desk C, you write into the appropriate boxes:

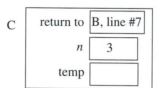

At desk C, you begin the instructions again from the start: 3 is greater than 1 and you must perform line #7. You go to desk D, taking the arguments indicating a return to C, line #7, and the value of 2:

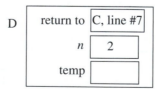

The same story is at desk D: 2 is greater than 1, and you pause at line #7. You go to desk E. At desk E, you find that n is equal to 1 and go to line #5 and write 1 into the temp box:

E   return to D, line #7

                 n   1

              temp   1

When you now come to the end of the instructions, you must take the value of temp and return to the indicated location—in this case, desk D, line #7. Arriving back at desk D, *you continue where you left off* at line #7. The calculation of *n* (2 at desk D) times 1 (just 1) is written into temp, and you have completed the instructions at desk D:

D   return to C, line #7

                 n   2

              temp   2

You memorize the value of temp and return to the indicated location (C, line #7) to report that the factorial of *n* (2) is 2. Arriving back at desk C, you continue where you left off, at line #7. The product of *n* (3 at desk C) times 2 is written into temp and you are finished at desk C:

C   return to B, line #7

                 n   3

              temp   6

You report back (desk B, line #7) that the factorial of *n* (3) is 6. Back at desk B, you continue where you left off at line #7. The product of *n* (4 at desk B) times 6 is written to temp and you are finished at desk B:

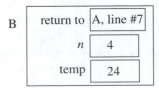

B   return to A, line #7

                 n   4

              temp   24

You're almost done. You report back to desk A that the factorial of *n* (4 at desk B) is 24. At desk A, you continue at line #7 and calculate *n* (5) times 24 and write 120 into temp. Completing the instructions, you finally report back to the boss that *n* factorial (5) is 120.

One small difference between this analogy and how the computer actually executes this method to calculate `Fact(5)` is that the desks do not contain predrawn and labeled boxes on paper. Each time the system goes to a new desk, (so to speak), it must get out a clean sheet of "workspace" memory and draw the boxes before filling them in. With that minor symbolic change, this is analogous to how the computer would execute this method: Each time a method is called (recursively or not), the system sets up a new workspace of memory for local variables and parameters needed by that method—a clean sheet of paper, so to speak. Parameters are filled in, the return location is noted, and execution begins at the top. There is only one copy of the instructions, but there can be many different workspaces. Only one workspace is used at a time. When a method returns, it goes back to the workspace from which it was called.

KEY TERM
call tree

Often, to debug or verify a recursive method, it is useful to diagram a solution in a manner similar to that just shown. To simplify the process and eliminate the need for textual descriptions (such as those used in the above example), labeled arrows are usually employed. This diagram is known as a method *call tree* (Figure 10.1). The reason the term *tree* is used will become clearer in the following examples. The methods for building a call tree are:

1. When a method is called, draw an arrow from the calling to the called method. Label this arrow with the line number to be returned to (using the # symbol) and the values of arguments being passed.

2. When a method returns, draw an arrow back to the original method being returned to. Label this arrow with the value being returned.

The complete call tree for the `Fact(5)` example is given in Figure 10.1. The line for return in the first call to `Fact()` from some other method or the `main()` method is not important because this is not a recursive call. Each box in the diagram represents the variables of a workspace for a single method execution. Inside a box are the variables and parameters for a method.

CONCEPT
problems have both
kinds of solutions

The factorial problem also has a simple iterative solution that could have been used. In fact, the following is universally true: *For every recursive rule, there is an equally valid iterative rule. For every iterative rule, there is an equally valid recursive rule.*

In many cases, the iterative rule is easier to state and may be much more obvious to the programmer. There are some problems, however, where the recursive rule is easier to state! (The iterative rule for the **Maze** solution may be very difficult to see or state.) The programmer who is familiar with both approaches is in a stronger position to choose the one most appropriate. Some problems have very easy recursive solutions but have iterative solutions that are very complex and involved. Some problems are the other way around. You need both methods in your skills for problem solving.

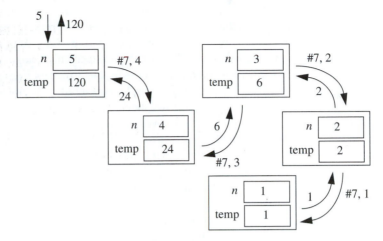

Figure 10.1   Call tree for the method call `Fact(5)`

It is possible that a method may contain more than one call to itself. Consider the rule for the Fibonacci series. A term in the series is defined as the sum of the previous two terms. The first two terms of the series are 1 and 1:

```
Fib(n)  =   1   if n <= 2
           or   Fib(n-1) + Fib(n-2)     if n > 2
```

The series starts out as follows:

```
1,   1,   2,   3,   5,   8,   13,   21,   34,   55,  . . .
```

Given any two successive terms in this series, it is a simple matter to calculate the next term. The other way around, however, is not as simple a task: Given a single term, calculate the previous two terms. More simply stated: Given a value of n (the term position in the series), calculate the term. Since the rule is a useful recursive definition, we can write a method to calculate any Fibonacci number for a positive value of n (Listing 10.III):

Listing 10.III

```
   // Fib()   Returns the Fibonacci number corresponding to n
1  //   IN:   n is a positive integer
2  public static int Fib (int n)
3  {   int temp;
4      if (n <= 1)
5          temp = 1;                            // trivial case
6      else
7          temp = Fib(n-1) + Fib(n-2);          // recursive case with two calls
8      return (temp);
9  }
```

Once again, the method is just a restatement of the rule. Note that both required characteristics of a useful recursive rule are present; each recursive call is for a simpler Fibonacci number (one closer to the trivial solution), and the trivial solution is not a recursive call. The call tree for the method call `Fib(5)` is given in Figure 10.2. Since each method call returns to line 7 (except the first call), the line numbers are left off this diagram for simplicity. Only the arguments passed and the values returned are given as arrow labels.

Note that there are two arrows out of each workspace box as a result of the two recursive method calls made. (In this case, the diagram really does look more like a tree.) As a result, each workspace has two arrows returning to it. The values being returned are then added together at line 7 (of Listing 10.III). Each method returns a single result: the Fibonacci number corresponding to the value of n within the method.

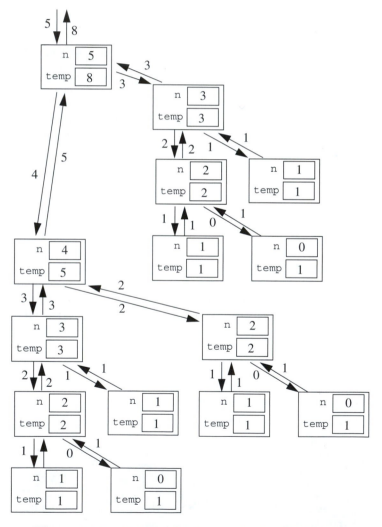

Figure 10.2 Call tree for the method call `Fib(5)`

Let's go back to the `Fib()` method of Listing 10.III and add an output statement at the beginning and end of the method. To simplify this diagram, we will not list the returning line number with the call arrow because it is always the same (line #7):

```
public static int Fib (int n)
{   int temp;
    IO.showValue("preparing to calculate Fibonacci ", n);
    if (n > 1)
         temp = Fib(n-1) + Fib(n-2);
    else temp = 1;
    IO.showValue(" value  is ", temp);
    return (temp);
}
```

When this method now executes, these output messages document the progress of the system through the numerous recursive calls. If this method were called as `Fib(5)` again, the following output diary would result:

```
preparing to calculate Fibonacci 5
preparing to calculate Fibonacci 4
preparing to calculate Fibonacci 3
preparing to calculate Fibonacci 2
preparing to calculate Fibonacci 1
  Fibonacci 1 is 1
preparing to calculate Fibonacci 0
  Fibonacci 0 is 1
  Fibonacci 2 is 2
preparing to calculate Fibonacci 1
  Fibonacci 1 is 1
  Fibonacci 3 is 3
preparing to calculate Fibonacci 2
preparing to calculate Fibonacci 1
  Fibonacci 1 is 1
preparing to calculate Fibonacci 0
  Fibonacci 0 is 1
  Fibonacci 2 is 2
  Fibonacci 4 is 5
preparing to calculate Fibonacci 3
preparing to calculate Fibonacci 2
preparing to calculate Fibonacci 1
  Fibonacci 1 is 1
preparing to calculate Fibonacci 0
  Fibonacci 0 is 1
  Fibonacci 2 is 2
preparing to calculate Fibonacci 1
  Fibonacci 1 is 1
  Fibonacci 3 is 3
  Fibonacci 5 is 8
```

You will quickly observe from this diagram that the process of determining the value to be returned from the first method call of Fib(5) is not at all efficient. Notice that many of the method calls are exact duplicates. The call to Fib(1) was made five times! The call to Fib(0) was made three times. An iterative solution to this problem would probably run much faster. Some will tell you that this is almost always the case; a recursive solution will usually be less efficient that an iterative solution. With a good optimizing compiler, however, that is not as true as it once might have been. You will find that many recursive solutions will be approximately as efficient as a good iterative solution. Some recursive solutions may even be more efficient than iterative solutions.

EXPERIMENT

Would the Fib() method run faster if you were to test whether a call was necessary before making a recursive call? For example:

```
int a, b;
  if ((n-1)>1) a = Fib(n-1); else a = 1;
  if ((n-2)>1) b = Fib(n-2); else b = 1;
temp = a*b;
```

A simple way of timing a method is to call it in a large loop from the main() method (perhaps thousands of times). One execution is the time required for the loop divided by the number of iterations.

Regardless of which solution would run faster, this recursive method was very easy to write. Frequently, a judgment call must be made regarding which is more important in a particular project: class execution time or programmer development time. Quite often, programmer development time is the more important aspect of a project budget.

10.4 Binary search

Let's return now to the binary search rule developed at the beginning of the chapter. To support this rule, we will first implement a simple method of calculating the middle of an array. Suppose we define the first index of the array as first and the last index of the array as last. We will define the middle index as:

```
middle = (last - first) / 2 + first;
```

Since these are integer values, the division will result in a truncation and the final middle result will be integer as well. Now we will express the method with *four* arguments: the name to be found, the array to be searched, and the first and last indexes of this array. In this manner, the method is more general than if we were to simply assume that every array is to be searched from index 0. The trivial case for this rule is when the name is found at the `middle` position. For this example, we will assume the name is always in the array. The method will return the index of the cell where the name was found (Listing 10.IV):

Listing 10.IV

```
// Find ()  A binary search of an array. Returns the index of the
//  cell matching the search name.
//    IN: name is a string to be found and must be in the array
//        array is a string array to be searched (contains >1 name)
//        first, last are beginning and ending indexes of the search

public static int Find (String name, String[] array, int first, int last)
{   int middle, found;
    IO.showMessage ("searching from " + first + " to " + last);
    middle = (last - first) / 2 + first;
    if (name.equals(array[middle])) found = middle;
    else
    {   if (name.compareTo(array[middle]) < 0)
            found = Find (name, array, first, middle-1);
        else found = Find (name, array, middle+1, last);
    }
    return (found);
}
```

Again, the method is simply a restatement of the recursive rule and is easy to write. No iteration loops were needed. The bold output statement at the top of the method will serve to document the progress of the method during testing. Now suppose we have the following disk file containing a list of names:

namelist.txt:

Ann
Bill
Carl
Dan
Eve
Fred
Gary
Hal
Ian
Julio

The following test class could be used to verify the `Find()` method:

```
// Perform a binary search of the names in file "namelist.txt"

public class BinarySearch
```

```
{   final int NUMNAMES = 10;
    public static void main(String[] args)
    {   String[] name_array = new String(NUMNAMES);
        String name;
        DiskInput infile = new DiskInput( );
        infile.open("namelist.txt")
        int n;
        for (n=0; n<NUMNAMES; n++)
            name_array[n] = infile.readString();
        name = IO.readString(" enter name to be found: ");
        IO.showValue (" found at index ",
            Find (name, name_array, 0, NUMNAMES-1) );
    }

    public static int Find(... copied from Listing 10.IV ...

}
```

Let's demonstrate this test application to find Fred:

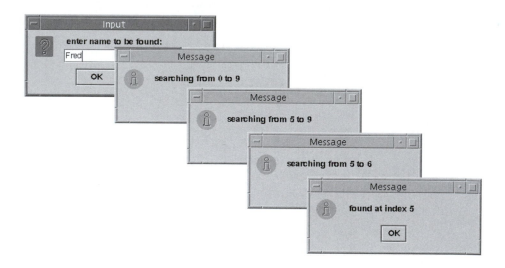

10.5 Example project

Up to this point, all the problems we have looked at had both iterative and recursive solutions that were relatively easy to see and understand. As mentioned earlier, however, there are problems where iterative solutions are not particularly easy to develop *but recursive solutions are natural*. Refer back to the **Maze** problem at the beginning of this chapter.

This problem requires a programming solution to finding a path through an arbitrary **Maze**. For simplicity, we assume the **Maze** object has an array of 10 by 10 characters. A wall or filled space is represented with the * character. Open spaces are marked with p. The goal in the maze is marked with the letter g. We assume that all outside cells are walls. The path must make vertical and horizontal movements; no diagonal jumps are allowed. Let's assume the following is in the file "maze.txt". This could be used to represent the data of a Maze object:

```
**********
*p**p**pg*
*pppp*pp**
***pp*ppp*
*ppp****p*
***pppppp*
*ppp******
***p****p*
***pppppp*
**********
```

Let's start by creating the **Maze** class (Listing 10.V):

Listing 10.V

```
public class Maze
{   private char[][] array;                      // maze array
    private String path = "";                    // solution path

    public Maze (String filename)
    {   array = new char[10][10];
        DiskInput infile = new DiskInput();
        infile.open (filename);
        for (int row=0; row<10; row++)           // read in the maze from a file
        {   String s = infile.readString();
            for (int col=0; col<10; col++)
                array[row][col] = s.charAt(col);
        }
    }

    public char getCell (int row, int col)       // return an array cell
    {   return array[row][col];
    }

    public void setCell (char c, int row, int col)   // set an array cell
    {   array[row][col] = c;
    }

    public void addToPath (int x, int y)         // add a position to the solution path
    {   path += ("\n" + x + ", " + y);
    }

    public String getPath()                      // return the current solution path
    {   return path;
    }
}
```

The constructor for this class accepts a **String** filename to open a disk file and read in the array that represents the **Maze** data. After creating a **Maze** object (and thus filling it from disk), there are several helper methods available. The first two deal with individual maze cells: getCell() to examine the content of one maze cell and setCell() to set the content of one maze cell. The **Maze** object also contains a **String** variable called path that contains the solution to the maze. Initially, that path is empty. The helper method addToPath() allows a maze position to be added to path, and getPath() returns the current path.

Now let's write the main() method. This does not really need to do any solving work; it only interacts with the user. The user should be able to specify a starting cell row and col position (which must contain a p) and then see the application output a path to the goal (Listing 10.VI). We'll put in a stub for an *additional* helper method we'll call Solve() that will be responsible for the actual path solution. We'll assume it returns a 1 if it found a path and a 0 if it did not find a path:

Listing 10.VI

```
public class SolveMaze
{
    public static void main (String[] args)
    {   int startx, starty;
        Maze maze = new Maze ("maze.txt");
        startx = IO.readInt ("Enter starting row position: ");
        starty = IO.readInt ("Enter starting col position: ");
        if (Solve(maze, startx, starty) > 0)
            IO.showMessage (maze.getPath());
        else
            IO.showMessage ("maze has no solution.");
        System.exit(0);
    }

    private static int Solve (Maze m, int row, int col)
    {
            // to be written later . . .
    }
}
```

This problem has an iterative solution, but it is quite involved and difficult for most to envision. The recursive solution is quite simple!

The concept is this: The entire problem does not need to be addressed; we must address only the decisions and actions for a single cell. Suppose you were an explorer placed arbitrarily within the maze and tasked to report back whether your cell was part of a new path solution. There are several trivial situations that might occur:

1. If your cell contains a g, report "YES".

2. If your cell contains a *, it cannot be a part of a new path; report "NO".

3. If your cell has previously been visited and contains footprints, it cannot be part of a new path; report "NO".

If none of these trivial solutions occur, it is possible that your cell could be part of a new path. In this case, *send out four cloned assistants*, one in each direction. If any assistant reports back that the cell he visited is part of a new path, report in turn to your boss that you are also part of this new path.

How do these assistants know if they found a new path? You might say, "That's not my problem. I only know that if I'm on a path, one of them is closer to the goal than me." In other words, the assistants have a simpler problem to solve. You are beginning to think recursively!

The implementation is now *a restatement of the recursive rule* developed earlier. We will define the letter f to represent a footprint. Here's the replacement for the Solve() stub (Listing 10.VII):

Listing 10.VII

```
private static int Solve (Maze m, int row, int col)
{
    int success = 0;
    switch (m.getCell(row, col))
    {   case 'g' :   success = 1; break;
        case '*' :   success = 0; break;
        case 'f' :   success = 0; break;
        default  :   m.setCell('f', row, col);              // leave a footprint..
                     success = Solve(m, row+1, col) +
                         Solve(m, row-1, col) +
                         Solve(m, row, col+1) +
                         Solve(m, row, col-1);
                     break;
    }
    if (success > 0)
        m.addToPath(row, col);
    return (success);
}
```

That's all there is to it! When we execute this class to solve the maze in file "maze.txt" from the starting position of row 8, column 4, the following dialogs occur:

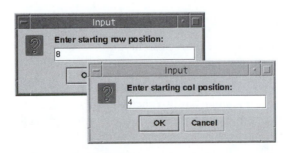

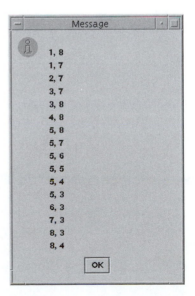

Notice that the path is printed backward. That makes sense if you think about it for a minute. Each explorer is also an assistant to the explorer who sent him out. The first assistant to actually determine that he is on the new path is the one that finds himself at the goal. As a result, that is the first cell location printed. There are lots of other explorers waiting to hear if their assistants have found a path. This assistant that found the goal then reports back to the explorer that sent him. That explorer now understands that he also is on the path, and that cell location is printed. He in turn reports back to the explorer that sent him and so on until the first explorer sent out by the public `Solve()` method reports back to the application.

EXPERIMENT

In the **Maze** implementation, the recursive method first marks a footprint before sending out assistant explorers. What would occur if the footprint were only marked just before the explorer returned to report?

If you plot the path in the maze, you will also see that the path is not necessarily the shortest path possible. However, it is a valid path. Try the class with a number of different starting positions and convince yourself that it works. Now, take 30 minutes or so and try to come up with an idea for a programming solution that does not involve recursion. Don't waste more time than that; it's a tough problem without recursion. The exercise will, however, help you appreciate the fact that some problems are more appropriately solved with recursive rules.

10.6 Summary

KEY TERMS   Only a few new terms were introduced in this chapter. They are quite important to this new concept of recursion, however:

1. *recursion*—an algorithm approach for solving a problem by reapplying a rule. A useful recursive algorithm has two characteristics: At least one application of the rule toward a trivial problem must not be recursive. A recursive application of the rule should be applied toward a simpler problem.

2. *binary search*—a method of searching a list by continually dividing a list into two halves and subsequently eliminating one half until the item is found.

3. *recursive method*—a method that calls itself or is called by another method before it returns.

4. *call tree*—a diagram of recursive calls showing arguments passed, individual workspaces with local variables, and values returned.

CONCEPTS   A recursive method generally will not contain a loop. Usually, a recursive method consists of an `if-else`. In the `if` section, the trivial cases are tested. In the `else` section, the recursive call is made with a simpler problem. A recursive method must always have two components or characteristics. First, the method will invoke itself—each time with a set of parameters that are closer to a trivial solution. Second, the method will contain a trivial case or base case, where a solution can be immediately returned without another recursive call.

For every recursive rule, there is an equally valid iterative rule. For every iterative rule, there is an equally valid recursive rule. The best rule to use may depend on which is easier and faster to implement and perhaps which is more efficient.

10.7 Exercises

Short-answer questions

1. What are the two characteristics of a useful recursive rule?
2. What two components or characteristics are found in a recursive method?
3. A _____ _____ is a paper-and-pencil diagram useful in designing and debugging a recursive method.
4. The _____ _____ algorithm is a method of searching an ordered list by continually dividing the remaining list in half and subsequently eliminating one of the halves from consideration until an item is found.
5. What might occur if a recursive rule does not contain a trivial solution?
6. For every iterative rule, there is an equally valid _____ rule.
7. Each recursive method in Java will often take the form of what common statement?
8. What is the purpose of drawing a call tree?
9. Are there some problems for which an iterative solution is not possible? Are there some problems for which a recursive solution is not possible?
10. State a useful recursive rule (in English) for the multiplication of two integer values. Tip: Suppose you wish to multiply 7×23. Would you be able to calculate the result without using multiplication if you knew the answer to 6×23?
11. State a useful recursive rule (in English) for outputting the characters in a `char` array. You may assume the string ends with the null \0 character. Tip: If you output the first character in the string, would outputting the rest of the string be a simpler problem?
12. Refer to the method `Fact()` of Listing 10.I. Draw the call tree for the following method call:

```
int n = Fact(6);
```

13. Refer to the method `Fib()` of Listing 10.III. Draw the call tree for the following method call:

```
int n;   n = Fib(3);
```

14. The value of sin(x) can be calculated (in radians) for positive values of x using the following series formula:

$$\sin(x) = x\left(1 - \frac{x^2}{1^2\pi^2}\right)\left(1 - \frac{x^2}{2^2\pi^2}\right)\left(1 - \frac{x^2}{3^2\pi^2}\right)\cdots$$

Each succeeding series term will be closer and closer to 1.0, and the series converges to a correct answer. For example, when the absolute value of a new term is within 0.01 of 1.0, you can assume the series is correct to within 0.05. Write a useful recursive rule (in English) for calculating the value of sin(x) to within 0.05.

15. Suppose a sorted array of 64 names must be searched using the binary search algorithm. What is the worst case number of names that must be compared to find a particular name?

16. The `Fact()` method of Listing 10.I is not particularly efficient. Write a better recursive rule (in English) so that recursive calls are not made if $n <= 3$. By drawing a call tree for `Fact(5)` for this new rule, determine how many recursive calls would be avoided.

17. The `Fib()` method of Listing 10.III is not particularly efficient. Write a better recursive rule (in English) so that recursive calls are not made if $n <= 3$. By drawing a call tree for `Fib(5)` for this new rule, determine how many recursive calls would be avoided.

18. Draw a call tree for a `Find("Hal", list, 0, 9)` call using Listing 10.IV and the same name list used in the chapter example.

19. Draw a call tree for a `Find("Carl", list, 0, 9)` call using Listing 10.IV and the same name list used in the chapter example.

20. The maze implementation of Listings 10.V through 10.VII in this chapter is not particularly efficient. For example, an explorer sends out all four assistants at once. Would it be more efficient to send out one assistant (say, to the left) and then await his report? If successful, there would be no need to send out the other three assistants. Write a better recursive rule (in English) for a more efficient approach.

Projects

1. Refer to Short-Answer Question 10. Implement this recursive rule for multiplication as a method. Provide a `main()` method to call this method for a variety of multiplication problems to test your implementation.

2. Implement a `Sin(x)` method using the useful recursive rule developed for Short-Answer Question 14. Provide a `main()` method to call this method for a variety of appropriate values of x to test your implementation.

3. The `Fact()` method of Listing 10.I is only capable of handling fairly small integers because the computer may quickly run out of workspace memory. Determine by experimentation the largest value of n for which your computer will calculate `Fact()`.

4. Implement the improved recursive rule of Short-Answer Question 16. Write an appropriate driver `main()` method to test your implementation for several values of n. Compare the number of recursive calls made with your implementation to those made by the method of Listing 10.I.

5. Implement the `Maze` classes of Listings 10.V through 10.VII in this chapter. Extend the size of the maze to 20 by 20 characters.

6. The maze implementation of Listings 10.V through 10.VII in this chapter is not particularly efficient. For example, an explorer sends out all four assistants at once. Would it be more efficient to send out one assistant (say, to the left) and then await his report? If successful, there would be no need to send out the other three assistants. Modify the implementation to effect this change. Test your implementation against the implementation in this chapter for several different starting points to determine which makes the fewest recursive method calls.

7. The maze implementation of Listings 10.V through 10.VII in this chapter does not always find the *shortest* path to the goal. Suppose you knew that the goal was always up and to the right of the starting position. (It still may require a path that goes left or down for parts of the path to reach the goal.) Modify the implementation to take advantage of this fact. Test your implementation against the implementation in this chapter for several different starting points to verify that the shortest path is always chosen if this fact is true.

8. A palindrome is a word or phrase (with punctuation and blanks removed) that is spelled exactly the same forward or backward. Some examples are "level" and "deed" and, of course, the first sentence ever spoken: "Madam, I'm Adam" (madamimadam). You've seen this problem as a project in a previous chapter. For this project, write a *recursive* method that accepts a string parameter in a `char` array and returns 1 if the string is a palindrome (0 otherwise). Tip: The first character must match the last, the second character must match the second to last, and so on.

9. The *greatest common divisor* of two integers x and y is defined as the largest integer that divides both x and y evenly. Euclid's algorithm states that this $GCD(x, y)$ is
   a. y, if y divides x evenly
   b. otherwise it is $GCD(y$, remainder of x divided by $y)$
   Write a method `GCD()` to calculate this value and test it with an appropriate driver application.

10. Creative Challenge: The Towers of Hanoi problem is a tradition in the computer sciences. Normally, these Creative Challenge projects involve some aspect of a problem you probably do not yet know how to completely solve. Not this time. You have all the tools you need to attack this one. It is not a trivial problem, however, and it involves learning to think recursively. (There is an iterative solution to this problem, but it is quite complex and requires that you first understand the recursive solution.) When you are finished, you will be surprised at how short and concise the solution is.

   There are three pegs and N differently sized disks. Each disk has a hole so that it will fit over a peg. Initially, all disks are on the first peg in size order such that the largest is on the bottom and the smallest is on top. The goal is to move all disks from the first peg to the last peg following two simple rules:

a. Only one disk may be moved at a time.

b. A larger disk may never be placed on a smaller disk.

Tip: A problem involving only one disk is trivial. So is the problem of moving only two disks. Suppose the pegs are labeled A, B, and C. To move two disks from A to C:

move the top disk from A to B

move the top disk from A to C

move the top disk from B to C

Now suppose the problem involved moving three disks. If you could move two disks to an intermediate peg, move the bottom disk to the destination peg, and then move the two disks from the intermediate peg to the destination, you would have it. Moving two disks requires the separate steps to move them one at a time, but that is a trivial problem. So, we have expressed a complex problem (three disks) into two trivial problems (two disks and one disk).

What about moving four disks? Move three disks to the intermediate peg, move the bottom disk to the destination, and finally move the three disks on the intermediate peg to the destination. We have expressed the problem in a simpler recursive problem (three disks) and a trivial problem (one disk).

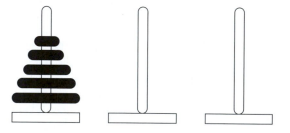

Programming
with `Swing`

Up to this point, our display output has consisted of fairly simple display boxes. Our keyboard input has allowed only single text lines of user response. Both of these have been generated with the `IO` class provided with this text. You have seen fairly sophisticated user interfaces with buttons for mouse click input, menus, and so on in other program classes. In this chapter, you will learn how to produce some graphical user interfaces much more capable than those using the simple `IO` class. We'll do this with the `Swing` package available in the standard Java library.

11.1 Swing

KEY TERM
graphical
user interface

The `Swing` package is part of the Java library in Versions 1.2 and higher. Basically, it is a set of classes to support *graphical user interfaces*, or GUIs. GUI is usually pronounced "gooey." Providing the user with buttons, menus, and formatted display windows is a powerful tool in developing programs that are easy and intuitive to use. Although virtually all windows features you have seen in other programs can be done with the `Swing` package, this chapter will only introduce a few of the fundamental features and classes. (Entire books have been written on just this package.)

There are other Java packages available for GUI support. Some are even part of the Java library, such as the Abstract Windows Toolkit, or **AWT**. **Swing** is generally considered one of the more modern of these and is certainly the easiest to learn and use. **Swing** is actually a part of a larger package called the Java Foundation Classes, or **JFC**. This larger package is beyond the scope of this text. For now, it is interesting to know that **Swing** is a part of the **JFC**.

To import the **Swing** package, the following line is used:

```
import javax.swing.*;
```

KEY TERMS
window, button, menu

Before we get into GUI development using **Swing**, let's review some of the basic terminology of windows programming. A *window* is a self-contained display area within a frame and with a title at the top. It often can be minimized to an icon. A *button* is a symbol within a window that may be mouse clicked by the user. Clicking a button corresponds to a request for some program action by the user. A *menu* is a type of table with multiple choices. Choosing a menu option with the mouse may be a request for some program action or it may be a way of specifying class input from a list of possible choices.

In learning to develop a GUI for a program class, we need to be aware that this type of user interaction is fundamentally different from what we have previously done with the **IO** class. Up to this point, all our input operations have been done *sequentially*. If a class needed two pieces of information from the user, it would provide two sequential input boxes with prompts for the needed information—one after the other. The user was restricted to entering the information, as prompted, into one window at a time.

On the other hand, a GUI usually presents multiple types of input that can be selected by the user. If two buttons are presented in a window for example, the class must be ready to respond to either button. Our `readInt()` method from the **IO** class, for example, was expected to return the integer entered by the user—and only that. Actually, however, the input window had two buttons available for the user: OK and Cancel. You have seen that if the user selects the Cancel button, the class aborts. We didn't have to worry about that option in our programming. When we design more complex GUIs, however, our software must be ready to accept any of the presented possible inputs that the user may select.

Another way of looking at it is to recognize that our previous programs have all been under the control of `main()`. Our `main()` method determined which helper methods would be executed and when, with input requests by the user. When using **Swing**, we will still have a `main()` method to generate the GUI, but it will then turn class control over to the user. Our `main()` method will only set up the GUI. From that point on, the user selections and mouse inputs will determine which method is executed and when. (If this seems a bit confusing, don't worry and don't feel alone. Nobody else understands it at first. We will try to simplify this concept in the first couple of examples.)

KEY TERMS
event, event programming

The act of the user in choosing a button or menu option with the mouse triggers what is known as an *event*. Programs that have GUIs with more than one input option are developed using what is known as *event programming*. Let's start with buttons.

Basically, this means that for each button option in the GUI, the programmer provides a method. When the user selects the button with the mouse, the associated method is automatically executed.

Here is a symbolic or corollary example. Suppose you wish to set up a lemonade stand. Once you have initialized your stand, you simply wait for events to happen. Until an event happens, you are pretty bored. There are two possible events:

1. a customer arrives and requests service, or

2. a supplier arrives with more product and requests service.

For a customer event (or request), you spring into action and pour a glass of lemonade, receive payment, and make change. For a supplier event, you spring into action to sign the invoice and store the product. All your actions are event driven. If several customers and suppliers arrive at the same time, they queue up and wait their turn.

A GUI application is very similar. Here, the events are user mouse clicks, menu choices, and keyboard actions. A particular event causes a particular method to be invoked to accomplish some task.

11.2 Window components

A Java window may be thought of as having two components (Figure 11.1). The frame border is usually pretty much the same for all Java windows on your computer. The color and detailed image of the border may change from one computer to the next, but the components of the border are the same. They consist of the menu button (upper left corner), the title (center), and minimize/maximize buttons (upper right). You've used this standard window before—the **IO** class generated these, and they are a part of other programs and the operating system that you use—so we won't review the menu and minimize/maximize operations. The important point to recognize is that all the programming to generate and manipulate this window is a basic or foundation part of **Swing**.

KEY TERM
content pane

The second component is the area where the contents of the window are placed. This is called the window or frame *content pane*. To customize our GUI, we'll need to specify the following:

1. the title of the frame border,

2. the initial size of the window, and

3. the components to be added to the content pane.

standard frame boarder

frame content pane

Figure 11.1 The standard Java window

Initially, we'll accept the default characteristics of the basic window (e.g., color, size, and position).

Creating a standard window

A window can be declared using the **JFrame** class and created as follows:

```
JFrame name = new JFrame ( title );
```

Syntax form

Table 11.1 presents some of the basic helper methods of this class that may be used to specify the needed customization items mentioned earlier.

We'll ignore the addWindowListener() method for the moment. With this knowledge, we are ready for our first attempt to create a Java window. Notice that the following code imports several packages. In general, these three import lines are needed for a **Swing** class. Notice also that the following class is marked WRONG! You'll see in a minute what the problem is:

```
// a class to demo Swing
```

WRONG!

```
import javax.swing.*;
import java.awt.*;
import java.awt.event.*;
```

Table 11.1   JFrame helper methods

JFrame method	action
setVisible (option);	set whether the window is currently visible (true) or hidden (false).
setSize (width, height);	set the initial size of the window (in integer pixels for height and width).
setTitle (some_string);	change the title of a window.
addWindowListener (listener);	register a listener class.

```
public class WinDemo
{  public static void main(String[] args)
   {  JFrame w = new JFrame ("this is a demo");
      w.setSize (300, 150);
      w.setVisible(true);
   }
}
```

When you compile and run this class, you do in fact create the window you expect (see Figure 11.1). Test the maximize and minimize buttons—they work as expected even though you did not write any Java code to support these actions. Notice that the window can be dragged or moved and resized. Now try the menu buttons. They all seem to work except the CLOSE option. When you click this menu option, the window goes away, but the class continues to run! This can be very confusing. We don't have any way (other than perhaps Ctrl + C) of terminating the class.

The reason for this is subtle. Remember the earlier analogy? This main() sets up a window and makes it visible but then goes to sleep. The above class does not have a System.exit(0) statement, and this is what we want. If we were to add a System.exit(0) statement at the end of main(), the class execution would again create the expected window but then terminate and destroy the window before we had a chance to use it (or probably even see it on a fast computer).

The concept to recognize is that after setting up the window, main() has turned over any further method calls to the **Swing** system. Further method calls will be made in response to the user selecting a button or a menu option. There are default methods to respond to all the menu options and buttons. Unfortunately, the default method that is invoked in response to the CLOSE option event closes the window but does not terminate the sleeping main(). If we want that to occur also, we must overload the default method with our own.

To do this, we must create a class that inherits the default class (with the default methods), which sounds a bit convoluted. In practice, this is what we need (Listing 11.I):

Listing 11.I

```
// a class to overload the default JFrame listeners
import java.awt.*;
import java.awt.event.*;

public class FrameListener extends WindowAdapter
{ public void windowClosing (WindowEvent e)
   {    System.exit(0);
   }
}
```

As you have previously seen, the phrase extends WindowAdapter implies that this new class we are creating (I called it **FrameListener**) has all the information variables and helper methods of the **WindowAdapter** class. The method we wish to overload (or replace) is the windowClosing() method, so we simply provide our own. Our windowClosing() method does the needed System.exit(0) call. We're not done yet. Here's the correct version of the **WinDemo** class demonstration (Listing 11.II):

Listing 11.II

```
// a class to demo Swing
import javax.swing.*;
import java.awt.*;
import java.awt.event.*;

public class WinDemo
{  public static void main(String[] args)
    {  JFrame w = new JFrame ("this is a demo");
       FrameListener listen = new FrameListener();
       w.addWindowListener (listen);
       w.setSize (300, 150);
       w.setVisible(true);
    }
}
```

Notice that we added two extra statements. The first creates an instance or object of type **FrameListener** (our new class from Listing 11.I). The second statement calls a member method of the **JFrame** class called addWindowListener(). This registers the **FrameListener** object listen as the default class to invoke in response to the **JFrame** events associated with the top frame buttons and menu options. Now, when the CLOSE menu option is selected, the closeWindow() method of our **FrameListener** object listen is called. This performs the System.exit(0) (which also closes the window) to terminate the class execution.

Confusing? Of course. That is why the first 10 chapters of this text simply used the **IO** class provided in Appendix A. I'll bet you are wondering if the **IO** class is just a wrapper that uses **Swing**. Of course!

There are a number of other default methods in the **WindowAdapter** class. At this point, we will accept the defaults. It is important to recognize, however, that nowhere did you directly invoke the windowClosing() helper method. It was invoked by the user or, more correctly, by Java in response to a user action.

Let's go back and look at the setSize() method of **JFrame**. What does a height of 150 and a width of 300 actually mean? Certainly, they are not measurements in inches or centimeters. Sizes in Java are measured in pixels. A pixel is a dot, or *picture el*ement—the smallest thing your screen is capable of showing. A 1024×760 resolution display means that the screen can show up to 1024 pixels in a line and up to 760 lines of pixels to fill the display. As such, a low-resolution screen will show a window of 150×300 much larger than a high-resolution screen. In any case, the image of the window will be pretty much the same.

Adding content to a frame

KEY TERM
container

Now we need to add some content to our basic window. We'll focus on three different possibilities: a label, a button, and a text area. With these three basic components, you can design some very versatile GUIs. To add content to the window, we need a reference to the content area. Formally, this is called a *container*, and there is a **Container** class. You will want to think of a window as having a container for window content. That isn't strictly correct, but it is a good way of thinking about it. The **JFrame** class has a method to return a reference to the container of the window:

```
Container name = winname.getContentPane ( );
```

Syntax form

Notice that we don't need to create a new **Container** object. One already exists within the **JFrame** object or window we have already declared. The getContentPane() method simply returns a reference to this **Container** for us to use. Here are the basic helper methods of the **Container** class that we can use to customize our window (Table 11.2).

If you wish to change the background and foreground colors of a window, here is a set of recognized color constants from the **Color** class. You can generate your own colors, but these predefined constants are usually adequate:

Color.black	Color.blue	Color.cyan
Color.darkGray	Color.gray	Color.green
Color.lightGray	Color.magenta	Color.orange
Color.pink	Color.red	Color.white
Color.yellow		

Table 11.2   Container class methods

Container method	action
add (*window_object*) ;	add this window object to the content pane.
add (*window_object, location*) ;	add this window object to the content pane at this location.
setBackground (*some_color*) ;	set the background color of the content pane.
setForeGround (*some_color*) ;	set the foreground color of the content pane.

Table 11.3 JLabel helper method

JLabel method	action
setText (*some_string*);	change the text of a label.

The three components we wish to add to our content pane are *window objects*: A label, a button, and a text area are window objects (along with many others). To create a label object, we'll use the **JLabel** class:

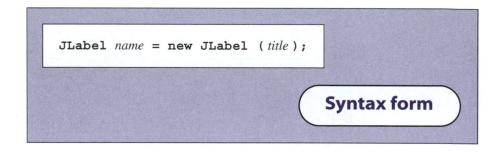

```
JLabel name = new JLabel ( title );
```

Syntax form

One useful helper method of this class allows you to change the string associated with a label after the label has been displayed (Table 11.3).

Let's modify our simple demonstration to display the label Hello World! (Listing 11.III):

Listing 11.III

```
// a class to demo Swing
import javax.swing.*;
import java.awt.*;
import java.awt.event.*;

public class WinDemo2
{  public static void main(String[] args)
   {  JFrame w = new JFrame ("this is a demo");
      FrameListener listen = new FrameListener();
      w.addWindowListener (listen);
      Container pane = w.getContentPane();
      JLabel label = new JLabel (" Hello World!");
      pane.add (label);
      w.setSize (300, 150);
      w.setVisible(true);
   }
}
```

Notice that we added the label to the content pane prior to setting the window as visible. Usually the last thing you will do is call `setVisible()`. Now when we run this class, the screen displays:

Suppose we wish to add two labels to a pane? Consider the following modifications to Listing 11.III:

```
.  .  .
Container pane = w.getContentPane();
JLabel label = new JLabel (" First Label!");
pane.add (label);
JLabel label2 = new JLabel (" Second Label!");
pane.add (label2);
.  .  .
w.setVisible(true);
```

When you execute this class, the effect you see may depend on the particular computer you are using. On my computer, for example, I don't see both the expected labels. I see only the last label added:

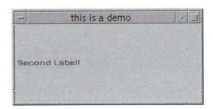

The reason is simple: The second label was added over the top of the first. We have the option when adding something to a container pane to specify one of five possible positions within the pane. These positions are defined by the following constants:

```
BorderLayout.NORTH
BorderLayout.SOUTH
BorderLayout.EAST
BorderLayout.WEST
BorderLayout.CENTER
```

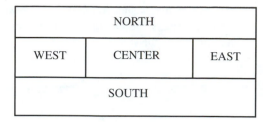

Figure 11.2   Five-location grid for the default layout manager

KEY TERM
Layout Manager

These five positions are a simple grid (Figure 11.2). If all five positions are not utilized, Java is free to take up the unused space with the grids that are utilized. The format of a pane is managed by a *Layout Manager* method. This method controls what goes where. There are a variety of different layout managers that can be used with a window, but we'll accept the default layout manager and these five simple grid locations. The location of an object being added to a container pane is given as the second argument in the add() method (see Table 11.2).

The following will produce a window with the two labels we desired:

```
Container pane = w.getContentPane();
JLabel label = new JLabel ("First Label!");
pane.add (label, BorderLayout.NORTH);
JLabel label2 = new JLabel (" Second Label!");
pane.add (label2, BorderLayout.SOUTH);
```

Now let's add a button to our simple demo. The **JButton** class is also a window object:

```
JButton name = new JButton ( title );
```

Syntax form

There are two important methods associated with using buttons (Table 11.4). The setText() method allows us to label or name a button with text. While a **JLabel** object is just a text label, a **JButton** object allows some user action. As

Table 11.4 `JButton` **helper methods**

JButton method	action
addActionListener (**this**);	indicate that the method `actionPerformed()` of this class is to be invoked for a button event.
setText (*some_string*);	change the title of a button.

such, we must specify or register an event handler with the button. This is the method we wish to be invoked when the user selects or clicks this button. To register an event handler method, we use the `addActionListener()` method of **JButton**.

KEY TERM
this

The argument **this** is actually a keyword in Java. It always references the current class object. In other words, it stands for `this` object. This statement indicates that we wish the method `actionPerformed()` to be invoked when the user chooses this particular button. Of course, we now need to write an `actionPerformed()` method to add to our class.

A **static** main() object is not associated with **this**. Only objects that are created with the keyword **new** have an associated **this**. At this point, let's modify our demonstration to form the framework of a general window GUI. If we make a class to display a GUI window, we can have more than one window for a given application. We'll call this a **Gui** class. Each **Gui** object will represent a new window. The simplest approach is to recognize that our **Gui** class is really just a **JFrame** class with some added capability. In other words, we can easily inherit the **JFrame** class using the keyword **extends**. To add an event handler, we specify that this class **implements ActionListener**. So, we can say that a **Gui** is a **JFrame** with an added `actionPerformed()` method that provides an event handler for **Gui** events.

```
// a class for a graphical user interface window
import javax.swing.*;
import java.awt.*;
import java.awt.event.*;

public class Gui extends JFrame implements ActionListener
{ public Gui (String title)
   {    setTitle (title);
        FrameListener listen = new FrameListener();
        addWindowListener (listen);
   }
  public actionPerformed (ActionEvent e)
  {
  }
}
```

Once again, note that nowhere does the code invoke `actionPerformed()`. It is invoked by the user—that is, by Java in response to a user event. Now we're ready to do a GUI with some action. In the following demo, we'll present the user

Table 11.5   `ActionEvent` class helper methods

`ActionEvent` method	action
`getActionCommand()`	return the string associated with the action (default is the object title).
`setActionCommand()`	change the string associated with the action.

with a button with the title `"CLICK ME!"`. When the user clicks this button, we'll change the text title of the button to `"CLICKED!"`

When the `actionPerformed()` method is invoked in response to a mouse click event, the parameter e will be set by Java to represent the action associated with that event. There are two important helper methods of the **`ActionEvent`** class (Table 11.5).

In this case, the value returned by `getActionCommand()` will be the button title that is the action string default value (Listing 11.IV):

Listing 11.IV

```java
// a demonstration GUI with a button
import javax.swing.*;
import java.awt.*;
import java.awt.event.*;

public class Gui2 extends JFrame implements ActionListener
{ private JButton button = null;

  public Gui2 (String title)
  {    setTitle (title);
       FrameListener listen = new FrameListener();
       addWindowListener (listen);
       Container pane = getContentPane();
       JLabel label = new JLabel ("try this button:");
       pane.add (label, BorderLayout.NORTH);
       button = new JButton ("CLICK ME!");
       pane.add (button, BorderLayout.CENTER);
       button.addActionListener (this);
       setSize (300, 150);
  }

  public void actionPerformed (ActionEvent e)
  {    if (e.getActionCommand().equals("CLICK ME!"))
           button.setText ("CLICKED!");
  }
}
```

To demonstrate this class, the following simple `main()` driver class might be used. This driver creates a **Gui2** and then goes to sleep. The **Gui2** object terminates the class using the `CLOSE` option of the frame border window:

```
public class TestIO
{  public static void main (String[] args)
    {    Gui2 gui = new Gui2 ("Demo of a button");
         gui.setVisible(true);
    }
    }
```

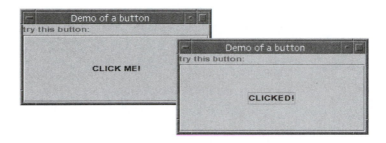

The bottom line is this: The **Gui** and **FrameListener** classes can be used to form the boilerplate for fairly versatile GUI development. They provide as much versatility as you will need for rest of this text. We can do this because all GUIs are basically simple variations on a basic theme. All we need to do for customized GUIs is to add components (and event handlers) to the contents pane of the basic **JFrame** object. Are there other ways to build GUIs? Yes because Java is very versatile. It isn't important to learn all the ways of doing something at the start. It is much more important to learn one way of building a GUI and then investigate other models in the future.

Finally, you need to learn how to do input and output with a window using the **JTextArea** class:

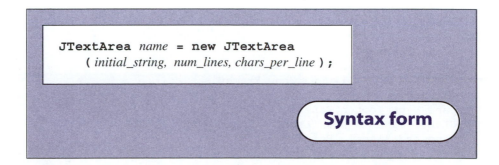

```
JTextArea name = new JTextArea
        ( initial_string, num_lines, chars_per_line );
```

Syntax form

Table 11.6   JTextArea class helper methods

JTextArea method	action
getText()	return the string currently displayed.
setText()	set the string to be displayed.

In this syntax, *initial_string* is the value we initially wish to have displayed within this text area, *num_lines* is the number of text lines to be available, and *chars_per_line* is the maximum number of characters that can be displayed per line. You have used this class before—when you invoke the IO.readInt() method, a **JTextArea** of one line is displayed (initially blank) for the user to type in a string representing an integer (Table 11.6).

We don't have a **Swing** class available for a numeric area (which might be named JIntArea or JDoubleArea) unless we design one. So if we need to do numeric input, it involves two steps: using a **JTextArea** for textual input and then converting the string into a number.

For example, here's an application that prompts the user to enter a number and then displays the square root of that number when the user clicks the OK button. If the user clicks the CLEAR button, the window cleans up for the next number entry (Listing 11.V):

Listing 11.V

```
// window GUI to calculate the square root of an input number
import javax.swing.*;
import java.awt.*;
import java.awt.event.*;

public class SquareRoot extends JFrame implements ActionListener
{
  private double root;
  JTextArea text = null;
  Container pane = null;
  JLabel answer = null;

  public SquareRoot()
  {setTitle ("Square Root Calc");
   FrameListener listen = new FrameListener();
   addWindowListener (listen);
   pane = getContentPane();
   JLabel label = new JLabel ("Enter a number: ");
   pane.add (label, BorderLayout.WEST);
   text = new JTextArea ("", 1, 10);
```

```
    pane.add (text, BorderLayout.CENTER);
    JButton okbutton = new JButton ("OK");
    pane.add (okbutton, BorderLayout.EAST);
    okbutton.addActionListener (this);
    JButton clearbutton = new JButton ("CLEAR");
    pane.add (clearbutton, BorderLayout.NORTH);
    clearbutton.addActionListener (this);
    answer = new JLabel ("");
    pane.add (answer, BorderLayout.SOUTH);
    setSize (300, 150);
  }

  public void actionPerformed (ActionEvent e)
  { if (e.getActionCommand().equals ("OK"))
    { String s = text.getText();
      root = Math.sqrt(Double.parseDouble(s.trim()));
      answer.setText ("answer is: " + root);
    }
    if (e.getActionCommand().equals ("CLEAR"))
      { text.setText("");
        answer.setText ("");
    }
  }
}
```

Let's look at what this class does. First, note that the setup and display of the window GUI takes place in the class constructor. This approach is very common and convenient. The window consists of five components: two **JLabel**s, a **JTextArea**, and two **JButton**s. Next, notice that some components of the window are declared as class members (text, pane, and answer). This is because they need to be referenced or used in both the constructor and the actionPerformed() methods.

The label in the SOUTH position is initially empty (""). This holds or reserves the position but doesn't display any text. Both the buttons register the same actionPerformed() method of this class to be invoked when a user action occurs. Suppose we execute this class with the following driver class:

```
public class TestIO
{
    public static void main (String[] args)
    {   SquareRoot gui = new SquareRoot ();
        gui.setVisible(true);
    }
}
```

Table 11.7   JPanel class helper methods

JPanel method	action
add()	add a window object to a grid location.

Initially, we see the window established by the constructor. When the user enters a number in the text area and mouse clicks OK, the label in the SOUTH position is changed to show the result of the calculation:

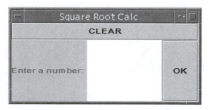 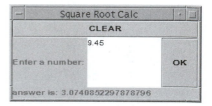

Subgrids

As you would expect, many GUIs are made up of more than five components, and many should be organized in more effective ways than the default five-location grid. Fortunately, each of the five grid locations can itself be another subgrid. In other words, we can have grids within grids. A subgrid is declared as a **JPanel**:

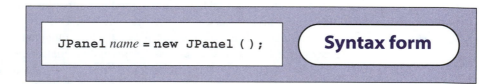

```
JPanel name = new JPanel ( );
```
Syntax form

We can form complex GUIs by creating **JPanel**s, filling the five grid locations, and then adding these **JPanel**s to the main **Container**. The example given later (Listing 11.VII) shows a nicely compound GUI using **JPanel**s. The **JPanel** class is quite simple and only one helper method is important at this point (Table 11.7).

11.3   Example project

Let's do a significant example GUI. How about a four-function calculator? We'll start with a diagram of how we would like the GUI to appear:

We would like this calculator to be used just like any simple (cheap) calculator. For example, to add two numbers the user would enter the number into the display, click the + button, enter the second number into the display, and then click the = button. The result should then be displayed.

Obviously, this design is not in the default five-grid format. We can think of it as two grids: The `center` grid contains the display label and text area while the `south` grid contains the five buttons. Now think of each of these as being a **JPanel** *with its own five grids*. In the `center` **JPanel**, we'll place the `Display:` label on the WEST side and the text area on the EAST side.

In the `south` **JPanel**, we'll group the four function buttons into two sub-**JPanel**s called `southwest` and `southcenter`:

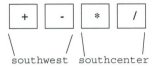

Now we have the following diagram of window object locations:

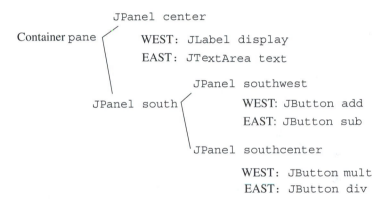

We don't need all five grid locations in each **JPanel**. Those not utilized are simply not there. This gives us the following layout:

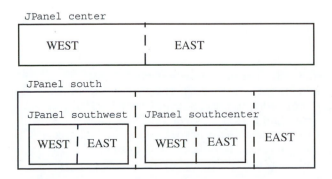

The constructor for our **Calculator** class will generate the GUI according to this diagram. As is often the case, this represents the bulk of the programming needed for this application. All of the actual work of the calculator GUI actions will be handled by the actionPerformed() method. Look at the Listing 11.VI constructor. We'll explain the events and actions after.

Listing 11.VI

```
// A simple 4-function calculator
import javax.swing.*;
import java.awt.*;
import java.awt.event.*;

public class Calculator extends JFrame implements ActionListener
{
  private double value;
  JTextArea display = null;
  char action;

  public Calculator()
  { setTitle ("Calculator");
    FrameListener listen = new FrameListener();
    addWindowListener (listen);
    Container pane = getContentPane();
    JLabel label = new JLabel ("Display: ");
    display = new JTextArea ("", 1, 10);
    JButton plus = new JButton ("+");
       plus.addActionListener (this);
    JButton minus = new JButton ("-");
       minus.addActionListener (this);
    JButton mult = new JButton ("*");
       mult.addActionListener (this);
    JButton div = new JButton ("/");
       div.addActionListener (this);
    JButton equal = new JButton ("=");
       equal.addActionListener (this);

    JPanel southwest = new JPanel();
    JPanel southcenter = new JPanel();
    JPanel center = new JPanel();
    JPanel south = new JPanel();
    southwest.add (plus, BorderLayout.WEST);
    southwest.add (minus, BorderLayout.EAST);
    south.add (southwest, BorderLayout.WEST);
    southcenter.add (mult, BorderLayout.WEST);
    southcenter.add (div, BorderLayout.EAST);
    south.add (southcenter, BorderLayout.CENTER);
    south.add (equal, BorderLayout.EAST);
    center.add (label, BorderLayout.WEST);
```

```
    center.add (display, BorderLayout.EAST);
    pane.add (center, BorderLayout.CENTER);
    pane.add (south, BorderLayout.SOUTH);
    setSize (300, 100);
  }

  public void actionPerformed (ActionEvent e)
  { String button = e.getActionCommand();
    double newvalue = Double.parseDouble(display.getText());
    if (button.charAt(0) == '=')
    {  switch (action)
       {  case '+':   value = newvalue + value;
                      break;
          case '-':   value = newvalue - value;
                      break;
          case '*':   value = newvalue * value;
                      break;
          case '/':   value = newvalue / value;
                      break;
       }
       display.setText(""+value);
    }
    else
    {  action = button.charAt(0);
       value = newvalue;
       display.setText ("");
    }
  }
}
```

To use this class, we'll need a simple main() driver class to allocate an instance of a **Calculator** object (Listing 11.VII):

Listing 11.VII

```
public class TestCalculator
{
   public static void main (String[] args)
   {  Calculator gui = new Calculator ();
      gui.setVisible(true);
   }
}
```

Look at the actionPerformed() method of the **Calculator** class of Listing 11.VI. This is where the calculator operations are actually performed. In the first step, this method retrieves and saves the **String** associated with the action and the current number in the text area:

```
String button = e.getActionCommand();
double newvalue = Double.parseDouble(display.getText());
```

Next, the method uses the first character of the action **String**—all buttons are unique in the first (and only) character. If the button clicked is a math function, the action takes these steps:

1. the current number in the text display is saved as value.

2. the first character of the String is saved as action.

3. the text area display is cleared.

In other words, clicking the plus button doesn't perform an addition. It just causes the current display to be saved. When the button clicked is the equal button, the method does the actual plus calculation and shows this result in the text area. Here's an example of 5.2 + 3.5 = :

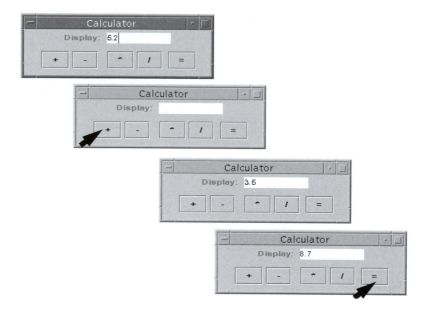

This simple demo does not handle errors very well. If the user types a nonvalid number, the class fails. If the user clicks an operation before entering a number, the class fails. It will handle sequential operations, however, as long as you click the equal button for each subexpression. Here's the result of 5 * 3 = + 7 = :

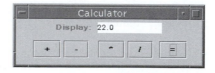

11.4 JOptionPane **class**

Now that you know how to form a GUI display or input window, you may be thinking that most Java GUIs do basically the same thing. In fact, the **IO** class provided by this book has been used in nearly all the Java applications you have written so far. The GUI methods available with the **IO** class are somewhat limited to a message display (showMessage()) and methods to do input (e.g., readInt()). These GUIs obviously contain **JButton**, **JLabel**, and **JTextField** objects. They just don't require the same level of detail as GUIs developed earlier. In other words, the **IO** class doesn't allow you as much control over the positions and number of GUI objects, but it is certainly simpler to use than forming GUIs from the **JButton**, **JLabel**, and **JTextField** objects.

The **IO** class is not in the standard Java library—it was provided with this book as a simplified way of learning Java. It was developed from the **Swing** library, however, using the **JOptionPane** class, which is in **Swing**. Let's look briefly at the **JOptionPane** class.

The **JOptionPane** class of the **Swing** library allows you to form one of four basic GUIs. We'll look at two of these: a window to display a message and a window to input a **String** value from the user.

showMessageDialog()

A display window consists of four components: a title, an icon, a message, and an OK button.

The purpose of the display is to show a message to the user and then wait until the user clicks the OK button. There are several variations of the showMessageDialog() method—two of which are described here.

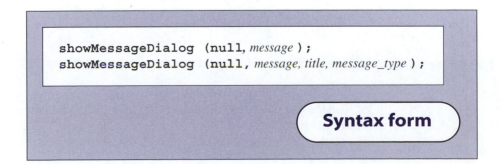

```
showMessageDialog (null, message );
showMessageDialog (null, message, title, message_type );
```

Syntax form

Table 11.8 Defined *message_type* constants for JOptionPane

name	related icon
JOptionPane.PLAIN_MESSAGE	*no icon*
JOptionPane.INFORMATION_MESSAGE	the i symbol
JOptionPane.ERROR_MESSAGE	*system dependent*
JOptionPane.QUESTION_MESSAGE	the ? symbol
JOptionPane.WARNING_MESSAGE	the ! symbol

The first argument to the method can always be the reserved word **null**. (This is actually a placeholder for a parameter that is not being used and beyond the scope of this text.) The *message* is the **String** or literal to be displayed within the dialog. The window *title* is the **String** or literal that you wish to be displayed in the title bar of the dialog window.

The icon presented in the window depends on the *message_type* argument. This is just an integer, and there are a number of predefined or global **static final** identifiers that can be used in this position as described in Table 11.8.

In the first syntax form, the default message type is JOptionPane.INFORMATION_MESSAGE (with the associated i or information icon) and no title.

showInputDialog()

The input dialog box is intended to solicit input from the user. The window consists of five components: a title, a label, a text field for user input, an icon, and finally, an OK and a Cancel button.

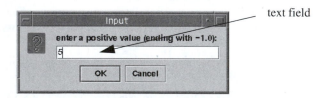

The label is simply the text you would like to use as a prompt. When the user chooses the OK button, the window disappears and the information entered by the user is returned to the calling method as a **String**. The default message type is JOptionPane.QUESTION_MESSAGE with the associated ? icon.

There are two convenient ways of invoking the `showInputDialog()` box:

```
showInputDialog (null, prompt_message );
showInputDialog (null, prompt_message, title,
                    message_type );
```

Syntax form

Just as before, the *title* and *message_type* are optional. They have the same meaning as in the `showMessageDialog()` method discussed previously. The *prompt_message* is the label you would like used to prompt the user for input. When this method returns after the OK button is clicked, the return value is whatever the user typed into the text field.

11.5 Summary

KEY TERMS   Quite a few terms were introduced in this chapter:

1. *graphical user interface (GUI)*—a window of menus, buttons, and other objects that allows a user to interact with the class using the keyboard and the mouse.

2. *window*—a titled and bordered area of the display under class control.

3. *button*—a graphical representation of a button that can be operated with the mouse.

4. *menu*—a list of choices with a selection chosen with the mouse.

5. *event*—a user mouse click or keyboard input.

6. *event programming*—providing a method to be invoked by Java as a result of an event and not as a result of a call from another method.

7. *content pane*—the area of a window within the border wherein GUI content is placed.

8. *container*—a reference to a window content pane.

9. *window object*—a GUI object that can be added to a content pane.

10. *Layout Manager*—the strategy used to place window objects in a GUI.

11. `this`—a reference to the current object.

CONCEPTS Using the **Swing** package from the Java library or Java Foundation Classes, several useful window objects can be instantiated and used in a GUI. You studied the following:

JFrame—a bordered and titled window in which window objects may be placed.

FrameListener—a class containing a `windowClosing()` method. A **JFrame** registers a **FrameListener** object so that when the user selects CLOSE from the border menu, this `windowClosing()` method will be invoked.

Container—a reference to a **JFrame** content pane.

JLabel—a labeled window object containing simple text.

JButton—a labeled window object that can be selected with the mouse. When selected, the `actionPerformed()` method of the registered event handler object is automatically invoked.

JTextArea—a window object containing a field where text can be displayed by the class or entered/modified by the user.

JPanel—a window object that is subdivided into a five-location grid. Window objects may be added to each grid location.

JOptionPane—a window containing a preset GUI formed with the **JLabel**, **JButton**, and **JTextArea** objects.

Let's summarize the steps that can be used to write a class for a graphical user interface, or GUI:

1. The class declaration should include **"extends JFrame implements ActionListener"**.

2. The class constructor should:
   a. declare and initialize a **Container** reference.
   b. declare a **FrameListener** object and add it to the frame using the `addWindowListener()` method.
   c. declare and initialize window objects; if the object can be associated with a user action, register the `actionPerformed()` method of this class as the event handler.
   d. add these window objects using the **Container** add method, indicating the appropriate position for the object.
   e. set the size of the frame using the `setSize()` helper method.

3. Declare a "public void actionPerformed (ActionEvent e)" helper method that should:
   a. test the action just performed by the user with the `e.getActionCommand()` helper method.
   b. perform the necessary steps associated with this action.

4. A driver class should declare an object of this class type and display the GUI for the user with the `setVisible(true)` helper method. The driver class `main()` method does not exit but waits for the **FrameListener** to exit the class as a result of a user CLOSE menu choice.

11.6 Exercises

Short-answer questions

1. The area of a **JFrame** into which you may add window objects is called the _____.

2. A _____ is a reference to a **JFrame** content pane.

3. The title of a **JFrame** window may be changed with the _____ helper method.

4. A **JLabel** object may be placed onto a content pane using the _____ helper method of a **Container**.

5. The text within a **JLabel** object can be modified using the _____ helper method.

6. In event programming, certain helper methods are not invoked directly by the code. Rather they are invoked automatically in response to a _____ _____.

7. When the user selects the CLOSE menu option, Java attempts to invoke the _____ method of the registered **FrameListener** object.

8. Briefly explain how a **JButton** object indicates which actionPerformed() method is to be invoked in response to a mouse click.

9. Within an actionPerformed() method, how can code determine which event triggered the method being invoked?

10. List the necessary import lines that should be placed at the top of a class using the **Swing** classes.

11. List the five grid locations available in the default Layout Manager.

12. Give a section of code that could be used to (a) create a **JLabel** with the text This is a label and (b) place this object in the SOUTH grid of the current content pane.

13. Give a section of code that could be used to (a) create a **JButton** object labeled CLICK ME, (b) register the class actionPerformed() helper method as the event handler, and (c) add the button to the NORTH grid of the current content pane.

14. Give a section of code that could be used to (a) create a **JTextArea** object initially displaying This is text and (b) add this object to the CENTER grid of the current content pane.

15. Give a section of code to empty or clear the **JTextArea** object created in question 14.

16. Assume the user has entered a valid integer into the **JTextArea** object of question 14. Give a section of code to replace this number with the next integer. In other words, add 1 to the value. If the current number is 25, this code segment should replace the text with 26.

17. Give a section of code that could be used to display a sequential list of four names as **JLabel** objects in a window. For example, give the code to create the following window display:

```
A list of names:

Fred Smith
Julio Gonzaga
Ahmed Mola
Janet Weinburg
```

18. Modify the section of code from question 17 to include a column of ages for the list of names. For example:

```
A list of names:

Fred Smith        21
Julio Gonzaga     22
Ahmed Mola        19
Janet Weinburg    30
```

19. Using the `IO.showMessage()` helper method, give a section of code that could be added to the `actionPerformed()` method registered with a GUI so that an error message is displayed if the user generates an event that is not expected.

20. Refer back to question 19. Give a section of code to be added to the `actionPerformed()` method registered with a GUI to generate the error message without using the `IO` class. In other words, produce your own warning message window class.

Projects

1. Develop a class named **MyIO** that could be used in a manner similar to the `IO.showMessage()` method. Demonstrate your class with the following driver code:

```
MyIO warning = new MyIO ("This is a warning");
```

This window should consist of the label `This is a warning` and an OK button. When the button is clicked, the window should become invisible.

2. Develop a class with a GUI consisting of a **JLabel** and two **JButton** objects named a and b. The **JLabel** object should show which of the two buttons was last selected. For example, if the user has last clicked a, the label should say `You selected button A`.

3. Develop a class that could be used to present a GUI to the user with **JTextArea** object and a **JButton** object. The user should be able to type a word into the GUI. A button click should cause the word to be replaced with the capitalized version in the display.

4. Create a class that will present a GUI to the user to enable the conversion of a Fahrenheit temperature to Celsius.

5. Improve the GUI of Project 4 so that it allows a temperature conversion in either direction. Present the user with two buttons: one to indicate a conversion to Fahrenheit and one to indicate a conversion to Celsius.

6. Create a GUI application that could be used to convert three currencies. Present the user with a **JTextArea** where an amount can be entered. Also present a way for the user to select the from currency name and the to currency name. Make up three different currency names and exchange rates for your test.

7. Modify the four-function calculator example in Listing 11.VI so that if the user clicks on a function button before entering a number, the button click is ignored.

8. Implement Project 8 of Chapter 9 (a spelling checker) with an appropriate GUI.

9. Design a simple *MineField* game with a GUI consisting of a grid of 5 by 5 buttons. The buttons should initially be unlabeled. Each time a button is clicked, the button is labeled. One of the buttons consists of the mine. The other buttons are labeled with ! if they touch the mine square and a blank if they do not. The trick is to click all the buttons without clicking on the mine.

10. Creative Challenge: Modify the four-function calculator example of Listing 11.VI to use postfix notation (as do many Hewlett-Packard calculators). In this notation, the operator is entered after the two operands. In other words, instead of entering 5 + 6 =, the user would enter 5 ENTER 6 +. There is no = operation, and the ENTER operation indicates that one number has been completed prior to entering the second.

12

Programming
with Applets

Up to this point, you have learned quite a bit about writing Java programs to be run by a single user. Java became famous, however, because of Its association with the Internet. In this chapter, you will learn how some Java programs can be invoked from a Web page.

12.1 Internet overview

KEY TERMS
Web page, server

Let's do a quick overview of the Internet. When you "surf the Net," you are retrieving *Web pages* from remote computers called *servers*. A Web page is just a display of information. When you access a Web page, the information associated with that page is downloaded over the Internet to your computer and displayed. The display may consist of text, graphics, images, menus, and so forth.

KEY TERMS
browser, URL

Retrieving a Web page for display is done with a web *browser*. A browser is a program that knows how to ask servers for Web pages; it then prepares the information supplied by the server for display on your computer. Each Web page has an address by which it is referenced or retrieved. This address is called the page Uniform Resource Locator (or Location), abbreviated *URL*. If you know the URL (address) of a page, you can ask your browser to communicate with the server for that URL to retrieve the specific page and form the display.

For example, the URL for the Utah State University Department of Computer Science Web page is http://www.cs.usu.edu/index.html and I can view the information associated with this page by starting my browser and entering this URL:

When I enter this URL into my browser and press the Enter key, my browser sends a message to the server for this page asking for the page contents. The server doesn't actually return a displayable image of the page—rather it returns coded information telling the browser how to construct the page. That turns out to be much more efficient and is applicable to many different types of computers. By having the server return coded information, each computer can generate a display according to its own capabilities.

KEY TERM
HTML

The method of coding page information is called *HTML*, or Hypertext Markup Language. The simplest way to think of HTML is to consider your word processor. When you save a word processor file, it contains more than the text of your document. It also contains information indicating how the document is to be formatted and displayed or printed such as what text is bold, what text is in what font, what graphics go where, and so on. HTML is similar in that it indicates how a document is to be formatted.

Here's a simple example to try. Create a disk file containing the following HTML (Listing 12.I) and name the file `first.html`:

Listing 12.I

```
<html>
<body>
<H1> This is my first web page! </h1>
<HB>
<H3> Created in 2002. </h3>
</body>
</html>
```

Now start your browser. If a Web page is located on your own computer, you do not need to have a server. The URL of the file will be the phrase `file://` followed by the directory path and filename. For example:

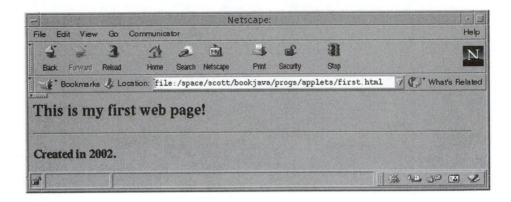

Let's look at the Web page. The first two lines

```
<html>
<body>
```

indicate that a Web page is beginning and that the following information represents the body of the page to be displayed. That's simple enough. The next three lines

```
<H1> This is my first web page! </h1>
<HB>
<H3> Created in 2002.</h3>
```

are the instructions for formatting the body of the page. As you have noticed, HTML commands or codes are enclosed in < > symbols. The code <H1> indicates that the following text is to be displayed in a large font. The </h1> code turns this formatting off or ends the code. The <HB> code indicates a solid line is to follow. The final code <H3> is for a small or normal size font. The ending lines

```
</body>
</html>
```

indicate that the body of the page and the Web page itself are ending.

The size of the large font, the appearance of the solid line, and so on are up to the computer and browser displaying the page. Different computers may display this page in a slightly different way, although all will follow the same format. There are many different formatting codes in HTML, and large books have been written on the language. You don't need to know everything, however, to generate some simple Web pages. Table 12.1 contains a few useful formatting codes.

There are many more HTML codes and capabilities—we'll leave those topics for another text and return to Java. Among the many features that may be in a Web page, one very interesting capability is the ability to insert the execution (input and

Table 12.1 **A few useful HTML codes**

code	action	ends with
<H1>	begin large text	<\h1>
<H2>	begin medium text	<\h2>
<H3>	begin small text	<\h3>
 	begin a new line (insert a Return)	*not needed*
<CENTER>	begin a centered section	<\center>
<HR>	insert a horizontal line	*not needed*
<P>	begin a new paragraph	<\p>

output) of a Java class! For example, consider the four-function calculator of Listing 11.VI. Here's a Web page with this calculator class embedded (Figure 12.1).

In other words, when a browser requests this Web page, the server will send the page HTML file and the calculator class to the browser. The browser can then display the page and run the class for the user. This nice little feature allows you to develop Web pages that not only display information but also interact in very interesting ways with the user. If a Java class is developed for a particular application, it can usually be embedded within a Web page with some minor modifications.

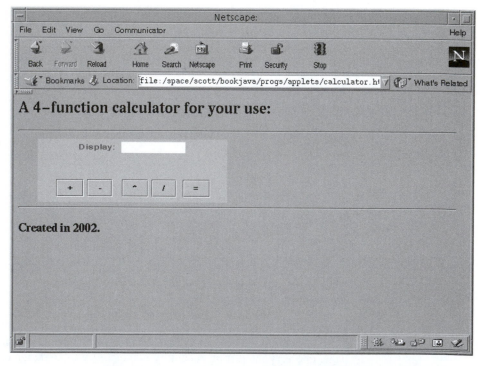

Figure 12.1 Calculator applet in a Web page

12.2 Applets

Let's look at how the **Calculator** class of Listing 11.VI was modified to be invoked from a Web page. We'll then look at how a Web page uses HTML to specify or create an instance of a Java class. A Java class that is intended to be invoked or instantiated from a Web page is known as an *applet*.

There are a variety of ways of designing applets. We'll use the **Swing** package we used in the previous chapter for GUIs. An applet should import the same libraries used in Chapter 11 for GUIs:

```
import javax.swing.*;
import java.awt.*;
```

If the applet has mouse events and buttons, you will also need the following:

```
import java.awt.event.*;
```

Technical Note: Not all browsers are up-to-date and capable of handling **Swing** applets. Netscape 4.x and Explorer 5.x versions are not, as they are installed. Netscape 6.x and Opera are. Remember that Java classes are interpreted on the computer running the application. In other words, the same Java class can be downloaded to any type computer and be executed or run as long as the computer has a Java interpreter. If you'll recall, this interpreter is called the Java Run-Time Environment, or JRE. Unfortunately, only Version 1.2 or higher versions of the JREs are capable of supporting **Swing**.

If your browser does not handle **Swing** applets, you have four options:

1. Install a newer browser.
2. Update the JRE on your computer with the Java plug-in.
3. Write applets without **Swing**.
4. Run applets using the appletviewer utility.

The first option is the simplest. Netscape 6.x and Opera are free and can be downloaded from:

http://www.netscape.com

http://www.opera.com

My experience is that Opera and Netscape can be installed on a computer that already has another browser without a conflict. In other words, you can have several browsers and choose which one you want to use. Opera may require you to click or double-click on an applet area to begin execution.

The second option is a bit more technical. It requires that you download a new JRE from Sun Microsystems, install it, and direct your browser to use `Swing` when such applets are invoked. Each time you create a Web page that invokes a `Swing` applet, you will need to modify it somewhat to instruct the browser to use the plug-in. This is explained later. The plug-in is free. Documentation and the download file can be found at:

http://www.java.sun.com/plugin

The third and fourth options are explained later in this text under 12.6 The appletviewer and 12.8 Older browsers.

Back to writing applets. We have written two types of classes in previous chapters. The first type contained a `main()` method. The second type of class did not and was intended to be created or instantiated from another driver class (containing `main()`). Listing 11.VI is an example of the latter. The **Calculator** class was instantiated in a simple driver class (Listing 11.VII):

```
public class TestCalculator
{
   public static void main (String[] args)
   {  Calculator gui = new Calculator ();
      gui.setVisible(true);
   }
}
```

All this driver class (**TestCalculator**) does is create a new **Calculator** and make it visible. The constructor of **Calculator** sets up the objects within the GUI. When the **Calculator** is made visible, the interaction with the user from that point on is via the **Calculator** buttons.

You may think of the Web page as taking over the responsibility of the driver class. The Web page creates a new **Calculator** and makes it visible. In our applets, we will not need a driver class, and there will be no `main()` methods.

Writing an applet is actually somewhat simpler than writing a GUI class. For one thing, you do not need to invoke a `setSize()` method because the size of the applet is determined by the Web page. Also, you do not invoke a `setTitle()` for an applet because they do not have a title. There is no need to do an `addWindowListener()` because the Web page browser is automatically the listener. When the browser page is replaced or the browser is stopped, the applet finishes.

There are two significant differences between the GUIs you learned to write in Chapter 11 and applets:

1. Rather than being based on **JFrame**, an applet is based on **JApplet**. In other words, the class declaration should extend **JApplet**:

```
class SomeClass extends JApplet
```

2. Rather than being set up in a constructor, the same operations for an applet are done in an `init()` method. An applet does not have a constructor.

Let's start with a GUI and then convert it into an applet. Here's a simple example of a GUI (similar to Listing 11.III) that simply displays the message Hello World! in a window:

```
// a class for a graphical user interface window
import javax.swing.*;
import java.awt.*;
import java.awt.event.*;

public class HelloGUI extends JFrame
{
  public HelloGUI ()
  { setTitle ("HELLO");
    FrameListener listen = new FrameListener();
    addWindowListener (listen);
    Container pane = getContentPane();
    JLabel label = new JLabel ("Hello World!");
    pane.add (label, BorderLayout.CENTER);
    setSize (300, 150);
  }
}
```

To convert this GUI to an applet, we start by eliminating the `setTitle()`, `addWindowListener()`, and `setSize()` method calls. (Since we don't add a listener, we can also delete the **FrameListener**.) Next, we change the name of the constructor to `init()`. Here's what we have now in file `HelloApplet.java` (Listing 12.II):

Listing 12.II

```
// an applet for a graphical user interface window: HelloApplet.java
import javax.swing.*;
import java.awt.*;

public class HelloGUI extends JApplet
{
  public void init ()
  { Container pane = getContentPane();
    JLabel label = new JLabel ("Hello World!");
    pane.add (label, BorderLayout.CENTER);
  }
}x
```

12.3 Invoking an Applet from HTML

We need one more HTML code in addition to those in Table 12.1 to add an applet to a Web page:

```
<APPLET   CODE = "classname" WIDTH = width
    HEIGHT = height > </APPLET>          .
```

Syntax form

The `APPLET` code specifies that at this position in the Web page, the named applet is to be invoked. This results in the GUI objects in the pane being displayed on the page. If you give the name of the applet class file, it should be in the same directory as the Web page. Here's the initial Web page for the **HelloGUI** applet (Listing 12.III):

Listing 12.III   Hello.html

```
<html>
<body>
<H1> A demonstration of an applet on a web page: </h1>
<HR>
<APPLET CODE = "HelloApplet.class" WIDTH = 300
   HEIGHT = 100> </APPLET>
<HR>
<H3> Created in 2002. </h3>
</body>
</html>
```

Technical Note: If you are using the Java plug-in with an older browser, you're not yet ready to reference this Web page with your browser. Some additional HTML codes need to be added to take advantage of the plug-in for **Swing**. Fortunately, you don't have to add them yourself. There is a simple utility that will do it for you called `HTMLConverter` that comes with the Java plug-in. To add the additional HTML codes for **Swing**, you may run the converter as a GUI or from a command line. The latter is probably the simpler approach:

```
% HTMLConverter Hello.html
```

Now we are ready to call up the browser. When the browser is given the URL for this Web page, the following is displayed:

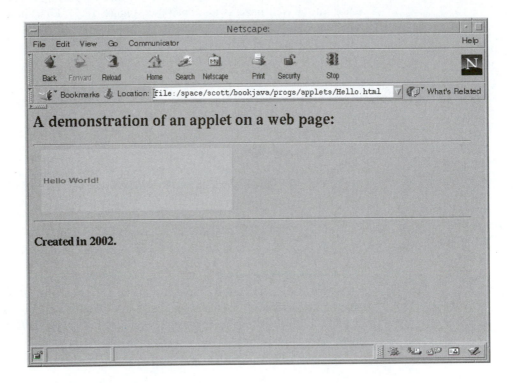

12.4 Converting Swing GUIs to Applets

If you have a working **Swing** GUI class (Chapter 11), we can summarize the steps to be taken to convert that class into an applet. Most of the conversion is removing lines from the GUI. The last two steps involve editing lines:

1. remove any calls to `setSize()`.
2. remove any calls to `setTitle()`.
3. remove any calls to `setWindowListener()` and the associated **FrameListener** creation.
4. edit the class declaration to `extend JApplet` instead of `extend JFrame`.
5. edit the constructor to `void init()` instead of `classname()`.

Now create an HTML file with an `<APPLET>` code at the position where you would like your applet displayed. (Add the extra HTML codes necessary for **Swing** using the `HTMLConverter` utility if you are using the plug-in.)

12.5 Example

Let's go back now and look at the complete files for placing our four-function calculator into a Web page as an applet (see Figure 12.1). First, here's the HTML file (Listing 12.IV):

Listing 12.IV   `Calculator.html`

```
<html>
<body>
<H1> A 4-function calculator for your use: </h1>
<HR>
<APPLET CODE = "CalculatorApplet.class" WIDTH = 300 HEIGHT = 100> </APPLET>
<HR>
<H2> Created in 2002.
</body>
</html>
```

Now, the **Calculator** class has an action listener for button events. The programming for this is the same as in our original GUI. In other words, the class for the applet is basically the same as the one developed in Listing 11.VI with the above five steps applied to the conversion to an applet (Listing 12.V):

Listing 12.V

```java
// A simple 4-function calculator as an applet
import javax.swing.*;
import java.awt.*;
import java.awt.event.*;

public class CalculatorApplet extends JApplet implements ActionListener
{
  private double value;
  JTextArea display = null;
  char action;

  public void init()
  { Container pane = getContentPane();
    JLabel label = new JLabel ("Display: ");
    display = new JTextArea ("", 1, 10);
    JButton plus = new JButton ("+");
       plus.addActionListener (this);
```

```
    JButton minus = new JButton ("-");
        minus.addActionListener (this);
    JButton mult = new JButton ("*");
        mult.addActionListener (this);
    JButton div = new JButton ("/");
        div.addActionListener (this);
    JButton equal = new JButton ("=");
        equal.addActionListener (this);

    JPanel southwest = new JPanel();
    JPanel southcenter = new JPanel();
    JPanel center = new JPanel();
    JPanel south = new JPanel();
    southwest.add (plus, BorderLayout.WEST);
    southwest.add (minus, BorderLayout.EAST);
    south.add (southwest, BorderLayout.WEST);
    southcenter.add (mult, BorderLayout.WEST);
    southcenter.add (div, BorderLayout.EAST);
    south.add (southcenter, BorderLayout.CENTER);
    south.add (equal, BorderLayout.EAST);
    center.add (label, BorderLayout.WEST);
    center.add (display, BorderLayout.EAST);
    pane.add (center, BorderLayout.CENTER);
    pane.add (south, BorderLayout.SOUTH);
  }

public void actionPerformed (ActionEvent e)
{ String button = e.getActionCommand();
  double newvalue = Double.parseDouble(display.getText());
  if (button.charAt(0) == '=')
  {   switch (action)
      { case '+':      value = newvalue + value;
                       break;
        case '-':      value = newvalue - value;
                       break;
        case '*':      value = newvalue * value;
                       break;
        case '/':      value = newvalue / value;
                       break;
      }
      display.setText(""+value);
    }
    else
    {   action = button.charAt(0);
        value = newvalue;
        display.setText ("");
    }
  }
}
```

12.6 The `appletviewer`

There is a quick way to test applet classes without the use of a browser. This approach is also handy if your browser is not capable of handling **Swing** applets. The Java system comes with a utility called `appletviewer` that is actually a small, minimal browser itself. To invoke this utility, use a command or a DOS window. Suppose your Web page (invoking the applet) is named `mypage.html`. The following

```
% appletviewer mypage.html
```

will start the `appletviewer` utility with the named Web page `mypage.html`.

The `appletviewer` utility is only capable of responding to the `<APPLET>` code, and the other HTML formatting codes are ignored. The net effect of this is that your applet is executed in a window, but the other text of the Web page is not displayed. The utility is simply a way to test the applet invoked from the Web page—not the Web page itself.

You do not need to add extra HTML codes with `HTMLConverter` to a Web page to use **Swing** with the `appletviewer` even if you have an older browser. The `appletviewer` is up-to-date. If we run the `appletviewer` with the Web page of Listing 12.V as follows

```
% appletviewer Calculator.html
```

we would see the calculator GUI without the associated Web page text.

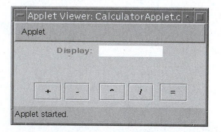

The applet class is fully functional—all the calculator buttons work. You just don't see the rest of the Web page.

The `appletviewer` can also be invoked directly from some integrated development environments. If you are using the Emacs system, you can run an applet by choosing the menu option JDE, Run Applet. If you are using TextPad, choose the Tools, Run Java Applet option. If you are using Forte, choose Load HTML File from the menu.

12.7 Additional applet features

Adding icons

An *icon* is simply a small graphic or picture used to represent some information you wish to convey to the user. Most icons have the file extension `.gif`. Although an icon is normally small, it really doesn't need to be. You can create your own icon images with the Microsoft `Paint` utility, a digital camera, a word processor, a graphics program, a scanner, or any number of other methods.

There are undoubtedly many icons already on your computer disk. If you are running a Windows operating system, click on `START` in the lower left corner of your screen. In the menu you see, click on `Find` and then on `Files and Folders`. Next, in the `named` box, enter `*.gif` and press the Enter key. You are asking Windows to find all the image files on your disk. Any of these files can be treated as icons.

For example, on my computer, there is an image file named `javalogo.gif` in my Java JRE directory:

This icon can be added to the front of a **Jlabel** object to be displayed as part of the label. To do so, use the following syntax:

```
ImageIcon icon_name = new ImageIcon ( image_filename );
    labelobject.setIcon ( icon_name );
```

Syntax form

Let's go back to the applet of Listing 12.II and modify it to associate this icon to a label to be displayed (Listing 12.VI):

Listing 12.VI

```
// an applet with an icon : JavaApplet.java
import javax.swing.*;
import java.awt.*;
```

```
public class HelloGUI extends JApplet
{
  public void init ()
  { setTitle ("Applet with an icon");
    Container pane = getContentPane();
    JLabel label = new JLabel (" Created with Java!");
    ImageIcon icon = new ImageIcon ( "javalogo.gif" );
    label.addIcon (icon);
    pane.add (label, BorderLayout.CENTER);
  }
}
```

Now if we execute this applet using the `appletviewer` utility, we see the label beginning with this little icon:

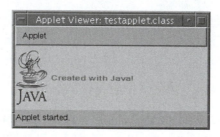

Just a note: An interesting source of icon images is other Web pages you encounter on the Internet. If you are using Netscape, you will find that each time you bring up a Web page, the image or icon files associated with the display are stored on your computer in a subdirectory called Cache. These files stay there when you are through with the browser. (Not forever, of course. When the directory reaches a certain size, the older images are replaced with newer ones. You can also clear the Cache subdirectory with an option in the browser.) You can often find a variety of nice little images to spruce up an applet.

Applet parameters

If you design a Java class with `public` methods, you would often expect that class to be invoked or instantiated from a number of other different applications. One class is reused for different applications as appropriate. The same is true for applets. To write a general class helper method, you used parameters. Parameters are also available for applets. In this case, however, the parameters are not being passed to the applet from another Java method but from the browser.

When an applet needs a parameter value from the browser, the browser determines the correct value from the Web page using the `<PARAM>` code:

```
<PARAM NAME = param_name  VALUE = " string_value " >
```

Syntax form

This code should be placed after opening the applet reference with the <APPLET> code and before closing the applet reference with </applet>. In other words, it must be between the <APPLET> and </applet> codes. Parameter values must be strings. The name given to a parameter must conform to Java variable naming rules.

Suppose we have an applet that can calculate the percentage of a number. In one Web page, we would like the user to enter a loan amount and then display the simple interest. The Web page might look like Listing 12.VII:

Listing 12.VII

```
<html>
<body>
<H3> Loan calculations at 12% </h3>
<APPLET CODE = "Percent.class" WIDTH = 200 HEIGHT = 100>
<PARAM NAME=percent VALU ="0.12">
<PARAM NAME=pupose VALUE="loan amount">
</applet>
</body>
</html>
```

In this Web page, we simply invoke the "Percent.class" applet and pass it two parameters: the parameter string "0.12" representing a percentage desired and the parameter string "loan amount" representing the purpose of the percentage. These two parameters are named percent and purpose.

Within the applet itself, you can retrieve the value of parameters using the getParameter() helper method of the **JApplet** (or **Applet**) class:

```
String variable_name = getParameter ( "parameter_ name" );
```

Syntax form

This method requires the name of the Web page parameter as a string and returns the **String** assigned as the VALUE of the parameter by the Web page. Now we can write the needed "Percent.class" applet (Listing 12.VIII):

Listing 12.VIII

```java
// Percent.java
import javax.swing.*;
import java.awt.*;
import java.awt.event.*;

public class Percent extends JApplet implements ActionListener
{
  private double value;
  JTextArea display = null;
  JLabel result = null;
  String percent_string;
  String purpose_string;

  public init()
  { Container pane = getContentPane();
    percent_string = getParameter ("percent");
    purpose_string = getParameter ("purpose");
    JLabel label = new JLabel ("Enter " + purpose_string);
    display = new JTextArea ("", 1, 10);
    result = new JLabel ("result is:                    ");
    JButton calc = new JButton ("calculate");
       plus.addActionListener (this);
    pane.add (label, BorderLayout.WEST);
    pane.add (calc, BorderLayout.CENTER);
    pane.add (result, BorderLayout.EAST);
    pane.add (display, BorderLayout.SOUTH);
  }

  public void actionPerformed (ActionEvent e)
  {    double percent_double = ParseDouble(percent_string);
       double x = ParseDouble(display.getText());
       x = x * percent_double;
       result.setText ("result is: " + x);
  }
}
```

OK, suppose later we need a Web page where users can enter a product price and have the Web page calculate the sales tax. We can simply reuse the same applet (Listing 12.IX):

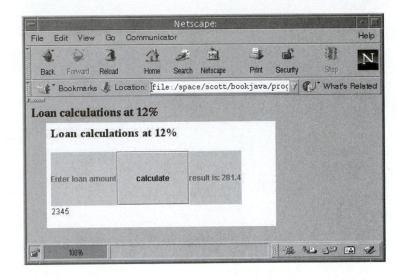

Listing 12.IX

```html
<html>
<body>
<H3> Sales tax calculations at 6% </h3>
<APPLET CODE = "Percent.class" WIDTH = 200 HEIGHT = 100>
<PARAM NAME=percent VALUE ="0.06">
<PARAM NAME=pupose VALUE="sales tax">
</applet>
</body>
</html>
```

In this case, we pass two different parameters to the **Percent** applet: a percent rate of 0.06 for sales tax and a purpose of `"sales tax"` for the prompt message.

Timers and dates

The **Timer** class is a part of **Swing** and can be used in applets and standalone Java applications. Think of it as learning some advanced Java features. Up to this point, you have learned how to handle mouse click events (Chapter 11). There are, of course, other events.

A **Timer** object can be programmed to automatically create an event according to a time interval:

```
Timer timer_name = new Timer ( num_milliseconds , this );
timer_name. start( );
. . .
variable_name. stop( );
```

Syntax form

The constructor for the **Timer** class creates a virtual alarm clock that generates an event after the indicated number of milliseconds has elapsed. It then resets for the next alarm event. The start() helper method turns the **Timer** on, and the stop() method turns it off. In between is a continuous stream of events that are spaced as indicated in time.

The this parameter in the **Timer** constructor indicates that the actionPerformed() method of the applet will be invoked each time the timer goes off. You will remember that this requires the applet to implement actionListener just as we did for button events.

Suppose we wish to create an applet that displays the current date and is updated every second while the user views the rest of the Web page. The **Date** class of the **util** package can be used to determine the current date and time:

```
Date date_name = new Date( );
```

Syntax form

A **Date** object can be concatenated with a string for display. For example:

```
Date new = new Date( );
String today = "Today is: " + now;
```

We now have enough information to write our applet. It will consist of a single label that is initialized to the current date. Every 1000 msec (1 sec), the label text will be automatically updated to show the new date (Listing 12.X):

Listing 12.X

```
// an applet class to test timers and dates
import javax.swing.*;
import java.awt.*;
```

```
import java.awt.event.*;
import java.util.*;

public class TimeTest extends JApplet implements ActionListener
{ private JLabel label = null;
  Container pane = null;

  public void init ()
  {
    pane = getContentPane();
    label = new JLabel();
    Date now = new Date();
    label.setText ("Date is: " + now);
    pane.add (label, BorderLayout.NORTH);
    Timer ticks = new Timer (1000, this);
    ticks.start();
  }

  public void actionPerformed (ActionEvent e)
  { Date now = new Date();
    label.setText ("Date is: " + now);
  }
}
```

When I tested this applet using the `appletviewer`, I saw the following display. Every second, the date would change. Try it!

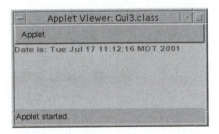

12.8 Older browsers

If you are designing an applet that you expect a variety of other computer users to access, it's a good bet that some of these other computers will have older browsers that are not capable of handling **Swing** applets. Remember, when a Web page is accessed, the HTML file and the applet class file are both downloaded to the user's computer. The applet class is interpreted on the user's computer and not on the computer where the applet was found.

One solution to this dilemma is to use an older library for applets. An applet class can extend `Applet` instead of extend `JApplet`. The **Applet** class is

Table 12.2   Some older style applet GUI objects for the `Applet` class

GUI object class	some useful methods	closest `Swing` object class
Label	setText()	JLabel
Button	setText()	JButton
	addActionListener ()	
TextArea	setText()	JTextArea
	getText()	

older than **JApplet** and does not require **Swing**. If a browser is capable of handling applets at all, it can probably handle this older version.

Instead of importing the **Swing** library, you should import the following library:

```
import java.applet.*;
```

The **Applet** class doesn't handle icons and images very well, but there are limited-feature labels, buttons, text fields, and so on for GUI objects. With the GUI objects you have learned so far, the transition is simple. You just leave off the capital J in front of each class. In other words, rather than declaring **JLabel** objects, you declare **Label** objects. These older GUI objects do not have the same capability or number of member methods as the **Swing** objects, but they are not too bad for simple applets (Table 12.2).

The **Applet** class has one other major difference: It doesn't have a content pane. In the **JApplet** class, you would add objects to the content pane of the window. In the **Applet** class, you add objects directly to the **Applet** itself. The best way to think of this is to consider the **Applet** class as a single pane in itself—not a class containing a pane (or many panes).

In Java, it's easy to get carried away with jargon like the above that might not be readily understandable to the new student. Here it is in a simple demonstration. We'll start with the applet of Listing 12.II using the more capable **JApplet** class. In this applet, the lines that are to be modified are commented out so they no longer have an effect. The replacement line (if any) is below the commented line and in italics (Listing 12.XI):

Listing 12.XI

```
// an applet from Listing 12.II modified to use the older Applet class
// import javax.swing.*;
import java.applet.*;
import java.awt.*;

// public class HelloGUI extends JApplet
public class HelloGUI extends Applet
```

```
{
    public void init ()
    { // Container pane = getContentPane();
      // JLabel label = new JLabel ("Hello World!");
      Label label = new Label ("Hello World!");
      // pane.add (label, BorderLayout.CENTER);
      add (label, BorderLayout.CENTER);
    }
}
```

Since we are not using **Swing**, there is no reason to add the extra HTML to the Web page with the HTMLConverter utility to use the plug-in. Here's the result with an older browser:

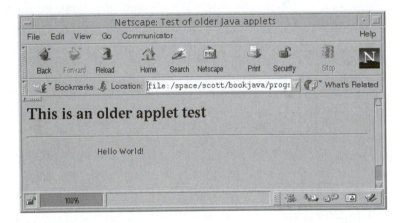

It doesn't look much different, does it?

12.9 Security with applets

We have an interesting issue to address when writing applets. Since they are actually to be executed on remote computers that access your Web page, they have the potential to do harm to someone else's computer.

If this doesn't bother you, consider that each time you access a Web page with your browser, you may be executing someone else's applet programs. If someone wants to infect you with a virus, the simplest approach is to have you run their infecting program on your computer. If someone wants sensitive information on your computer—financial data, email addresses, phone numbers, and so on—again the simplest way to get those data is to have you run their snooping program on your computer. Since a browser is downloading applets (and other similar executables) often without the user's knowledge, an applet might be considered dangerous.

For this reason, Java has been designed so that applets cannot read or write disk files on other computers. They can only interact with the user and generate displays. Other executables downloaded by your browser are often not so protected, and this is a common way of spreading a virus. Naturally, this limits what you can accomplish with an applet, which most feel is a good thing!

12.10 Summary

KEY TERMS   The terms introduced in this chapter deal with using Java on the Internet:

1. *Web page*—a display of information to be provided to a remote user, consisting of text, graphics, and possibly applets and other objects.

2. *server*—a remote computer and program capable of returning a Web page in response to a browser request.

3. *browser*—a local application program used to retrieve Web pages from servers and format a display for the user with the Web page content.

4. *URL*—the Universal Resource Locator or address of a Web page.

5. *HTML*—Hypertext Markup Language; used to specify the content and format of a Web page.

6. *applet*—a Java class capable of being downloaded and then instantiated or invoked by a browser.

7. *icon*—a graphic used to annotate information.

CONCEPTS   The chapter began with showing you how to write simple Web pages with a handful of useful HTML codes. In the previous chapter, you learned to develop Java classes and applications with GUIs using the **Swing** library or package. Your GUIs consisted of **JLabel**, **JTextField**, and **JButton** objects. In this chapter, you learned that an applet can also be constructed using these same objects. You learned that applets are invoked from a Web page using the HTML code of <APPLET>.

An applet is a helper class to a Web page. When an applet is referenced, the init() method of the applet is invoked. An applet may have objects that register a listener method to receive control when a GUI event occurs.

While GUI classes from the previous chapter extended the JFrame class, an applet extends either the **JApplet** or the older **Applet** class. There are five basic steps to converting a Java class GUI into an applet:

1. remove any calls to setSize().

2. remove any calls to setTitle().

3. remove any calls to setWindowListener() and the associated **FrameListener** creation.

4. edit the class declaration to extend JApplet instead of extend JFrame.

5. edit the constructor to void init() instead of "*classname*()".

You also learned that a **JLabel** may be associated with an icon and that an applet may be passed parameters from the parent Web page.

12.11   Exercises

Short-answer questions

1. The language of formatting codes used to specify the content of a Web page is abbrievated __ __ __ __.
2. A _____ is a computer and program used to supply Web pages to remote browser programs.
3. A _____ is a program used to request a Web page from a server and then format the page content for display.
4. A graphic used to annotate information is often called an _____.
5. The HTML code used to specify that the following text is to be formatted in a large font is _____.
6. The HTML code used to specify that the following text is to be formatted in a new paragraph is _____.
7. A standalone Java application with a GUI using the **Swing** library packaage extends the _____ class. An applet GUI using **Swing** extends the _____ class.
8. Name three methods of the **JFrame** class that are not needed in an applet extending the **JApplet** class.
9. Explain the three pieces of information or parameters that must be supplied in an <APPLET> code to invoke an applet.
10. Show the HTML code that might be used to execute an applet named test.class in a box 500 wide × 250 pixels high.
11. An applet can be tested without a fully capable browser using the _____ utility provided with the JRE.
12. Suppose an icon named picture.gif resided in the current directory. Show how this icon can be associated and displayed with the **JLabel** object named mylabel.
13. Consider the following applet instantiation or creation in a Web page. Show what should be added to pass the parameter named purchaser as the string Fred Smith.

    ```
    <APPLET CODE="invoice.class" HEIGHT=400 WIDTH=400>
    </applet>
    ```

14. If a Web page is developed using the <APPLET> code of question 12, show how the following variable could be set to the value passed in the <PARAM> code of the Web page:

    ```
    String webparam;
    ```

15. Briefly explain how you would convert an applet that extends **JApplet** to one that extends **Applet**.

16. Which class, **JApplet** or **Applet**, is more likely to be compatible with older browsers?

17. Which class of the **util** package can be used to determine the current time?

18. Give the Java code that might be used to create a **Timer** to produce an event every 5 sec.

19. Briefly describe the purpose of the implements actionListener phrase added to a class definition that intends to create **Timer** objects.

20. Suppose an applet has two **Timer** objects running at different rates. Speculate how an actionPerformed() method of the applet might distinguish between the two and determine which object created the event. Create a simple test for your hypothesis.

Projects

1. Construct a simple Web page to display your name and address information.

2. Construct a simple applet to provide an author's name to a Web page. Each time this applet is invoked, it should display your name and address.

3. Construct a simple Web page to use the applet created in Project 2. Show that this applet can be invoked from more than one Web page.

4. Demonstrate a Web page and applet to display an icon. You may use any .gif file you can locate.

5. Construct a simple applet to allow a user to enter two integer numbers and then display the sum of those integers. Demonstrate your applet with the appletviewer utility.

6. Construct a simple applet to display the current date. The date can be determined in Java using the **util** package and **Date** class. A **Date** object can assigned to a label or text field as if it were a string:

```
import java.util.*;
. . .
Date now = new Date();
```

7. Implement Project 2 of Chapter 11 as an applet and demonstrate it with the appletviewer utility.

8. Implement Project 3 of Chapter 11 as an applet and demonstrate it with the appletviewer utility.

9. Construct a Web page and applet to allow a user to convert between three different currencies. The GUI should allow the user to enter an amount and then click on a FROM currency choice and a TO currency choice. The applet should then display the converted value. You can easily find current exchange rates on the Internet or make them up for hypothetical currencies.

10. Creative Challenge: Implement a Web page and applet combination that shows the number of seconds since a button was last pressed. If a user does not press the button within 10 sec, the button should automatically disappear.

IO, DiskInput, and DiskOutput Classes

The **IO**, **DiskInput**, and **DiskOutput** classes are used extensively throughout this book. At this point, you know enough Java to write these classes yourself. It is helpful to look at how these classes are implemented because they are not part of the standard Java library. They were provided to allow you to begin writing useful and meaningful Java programs prior to learning the additional syntax and concepts that the standard Java library requires.

A.1 **IO class**

The **IO** class is based on the **JOptionPane** library of **Swing**. In fact, it is basically a simple wrapper for this useful library (Listing A.I). The basic methods of the **JOptionPane** class used in the **IO** class were explained in Chapter 12.

Listing A.I

```
import javax.swing.JOptionPane;

public class IO
```

```
{
  public static void showMessage (String s)
  { JOptionPane.showMessageDialog (null, s);
  }


  public static void showValue (String s, double d)
  { JOptionPane.showMessageDialog (null, s+d);
  }


  public static void showValue (String s, float f)
  { JOptionPane.showMessageDialog (null, s+f);
  }


  public static void showValue (String s, int i)
  { JOptionPane.showMessageDialog (null, s+i);
  }


  public static void showValue (String s, char c)
  { JOptionPane.showMessageDialog (null, s+c);
  }


  public static void showValue (String s1, String s2)
  { IO.showMessage (s1+s2);
  }


  public static double readDouble (String prompt)
  { String s;
    s = JOptionPane.showInputDialog (prompt);
    return (Double.parseDouble(s));
  }


  public static float readFloat (String prompt)
  { String s;
    s = JOptionPane.showInputDialog (prompt);
    return (Float.parseFloat(s));
  }


  public static int readInt (String prompt)
  { String s;
    s = JOptionPane.showInputDialog (prompt);
    return (Integer.parseInt(s));
  }

  public static char readChar (String prompt)
  { String s;
    s = JOptionPane.showInputDialog (prompt);
    if (s == null)
       return 0;
    else if (s.length () > 0)
       return s.charAt (0);
```

```
    else
        return '\n';
}

public static String readString (String prompt)
{ return (JOptionPane.showInputDialog (prompt));
}

public static String concatenate (String s1, String s2)
{ return (s1 + s2);
}

public static String concatenate (String s1, double d)
{ return (s1 + d);
}

}
```

Look at how the **JOptionPane** class is utilized and ask yourself if it is **static** or dynamic. That's right: It's **static**. We did not need to create an object and assign it to a reference variable. The class contains only constants and helper methods—as far as we are concerned. We only have one such object at a time.

A.2 IO **helper method descriptions**

Most of the helper methods consist of wrapper methods for the **JOptionPane** class of the **Swing** library. These wrappers are simplifications to allow the teaching of a principle without the need to teach new syntax and data types.

The IO.showMessage() method is a wrapper for

JOptionPane.showMessageDialog().

The IO.showValue() method has five overloaded matches or options. Each of these overloaded methods accepts a string message and a **float**, **double**, **int**, **char**, or **String** value to be displayed. This value is concatenated onto the end of the message string, and the JOptionPane.showMessageDialog() is called. It is the responsibility of the built-in concatenation operation to convert each value into a comparable string.

The IO.readString() method is also a wrapper for

JOptionPane.showInputDialog()

—they both do exactly the same thing.

The IO.readDouble(), IO.readInt(), and IO.readFloat() methods invoke the JOptionPane.showInputDialog() method to input a string from the user. The string is then converted into an appropriate numeric value using the static parse method of the Java numeric class. For example, the **String** variable *s* is converted to an integer value for return with the following:

```
return (Integer.parseInt(s));
```

Table A.1   Static numeric parsing methods

Static numeric class	Conversion from string to numeric type
Double	parseDouble (*string*) ;
Float	parseFloat (*string*) ;
Integer	parseInt (*string*) ;

As you will recall, each numeric data type has an associated static class with a parsing method to convert a string into that numeric type. Each of these parsing methods returns the appropriate numeric type. These are reviewed in Table A.1.

Inputting a character with IO.readChar() is a bit more complicated. Since the user is allowed to input a string with JOptionPane.showInputDialog(), this string must be converted to the appropriate single character. IO.readChar() assumes the following:

1. If the string entered by the user is empty, return the number code 0.

2. If the string is nonempty and of nonzero length, return the first character of the string.

3. If the string is nonempty but of zero length, return the \n character.

Other definitions could also be implemented. There is nothing special about these.

The IO.concatenate() method is just a wrapper for the + operator. The bottom line is that you didn't really need some of the IO methods after all! Teaching I/O concepts using the **IO** class allowed us to put off some of the syntax and data operations you were not yet ready to learn.

A.3 DiskInput class

The **DiskInput** class is based on the **BufferedReader** class in the standard library and explained in Chapter 9 (Listing 9.II). A **BufferedReader** object allows an application to open a disk file for line input. The two most useful helper methods are summarized in Table A.2.

This class and the associated helper methods are not static like the **JOptionPane** class. For simplicity, this method does not **extend** the **BufferedReader** class but declares a reference to such an object as a private class variable. (One could certainly implement **DiskInput** with inheritance.)

Table A.2   Useful BufferedReader helper methods

method	purpose	returns
readLine()	read the next file line.	a string
close()	close the file—no further input will occur.	*nothing*

Listing A.II

```java
import java.io.*;
public class DiskInput
{
    private BufferedReader input = null;
    private String s;
    public void open (String filename)
    { try
        {   input = new BufferedReader (new FileReader (filename));
        }
        catch (Exception e)
        {   IO.showMessage("file not found!");
            System.exit(0);
        }
    }

    public void close ()
    { try
        {   input.close();
        }
        catch (Exception e)
        {   IO.showMessage ("file closing error!");
            System.exit(0);
        }
    }

    private void readLine ()
    {   try
        {   s = input.readLine();
        }
        catch (Exception e)
        {   IO.showMessage ("incorrect input!");
            System.exit(0);
        }
    }

    public int readInt ()
    { readLine();
      return (Integer.parseInt(s));
    }

    public double readDouble ()
    { readLine();
      return (Double.parseDouble(s));
    }

    public char readChar ()
    { readLine();
      if (s == null)
          return 0;
      else if (s.length () > 0)
          return s.charAt (0);
      else
          return '\n';
    }

    public String readString ()
    {   readLine();
        return s;
    }
}
```

A.4 DiskInput helper method descriptions

The first helper method to examine is open(). This method creates or allocates a new **BufferedReader** object to do the actual disk input operations. This allocation in turn allocates a **FileReader** object to be associated with a particular filename. (We don't need to be concerned with the **FileReader** class—that is the responsibility of the person who wrote the **BufferedReader** class.) This allocation is within a **try-catch** block because it may fail if the file does not exist or is not openable.

The **DiskInput** class is dynamic (not static) because one might certainly wish to have more than one disk file being read at the same time.

When a **BufferedReader** object is allocated or created, the system finds the appropriate file on the disk and reads the first block of lines from the file into a scratch system memory area called a *buffer*. From that point on, each time your application desires a line from the disk file, it is actually read from the buffer. Each **DiskInput** object (with the private BufferedReader object) is associated with its own buffer.

There are two reasons for this approach. First, system memory can be accessed much faster than a disk file. Second, it is much faster for the computer to read N lines in one disk-access operation than it is to read one line in N operations. When the buffer is exhausted, Java automatically fills it again with the next block of lines from the file.

The close() method of **DiskInput** frees the system buffer. Although this is also nested in a **try-catch** block, there are very few situations where a close() method might fail.

The actual input operations from the **BufferedReader** object are done with the readLine() method of that class. This method simply returns the next line of the file. A line is defined as all text up to but not including the end-of-line character or \n. If you attempt to read beyond the end of a file, the catch block will receive control.

The other helper methods of **DiskInput** are very similar to the **IO** class. Instead of getting a line from the user, they get a line from the disk file using the **BufferedReader** readLine() helper method. Strings are again converted to numeric values using the static type classes of Java (refer to Section A.2).

By using the **DiskInput** class instead of **BufferedReader** directly, you were able to do disk input without first learning about **try-catch** blocks and exceptions.

A.5 DiskOutput class

The **DiskOutput** class is based on the **PrintWriter** class of the Java standard library explained in Chapter 9. Just like the **DiskInput** class, this class does not **extend** the **PrintWriter** class. For simplicity, we only define a private **PrintWriter** reference for each **DiskOutput** object.

Since we may wish to have more than one disk file open for writing at any one time, the **DiskOutput** class (and the nested **PrintWriter** class) are not **static**. The two useful methods of **PrintWriter** are summarized in Table A.3.

Table A.3   Useful methods of `PrintWriter`

method	purpose	returns
close()	flush the buffer to disk; deallocate the buffer.	*nothing*
println()	write a string to the buffer and then flush the buffer if it is full.	*nothing*

Listing A.III

```java
import java.io.*;

public class DiskOutput
{
  private PrintWriter output = null;
  private String s;

  public void open (String filename)
  { try
    { output = new PrintWriter (new FileOutputStream (filename));
    }
    catch (Exception e)
    { IO.showMessage ("file cannot be created!");
      System.exit(0);
    }
  }

  public void close ()
  { try
    { output.close();
    }
    catch (Exception e)
    { IO.showMessage ("file closing error!");
      System.exit(0);
    }
  }

  public void writeString (String s)
  { output.println (s);
  }

  public void writeInt (int i)
  { output.println (""+i);
  }

  public void writeDouble (double d)
  { output.println (""+d);
  }

  public void writeChar (char c)
  { output.println (""+c);
  }

}
```

A.6 DiskOutput class helper method descriptions

The open() method of **DiskOutput** allocates a new **PrintWriter** to do the actual disk output operations. This allocation in turn creates a new **FileOutputStream** to be associated with the filename. (We do not need to be concerned with the methods and use of the **FileOutputStream**—that was the responsibility of the person who wrote the **PrintWriter** class.) This allocation is done in a try-catch block because a failure exception may occur if the disk is write protected, is not in the drive, or for some other such reason.

Just as with the **DiskInput** class, the opening of a file causes the system to allocate a system memory buffer. Each time a writeInt() or similar method is invoked, the associated argument string is written to the buffer. When the buffer is full, it is then physically written to the disk. Also, when a file is closed with the close() method, the buffer is written to the disk (and deallocated).

So an application that crashes, fails, or otherwise does not reach the close() method of **DiskOutput** may leave some of the information still in the buffer and lost. For this reason, a file is not considered successfully written until the close() method is invoked.

The writeInt() and comparable methods closely resemble the similarly named methods of the **IO** class (refer to Section A.2).

Java Reserved Words

The following words are reserved in Java 1.2 and 1.3 and should not be utilized for variable, method, or class names.

abstract	boolean	break	byte	case
catch	char	class	const*	continue
default	do	double	else	extends
false	final	finally	float	for
goto*	if	implements	import	instanceof
int	interface	long	native	new
null	package	private	protected	public
return	short	static	super	switch
synchronized	this	throw	throws	transient
true	try	void	volatile	while

*Reserved but not actually utilized in current implementations.

ASCII codes

The following table represents the numeric codes used for the portion of the Java ISO Unicode standard for printable and other common characters.

ASCII table of characters and associated codes

char	dec	hex	char	dec	hex	char	dec	hex
NUL	0	00	+	43	2B	V	86	56
SOH	1	01	,	44	2C	W	87	57
STX	2	02	-	45	2D	X	88	58
ETX	3	03	.	46	2E	Y	89	59
EOT	4	04	/	47	2F	Z	90	5A
ENQ	5	05	0	48	30	[	91	5B
ACK	6	06	1	49	31	\	92	5C
BEL	7	07	2	50	32	]	93	5D
BS	8	08	3	51	33	^	94	5E
HT	9	09	4	52	34	_	95	5F
NL	10	0A	5	53	35	`	96	60
VT	11	0B	6	54	36	a	97	61
NP	12	0C	7	55	37	b	98	62
CR	13	0D	8	56	38	c	99	63
SO	14	0E	9	57	39	d	100	64
SI	15	0F	:	58	3A	e	101	65
DLE	16	10	;	59	3B	f	102	66
DC1	17	11	<	60	3C	g	103	67
DC2	18	12	=	61	3D	h	104	68

ASCII table of characters and associated codes

char	dec	hex	char	dec	hex	char	dec	hex
DC3	19	13	>	62	3E	i	105	69
DC4	20	14	?	63	3F	j	106	6A
NAK	21	15	@	64	40	k	107	6B
SYN	22	16	A	65	41	l	108	6C
ETB	23	17	B	66	42	m	109	6D
CAN	24	18	C	67	43	n	110	6E
EM	25	19	D	68	44	o	111	6F
SUB	26	1A	E	69	45	p	112	70
ESC	27	1B	F	70	46	q	113	71
FS	28	1C	G	71	47	r	114	72
GS	29	1D	H	72	48	s	115	73
RS	30	1E	I	73	49	t	116	74
US	31	1F	J	74	4A	u	117	75
space	32	20	K	75	4B	v	118	76
!	33	21	L	76	4C	w	119	77
"	34	22	M	77	4D	x	120	78
#	35	23	N	78	4E	y	121	79
$	36	24	O	79	4F	z	122	7A
%	37	25	P	80	50	{	123	7B
&	38	26	Q	81	51	|	124	7C
'	39	27	R	82	52	}	125	7D
(	40	28	S	83	53	~	126	7E
)	41	29	T	84	54	DEL	127	7F
*	42	2A	U	85	55			

Answers to Odd-Numbered Short Answer Questions

Chapter 1

1. volatile

3. declaration

5. literal

7. A semantic error is an error in logic or intent while a syntax error is an error in spelling or grammer.

9. a)

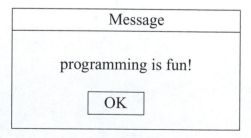

Message
programming is fun!
OK

b)

```
┌─────────────────────────────────────────┐
│                 Input                   │
├─────────────────────────────────────────┤
│            enter the cost:              │
│       ┌───────────────────────┐         │
│       │                       │         │
│       └───────────────────────┘         │
│     ┌─────────┐      ┌─────────────┐     │
│     │   OK    │      │   Cancel    │     │
│     └─────────┘      └─────────────┘     │
└─────────────────────────────────────────┘
```

c) (assume the value of variable 'cost' is 5.43)

```
┌─────────────────────────────────────────┐
│                Message                  │
├─────────────────────────────────────────┤
│                                         │
│          the cost is:  5.43             │
│            ┌─────────────┐              │
│            │     OK      │              │
│            └─────────────┘              │
└─────────────────────────────────────────┘
```

11. a) new_car_cost

    b) yards_gained

    c) distance_root

    d) ave_score

    e) pay_off_time

13. a) `x = (alpha * y * y + 3.0) / (4.0 - alpha) * pi;`

    b) `val = (x + y) * ( x - y);`

    c) `cost = rate * (value - 1.0);`

15. A decimal point will be assumed at the far right of the number entered.

17. A compiler does not know the programmers intent or the logic associated with a solution and cannot verify that a program class meets the programmer's desires.

19. The reserved words seen in Chapter 1 are public, class, static, void, main, and double. String, args, IO, showMessage, showValue, and readDouble have special meanings. You would not be wrong in considering these as reserved (at this point in your study), but they are technically not reserved. You will learn more of this concept as you progress.

Chapter 2

1. condition or conditional

3. definite or counted

5. before

7. indefinite

9. a) false

b) true

c) true

d) false

e) true

11.

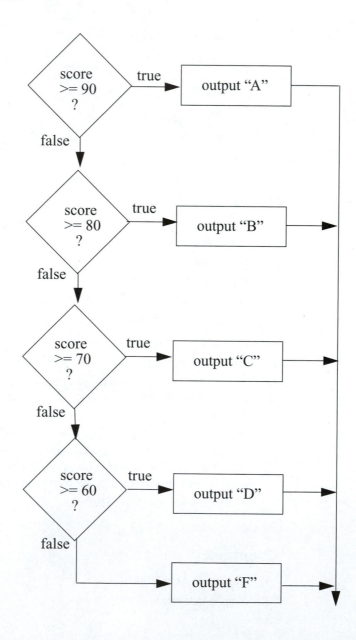

13. a) `if (cost < 0.0) IO.showMessage ("YES");`
      `else ;`

  b) `if (cost > 0.0)`
        `if (cost <= 100.0)  IO.showMessage ("YES");`
        `else ;`
     `else ;`

15. `count = 0.0;`
   `while (count < 25.0)`
   `{ value = IO.readDouble ();`
    `sum = sum + value;`
    `count = count + 1;`
   `}`

17. a) The parentheses are missing in the conditional statement.

b) The braces are missing around the two statements to be executed when the conditional statement is true.

19. `if (age < 100.0)`
   `if (age > 25.0)`
     `IO.showMessage ("YES");`
   `else IO.showMessage ("NO");`
  `else IO.showMessage ("NO");`

Chapter 3

1. (an) argument

3. An argument is a value passed to a helper method. A parameter is a helper method variable into which an argument value will be copied.

5. default library

7. double

9. A helper method should be declared above the method where it will be used or invoked.

11. `square_root = Math.sqrt (distance);`

13. The variable "cost" is declared twice—once as a parameter and once as a local variable.

15. `IO.showValue ("payment is:", Payment(52.0, 0.09));`

17. Classes are named beginning with an uppercase letter. Helper methods are named beginning with a lowercase letter. If a helper method consists of more than one word, the first letter of subsequent words (after the first) is capitalized. Variables are named using lowercase. Constants are named using all uppercase.

19. `import java.special.roots;`

Chapter 4

1. analysis, design, coding, testing, and maintenance.

3. During analysis, a programmer will attempt to determine the client's needs and requirements. Trade-offs and alternate approaches will be considered. Potential profit or savings will be determined. A budget and schedule will be formed. The goals and objectives of the class will be specified.

5. coding

7. During the maintenance state, a programmer will modify or enhance an existing class to meet the evolving needs and requirements of a client.

9. a) calculation

   b) condition

   c) counted loop

   d) input statements

   e) indefinite loop

   f) indefinite loop

11.
```
hours = IO.readDouble ("enter hours worked");
rate = IO.readDouble ("enter pay rate: ");
if (hours > 40.0)
```

```
(  calculate then display pay using overtime formula  )
```

```
else
```

```
(  calculate then display pay using regular formula  )
```

13.
```
number = IO.readDouble ("enter a positive value (ending with -1): ");
while (number > 0.0)
{
```

```
(  Input and sum a list of positive values  )
```

```
}
average = sum / count;
IO.showValue (" average is: ", average);
```

15.
```
hours = IO.readDouble ("enter hours: ");
rate = IO.readDouble ("enter pay rate: ");
if (hours <= 40.0)
```

```
{    pay = hours * rate;
```

Calculate pay based on the regular formula (no overtime).

```
}
else
{
```

Determine the amount of overtime worked.
Calculate pay using an overtime rate of 1.5 if the hours worked is less than or equal to 60 or using an overtime rate of 2.0 if the hours is greater than 60.

```
}
IO.showValue ("pay is: ", pay);
```

17.
```
output =   "table of powers \n";
output = IO.concatenate (output, " N 2 3 4 5 6\n");
while (N <= 5)
{
```

Build a display line called 'output' consisting of the first six powers of variable 'N'.

```
N = N + 1.0;
output = IO.concatenate (output, "\n");
}
    IO.showMessage (output);
```

19.
```
num_boxes = IO.readDouble();
cost_per_box = IO.readDouble();
```

Calculate the cost of the order: if the order exceeds $1000.00, reduce the order cost by 5%.

```
IO.showValue ("order cost is:", cost);
```

21.
```
plank = 0.0;
while (plank < 15)
```

```
        {
```

> Read the length, width, and thickness of this plank and calculate the number of board feet. Maintain a running sum of the board feet of all planks input.

```
            plank = plank + 1.0;
        }
    IO.showValue ("total board feet is:", total_board_feet);
23.  weight = IO.readDouble();
     while (weight > -1.0)
        {
```

> If this weight is over 150 lbs: sum the weight and maintain a count of the number of weights summed.

```
            weight = IO.readDouble ();
        }
        ave_weight = sum_weights / count;
IO.showValue ("average weight of customers over 150 lbs:", ave_weight);
25.  repair_time = 0.0;
     while (repair_time > -1.0)
        {
```

> Input the repair time for this repair. Sum this repair time and maintain a count of the number of repairs.

```
        }
        ave_repair = sum_repair_time / count_repairs;
    IO.showValue ("the average repair time is:", ave_repair);
```

Chapter 5

1. int
3. The characteristic is 3.0
5. Commas are not allowed in a number.
7. type, number or count
9. white spaces

11. a) 12

 b) 0

 c) 1

 d) 1

13. a) 5.76E-6

 b) 5.76E11

15. If a number too large for the range of a numeric variable is assigned, variable overflow will occur.

17. `int whole = (int) x;`

 `if (x = = whole) . . .`

19. A "yes" would be output for character letter values of "b", "c", "d", "e", and "f".

Chapter 6

1. braces

3. non-zero

5. the | operator

7. 10

9. the second (test) and the third (increment) expressions

11. 0, 0

 0, 1

 0, 2

 0, 3

 0, 4

 1, 1

 1, 2

 1, 3

 1, 4

 2, 2

 2, 3

 2, 4

 3, 3

 3, 4

 4, 4

13. a) false

 b) false

 c) true

15. int and char

17. If a default case is provided, it will be executed. Otherwise, none of the case options will be executed.

19. a) `a++;`

    b) `b *= 2;`

    c) `c += (++a);`

Chapter 7

1. object oriented programming

3. reference

5. buffer

7. instantiated or created

9. The assignment operator will only copy a reference to a dynamic object and not the object itself.

11. some_int

13. default constructor must be provided if any other constructors are defined.

15.
```
public class Course
{   private String teacher_name;
    private int location;
    private int student_count;
    public Course (String, int, int);
    public Course ();
    public void setName (String newname) { . . . }
    public void setLocation (int newlocation) { . . . }
    public void setStudentCount (int newcount) { . . . }
    public String getName () { . . . }
    public int getLocation () { . . . }
    public int getStudentCount () { . . . }
}
```

17.
```
public Fraction Abs ()
{ Fraction absval = new Fraction();
  absval.set(Math.abs(num), Math.abs(denom));
  return absval;
}
```

19.
```
public void set (double value)
{int whole = 1 / value;
//may result in small truncation inaccuracies
 num = 1;
 denom = whole;
}
```

Chapter 8

1. a) `int[] x = new int[10];`

   b) `float[] y = {5.6, 7.8, 9.1, 2.3, 4.5};`

   c) `String[] s = {"hello world", "hello world"};`

3. index or subscript

5. ordinal

7. This will result in an ArrayIndexOutOfBounds exception error message.

9. referencing an out-of-bounds cell and failing to specify an array index when referencing an array cell

11.
```
for (int x=0; x<20; x++)
        IO.showValue ("cell:", values[x]);
```

13.
```
for (int x=0; x<20; x++)
        sum += values[x];
```

15. `public void SomeFunc(int[] paramarray)`

17. the original cells are lost

19.
```
float[][] table = new float[2][3];
table[0][0] = 0.13;
table[0][1] = 0.52;
table[0][2] = 0.35;
table[1][0] = 0.26;
table[1][1] = 0.54;
table[1][2] = 0.2;
```

Chapter 9

1. index 15 (ignoring the hyphen used in typesetting)

3. thrown

5. package

7. text

9. `String.trim()`

11. the character "i"

13. `IO.showValue ("the number of characters in line is:", line.length());`

15. `IO.showValue ("the length of the sentence is:", sentence.length());`

17. Assuming a) the word can be anywhere within either string and b) the word is in String variable "word";

```
if (a.indexOf(word) >= 0 & b.indexOf(word) >= 0))
    IO.showMessage ("both strings contain the word");
```

19.
```
BufferedReader infile = null;

try

{   infile = new BufferedReader (new FileReader ("data.txt"));


}

catch (Exception e)

{    IO.showMessage ("FILE ERROR: " + e.getMessage());

    System.exit(0);

}
```

Chapter 10

1. Each useful recursive rule will invoke itself with a set of parameters that are closer to a trivial solution. Second, the rule will have a trivial case where a solution can be determined without another recursive application of the rule.

3. call tree

5. A recursive rule that does not contain a trivial solution may lead to infinite recursive calls.

7. a condition statement

9. All problems have both a recursive and iterative solution, although one may be much more complex than the other.

11. Assume the characters are indexed with variable 'n' (initially 0). I'll call this rule PrintChars():

   If the char at index "n" is '\0' stop.

   Otherwise, output this character and then PrintChars(n+1);

13. call tree for Fib(3);

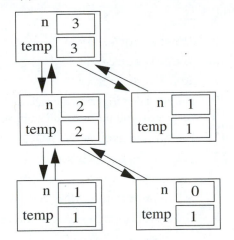

15. An array of 64 cells can be subdivided into two equal halves seven times until the remaining halves contain just one number each. So, worst case is seven name comparisons.

17. Recursive rule for Fib(n);

If n is <= 1, return 1.

else if n is 2, return 2.

else if n is 3, return 3

else return Fib (n-1) + Fib (n-2).

19. Call tree for Find ("Carl", list, 0, 9). For simplicity, I won't copy the list into each box.

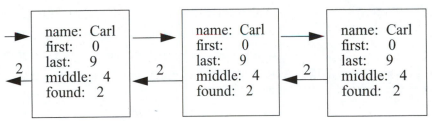

list: Ann
       Bill
       Carl
       Dan
       Eve
       Fred
       Gary
       Hal
       Ian
       Julio

Chapter 11

1. pane

3. JFrame.setTitle()

5. JLabel.setText()

7. actionPerformed()

9. The event that triggered the call can be determined by examining the text string associated with the method parameter using the getActionCommand() helper.

11. The five grid locations are NORTH, SOUTH, EAST, WEST, and CENTER.

13.
```
button = new JButton ("CLICK ME!");
        pane.add (button, BorderLayout.NORTH);
        button.addActionListener (this);
```

15. Assume the JTextArea object is 'area':
```
    area.setText(" ");
```

17.
```
JFrame thiswindow = new JFrame ("A list of names");
    Container pane = thiswindow.getContentPane();
    JLabel name1 = new JLabel ("Fred Smith");
    JLabel name2 = new JLabel ("Julio Gonzaga");
    JLabel name3 = new JLabel ("Ahmed Mola");
    JLabel name4 = new JLabel ("Janet Weinburg");
    pane.add (name1, BorderLayout.NORTH);
    pane.add (name2, BorderLayout.CENTER);
    JPanel south = new JPanel();
    south.add (name3, BorderLayout.NORTH);
    south.add (name4, BorderLayout.CENTER);
    pane.add (south, BorderLayout.SOUTH);
```

19. Assume the expected event commands are in strings "expected1" and "expected2":
```
public void actionPerformed (ActionEvent e)
{  if (e.getActionCommand().equals (expected1) . . .;
    else if (e.getActionCommand().equals (expected2) . . .
        else IO.showMessage ("UNEXPECTED EVENT");
}
```

Chapter 12

1. HTML

3. browser

5. <H1> *text to be large font* </h1>

7. **JFrame, JApplet**

9. The three parameters that must be supplied in an <APPLET> code to invoke the applet are the CODE, the WIDTH, and the HEIGHT values.

11. appletviewer

13. ```
    <APPLET CODE="invoice.class" HEIGHT=400 WIDTH=400>
    <PARAM NAME=purchaser VALUE="Fred Smith">
    </applet>
    ```

15. To convert an applet that extends **JApplet** to one that extends Applet, you should do the following steps;

    a) import the java.applet.* library

    b) convert the **Swing** library objects to simple applet objects by removing the preceeding 'J'—**JLabel** becomes **Label** and so on.

    c) Instead of adding objects to a context pane, objects are added directly to the Applet object itself.

17. the **Date** class of the **util** package.

19. The "implements actionListener" phrase is added to a class definition that will create **Timer** objects in order to allow Java to handle clock events that will continuously update the current time.
    ```

Index

Symbols

- operator 12, 25
- - operator 149, 161
! operator 140
! = operator 116, 130
% operator 151
&& operator 138, 160
* operator 12, 26
+ operator 12, 26
++ operator 149, 161
/ operator 12, 26
< operator 31, 53
<= operator 31, 53
== operator 116, 130
> operator 31, 53
>= operator 31, 53
{ } braces 34, 137, 160
| | operator 138, 160

A

abs 77
abstract 62
Abstract Windows Toolkit 290
access 61, 81
accumulating 40
accuracy 109
ActionEvent 300
add 295, 304
addActionListener 299
addition 13
addresses 3
addWindowListener 292
allocating variables 70
analysis 37, 102
Applet 317, 321, 335, 338
appletviewer 328
arguments 66, 80
array 197
array cell parameters 211
array declaration 197
array index ordering 222
array index out-of-bounds 206
array indexes 198, 222

array initialization 200
array parameters 207
array pointers 218
array referencing 197
array searching 212
array sorting 214
Arrays of objects 219
ASCII codes 351
assembly instruction set 2, 23
assignment 6
assignment statement 12
ASSUMPTIONS 211
auxiliary memory 1
AWT 290

B

backslash 8
base class 186, 191
basic components 88
basic instruction-set 3
binary file 168, 245
binary numbers 109
binary search 269, 278, 284
blanks 13
Block-local variables 156
boolean 126, 130
boolean operator 139, 159
brace symbols 6, 33
brackets 199
break 153, 160
browser 317, 338
buffer 174, 191, 346
BufferedReader 249, 344
bugs 15
button 290, 311, 336
byte 117

C

Cache 330
call tree 273, 284
CANCEL 290
Cancel 12, 38
carriage return 48, 53